ADJUSTING
TO
REALITY

THE INTERNATIONAL CENTER FOR ECONOMIC GROWTH is a nonprofit research institute founded in 1985 to stimulate international discussions on economic policy, economic growth, and human development. The Center sponsors research, publications, and conferences in cooperation with an international network of correspondent institutes, which distribute publications of both the Center and other network members to policy audiences around the world. The Center's research and publications program is organized around five series: Sector Studies; Country Studies; Studies in Human Development and Social Welfare; Occasional Papers; and Reprints.

The Center is affiliated with the Institute for Contemporary Studies and is headquartered in Panama; the administrative office is in San Francisco, California.

For further information, please contact the International Center for Economic Growth, 243 Kearny Street, San Francisco, California, 94108, USA. Telephone (415) 981-5353; Fax (415) 986-4878.

ICEG Board of Overseers

OTHER BOOKS BY ROBERT KLITGAARD

Tropical Gangsters

Controlling Corruption

Elitism and Meritocracy in Developing Countries

Data Analysis for Development

Choosing Elites

ADJUSTING TO REALITY

Beyond "State versus Market" in Economic Development

Robert Klitgaard

An International Center for Economic Growth Publication

ICS Press
San Francisco, California

Publication signifies that the Center believes a work to be a competent treatment worthy of public consideration. The findings, interpretations, and conclusions of a work are entirely those of the authors and should not be attributed to ICEG, its affiliated organizations, its board of overseers, or organizations that support ICEG.

Inquiries, book orders, and catalog requests should be addressed to ICS Press, 243 Kearny Street, San Francisco, California 94108, USA. Telephone: (415) 981-5353; Fax: (415) 986-4878; book orders within the continental United States: **(800) 326-0263.**

Distributed to the trade by National Book Network, Lanham, Maryland.

Cover design by Herman & Company
Index compiled by Patricia Ruggiero

Library of Congress Cataloging-in-Publication Data

Klitgaard, Robert E.
    Adjusting to reality : beyond "state vs. market" in economic development / Robert Klitgaard.
        p. cm.
    "An International Center for Economic Growth publication."
    Includes bibliographical references and index.
    ISBN 1-55815-147-8
    1. Developing countries–Economic policy.   2. Industry and state–Developing countries.   3. Privatization–Developing countries.   4. Economic development.   I. Title.
    HC59.7.K585   1991
    338.9–dc20   91-23177
                                                           CIP

For
Ronald MacLean Abaroa
of Bolivia, exemplar of the new wave of world
leaders who are striving for economic and
political freedom, just and efficient governance, and
solidarity among peoples and nations

CONTENTS

PREFACE

THE TRUE TEST OF CIVILIZATION, Boswell once said, is a decent provision for the poor. By that measure, economic analysis has been spearheading the civilizing process for some time, and it takes an exciting new turn in this volume by Robert Klitgaard. Poverty, Klitgaard argues, is—and should be—a principal concern of development strategists, but policy makers and analysts will continue to run from pillar to post in their search for a cure unless they can adjust their development schemes to reality.

Since the early 1950s, those schemes have been guided by two vastly different ideas about the role of the state in economic development. For a time, public planning and investment were extolled in many parts of the world, especially in former colonies that were eager to overcome the inequalities, exploitation, and elitism they had experienced under foreign powers and private enterprise. By the 1980s, however, disillusion had set in because the interventionist state had not promoted growth as expected. Instead, elitism and corruption had again become rampant as industries hid behind the state's protectionist policies and some countries succumbed to dictatorships.

Then came a move toward freer markets and greater emphasis on the private sector to ignite economic growth. As a result, the role of government has been shrinking in recent years. But the free markets are not magically solving the problems of the poor and underdevelopment. Free markets have weak institutional foundations in developing countries and thus tend to malfunction or not even exist. Peasants and the poor have not immediately benefited from the numerous economic reforms undertaken in the past decade.

In Klitgaard's view, the debate over markets versus govern-

ment intervention fails to get to the heart of the matter. It is not
enough to declare markets free or to rely exclusively on government
efforts. A new strategy is needed—one that recognizes the strengths
and weaknesses of each. The challenge, he says, is to make both the
market and the state work better.

But they cannot be made to work better as long as economic
theory, empirical research, and politicians pursue simple answers
such as "government intervention is bad (or good)." The time has
come, Klitgaard advises, to admit that both the market and the state
have functioned badly in most developing countries—not because
there is anything inherently wrong with the theory of the free market or of the efficient, benevolent state. The problem is that these
theories ignore the reality of the conditions in developing countries.

How, Klitgaard asks, can the government work efficiently in
conditions of adverse incentives, corruption, and overcentralization, and how can markets work well when there is no tradition of
enforcing contracts and property rights? And how can poverty be
eradicated when markets, the government, the press, and the legal
system overlook or misunderstand the ethnic dimensions of poverty
in the world? We must, Klitgaard urges, adjust to these realities.

The new approach to policy analysis that the author proposes
is based on two fundamental principles. One is that the proper
choice of economic strategies cannot be determined in the abstract
but depends on particular circumstances, which differ not only from
one country to another, but also from one time period to another. In
other words, the real environment must guide our policy decisions.
The other is that information is at the heart of the problems in the
real world of the developing countries. Market institutions cannot
work without information about prices, quantities, and quality; and
government institutions cannot work without information about
outputs and outcomes.

Klitgaard offers examples from Bolivia, Brazil, India, Indonesia, Malaysia, Pakistan, Peru, and the Philippines to make his
point—a defining characteristic of underdevelopment is that markets have poor information about the quality of goods, services,
risks, and people. But instead of proposing formal models to resolve
these problems, the author suggests creative ways in which the state
and citizens themselves can solve their own "inevitably unique
problems." One of the key tasks, in Klitgaard's view, is to ensure
that environments are rich in information.

This volume offers a broad framework for policy analysis that
moves us closer to intelligent solutions to the real problems of
the real poor in the modern world. The literature on economic devel-

opment will benefit greatly from this illuminating discussion of
the interrelationships between public policy and environmental
analysis.

Nicolás Ardito-Barletta
General Director
International Center for Economic Growth

August 1991
Panama City, Panama

AUTHOR'S PREFACE

IT WAS EARLY NOVEMBER of 1988. I had just departed the tiny and impoverished country of Equatorial Guinea, where I had been working with the government for almost two and a half years on an economic rehabilitation program. Three days later, I found myself in La Paz, Bolivia. The transition from the tropics to the world's tallest capital city was breathtaking. So were the country's problems.

I had worked in Bolivia for two months in 1985. That was the time of its remarkable structural adjustment program, a combination of inflation-fighting and free-market reforms that shocked the country and the world. Here was a nation whose revolution of 1952 had been watched and admired by many who favored state-led growth, nationalization, and land reform. But in August 1985, with inflation racing along at 20,000 percent, the newly elected government of President Victor Paz Estenssoro carried out a remarkable about-face. The same President Paz who had been the leader of the 1952 revolution now launched a new one, this time toward a free-market strategy of economic development.

But by 1988 the economy had not responded. Although inflation was under control, per capita production and consumption continued to fall. Private investment had not picked up. It was said that most of the poor were worse off than before Bolivia's New Economic Policy. As I write in early 1991, five and a half years after the reforms, roughly the same conclusions hold.

In this syndrome Bolivia is not alone. In many of the fifty or so countries that have been part of the unprecedented worldwide move toward free-market strategies of economic development, the results so far have been disappointing. Markets turn out not to function as well as the textbooks advertise. Cutbacks in public spending lead to increased poverty, particularly among disadvantaged

groups. I found it striking in countries as different as Equatorial
Guinea and Bolivia to hear people describe similar problems.

"Free markets have been declared, but they haven't yet
reached the poor." Markets for products, credit, and labor need to
be democratized. If not, only the rich and the foreigners will benefit
from structural adjustment. Part of the solution is getting government off the back of the small producer and business person. But
only part. Many of the markets the poor in developing countries face
are highly imperfect. What proactive roles should public policy play
to make markets work?

"Our government is crippled by inefficiency, corruption, and
overcentralization." Even after structural adjustment, the state performs many crucial functions. But a crisis grips public administration in many poor countries, and many people have lost confidence
in their governments. The streamlining and privatizing induced by
free-market reforms will help. But is there not also a need for better
incentives, anticorruption measures, and decentralization? For what
might be called the structural adjustment of government itself?

"We face ethnic (tribal, caste, communal) inequalities. We
probably always had them, but now they are impossible to ignore."
With freer markets and freer flows of information and moves toward
democracy, many countries find that ethnic inequalities and discrimination become a primary concern. We have become aware of
these issues recently in the Soviet Union and in Eastern and Central
Europe, but they are almost universal. Within most countries of
Latin America, Africa, and Asia, poverty is concentrated in certain
social groups, and prejudice is widespread. What can be done to
reduce economic and educational inequalities among groups?

These are some of the issues taking center stage in economic
policy making in the developing world. Notice that they go beyond
the debate over the relative powers of state and market in economic
life. During the 1950s and 1960s, most economists and aid donors
advocated an interventionist state that would mobilize and manage
the nation's resources. This was necessary, they argued, because
markets failed in developing countries. In the 1980s and 1990s, the
pendulum has swung the other way. Most economists and aid
agencies now argue that the private sector should take the lead in
economic mobilization and management. The argument now is that
governments fail in developing countries.

For what it is worth, I tend to agree with the latest swing of this
pendulum. But I believe the debate must go beyond state versus
market. The reality in developing countries is that neither market

nor government works well. The agenda now is to make both work better.

This book tries to move the new agenda forward in three ways. First, I hope the book will help induce a *shift of focus* in the debate on development policies. As I said, the debate has tended to be at the level of "the role of the state"—the balance (or blend or mix) of state and market. I try to move below this argument, from a macro to micro level of analysis and action. Beyond stabilization and liberalization, a host of microeconomic and institutional measures are needed to improve the market. Beyond reducing government's scope, we need to improve its management through the application of better incentives and information systems. And beyond declarations of nondiscrimination and equal rights, we need to rethink the policies that influence prejudice and inequality.

Second, the book exemplifies a *mode of policy analysis*. I don't mean that the book provides the first example or that it's a perfect one, only that it illustrates a useful way to do analysis that is at once mind-stretching and humble.

With what mode of analysis does it contrast? A few key policy makers and analysts meet behind closed doors. Excellent models of the economy are trotted out. Decisions are based on parameters such as the interest and exchange rates, tariffs, taxes, and public investment. The analysis and the decision making are macro and top down, often with decisive foreign involvement and funding.

What do I propose instead? The new agenda's questions about improving markets and governments are institutionally and culturally loaded. Their solutions will involve more participation by line officials, business people, and ordinary citizens. Analytically, the issues require micro-level rather than macro-level analysis—or so I contend. This book imports qualitative insights from areas of economics not often applied to development—the so-called new industrial economics (Chapters 3–5, 9), the new theory of the firm (the principal-agent model plus a little bit of the new labor economics, Chapters 7 and 8), and the economics of discrimination (Chapters 10–12). In each case, these models stress imperfect information and its corrosive effects on incentives.

From these models I derive a set of frameworks for policy analysis. There is no illusion here of a formal model from which optimal parameter values are derived under restrictive assumptions. Instead, the frameworks are designed to guide inquiry and stimulate debate, so that policy makers and citizens may be more creative in solving their own inevitably unique problems. Their purpose is heuristic. If they can stimulate more and better frameworks, all the better—for I recognize the partial and imperfect nature of those presented here.

The frameworks are complemented by case studies of successful or at least interesting efforts to deal with the problem at hand. Working through examples is the best way I know of fostering creative problem solving, and the book includes cases from Bolivia, Brazil, India, Indonesia, Malaysia, Pakistan, Peru, and the Philippines, plus shorter examples from many other countries.

Without wishing on a star, I would hope the book does one more thing: help us to *reconceptualize underdevelopment*. Past theories of economic development have focused on capital formation, getting prices right, class structure, center-periphery relations, and many other factors. Without denying their relevance, this book suggests a different cut. Information and knowledge are at the heart of development; underdevelopment is bound up with ignorance and uncertainty. More concretely, individuals and societies with the lowest levels of information and of information-processing capabilities will likely also be the poorest. This is a probabilistic statement, not a deterministic one, and it does not mean that information is everything nor that it alone explains malfunctioning markets, inefficient governments, and institutionalized discrimination. The reader will notice that the book's frameworks for policy analysis include many other factors. But I believe we will see in the next decade an explosion of interest in the informational bases of development, not only in economics but in other fields as well.

Thus, the seemingly disparate topics in the book are linked in several ways. They are emerging as crucial issues in the era after free-market reforms (although they have long been present). They go beyond the usual debates over state versus market, and they may provide a provocative if incomplete way of reconceptualizing the role of the state in economic development. They invite a different kind of policy analysis: one that is more participatory and open-ended, emphasizing frameworks and checklists and case studies more than formal modeling. They have at their core a problem of imperfect and asymmetric information, a fact that may in turn suggest new hypotheses about economic progress and backwardness.

ACKNOWLEDGMENTS

FOR ADVICE AND assistance of various kinds, I am indebted to Graham Allison, Nicolás Ardito-Barletta, Bruce Bushey, Ledivina Cariño, Nananda Col, Shantayanan Devarajan, Jorge Domínguez, Luisa Fernandes, John Haaga, Carlos Hassenbalg, Javed Haider, Donald Horowitz, Cord Jakobeit, Bruce Johnston, Ruth Katz, Marc Lindenberg, Vicky Macintyre, Ronald MacLean Abaroa, Liling Magtolis-Briones, Toemin Masoem, John D. Montgomery, Janet Mowery, Samuel Paul, Dwight Perkins, David Rossington, Thomas Schelling, Donald Snodgrass, Joseph Stern, Paul Streeten, Indro Suwandi, Raymond Vernon, Aaron Wildavsky, and Richard Zeckhauser. It was the inspiring teaching of William Fairley, Frederick Mosteller, Howard Raiffa, Thomas Schelling, Michael Spence, David Starrett, and Richard Zeckhauser that first suggested to me in various ways the importance of information, uncertainty, and incentives for understanding economic development, and this later became the theme of my own course at Harvard's Kennedy School of Government, "Policy Problems in Developing Countries." Many students helped me develop these ideas, especially three remarkable course assistants: Ronald MacLean Abaroa, Deborah Matthews, and Ana Teresa Gutiérrez San Martín.

The Russell Sage Foundation provided financial support for the drafting of early versions of several parts of the book in 1984–1985; special thanks to Marshall Robinson. The Hanns-Seidel Foundation invited me to Bolivia in 1988 and again in late 1990; I am particularly grateful to Hartwig Meyer-Norbisrath. Hanns-Seidel is also funding the Spanish translation and publication of this book.

I wrote a draft of most of the book during a year as a visiting scholar at the Rand Corporation in 1989–1990. Thanks to Charles Wolf, Jr., for making it happen and to James Hosek, Phyllis Pierson, and Patricia Williams for support. The final manuscript was produced as I overlooked the wintry coast of Maine, with the sole company of National Public Radio and the BBC. Thanks to Maureen White for making this monastic interlude possible.

Throughout this period, I have been blessed by Geralyn White's special brand of encouragement and inspiration. To her my gratitude and love.

BEYOND
"STATE VERSUS MARKET"

BOLIVIA'S THREE-TIME former president recently described some of the reasons for the Bolivian Revolution of 1952. "In the 1950s, business interests were very great but they had no creative functions, only big mining where the money left the country. In the countryside, there were property holders of the feudal type. The economy was therefore stagnant. In these circumstances it was essential for the state to play the leading role."[1]

So Victor Paz Estenssoro's first administration acted boldly. The government nationalized most of the country's mines, seized private lands and redistributed them to poor peasants, and formed new state-run enterprises. The state controlled most prices. It imposed high tariffs in order to protect, indeed to create, Bolivian industry. Public planning and investment, it was declared, were the keys to growth. The Bolivian Revolution of 1952 was widely admired and even copied around the globe.[2]

But look at what happened in 1985 when the same Victor Paz Estenssoro was elected president for the third time, at the age of seventy-eight. In a remarkable shift, his government declared a New Economic Policy that stabilized the economy, liberalized trade, and rolled back government intervention. Prices would henceforth be determined by domestic and international markets. The private sector, not the state, would play the leading role in economic development. In effect, Bolivia redefined the role of the state in development. And once again, Bolivia's example is being watched closely, sometimes being imitated, around the world.

President Paz Estenssoro reflected on this drastic change in the role of government. "Over time the state grew. It became inefficient and corrupt. It no longer played *its* role. In fact, it became a negative force. The state retarded the economy and, through deficits, created inflation that reached 25,000 percent when I took office in 1985. The intervention of the state created the conditions for corruption and bribes."

In this economic about-face, Bolivia has not been alone. Around the globe, a revolution in economic policy is under way. The Soviet Union and Eastern Europe are dramatic examples. But radical changes are also transforming the so-called developing countries.

By early 1991, more than fifty countries had received loans from the International Monetary Fund that were conditioned on promises to adopt free-market economic policies. Of these fifty, about three-quarters were receiving structural adjustment or sectoral adjustment loans from the World Bank, again conditioned on pulling back the interventionist state. "The objective of structural adjustment programs," observes a World Bank report in the starchy prose favored by that institution,

> is to restore rapid economic growth while
> simultaneously supporting internal and external
> financial stability. As such, these programs have
> macroeconomic and microeconomic aspects. The major
> macro objectives are to improve the external balance
> and domestic fiscal balance. An adjustment program
> thus commonly includes a combination of (1) fiscal and
> monetary policies to bring about overall demand
> reduction and (2) trade policies (mainly the exchange
> rate and import/export taxes and subsidies) to alter the
> relative incentives between tradable and nontradable
> goods. On the micro side, the major objective is to
> improve efficiency in the use of resources by removing
> price distortions, opening up more competition, and
> dismantling administrative controls (deregulation).
> Such programs include those for government
> expenditures and the management of public
> enterprises, including reductions in the government's
> presence in areas where private enterprise can operate
> more efficiently.[3]

Plainly put, structural adjustment means less government, freer trade, and more private enterprise.

These changes mark a sharp departure from previous practice

and theorizing about economic development. For years the pre-vailing wisdom advocated an interventionist state. The private sector, went the argument, would not muster the massive public investments needed for economic growth, and markets in poor countries did not work as economics texts said they should. Because of market failures, it was up to the government to mobilize economic resources and manage them. The state itself could substitute for inadequate capital, skills, and home demand, as the economic historian Alexander Gerschenkron showed for the Soviet Union.[4]

In contrast, today government is shrinking in both size and scope. The emphasis now is on the private sector's efficient use of resources to fire economic growth, whereas the state's role as mobilizer and manager is played down. As economies have grown over this century, the effectiveness of the state as a substitute for missing capital and institutions has declined; Gerschenkron has been updated.[5]

The pendulum of opinion has swung toward the market, but not because of new philosophical arguments or ideological conversion. Rather, disillusionment has set in. Bluntly put, in most countries the old strategy simply didn't work. Instead of promoting growth, the state botched economic mobilization and spawned inefficiency. Instead of redistributing resources to the poor and the powerless, the interventionist state too often coincided with elitism, corruption, and dictatorship. Some statistical studies indicate that in recent years more interventionist states have experienced lower growth rates, as well as less liberty, than states whose development strategies relied more on the private sector.[6]

"In my personal case," President Paz Estenssoro said during our discussion, "our neoliberal policies, as they are now labeled, of 1985 certainly have a philosophical justification." He showed me a volume of Friedrich von Hayek's. "But it was primarily a situation engendered by realities—the inflation, the complete economic disorder, the fiscal deficit, the bad loans of the Central Bank—and not a decision taken for philosophical reasons."

In the throes of our current disillusion with government in the third world, we may tend to forget past disappointments with the private sector. The pendulum of opinion had reasons for being where it was in the 1950s and 1960s. By then the new nations of Africa and Asia, as well as the poor countries that had been independent for years, had accumulated ample experience with the imperfections of the private sector. Even where the economic role of the state was negligible, growth was minimal in many countries.[7] Often, what was advertised as "capitalism" or "competition" turned out to

CARLOS FUENTES ON THE FAILURES OF BOTH CAPITALISM AND SOCIALISM IN LATIN AMERICA

"And we ourselves suffer hyperinflation, unemployment, rising indices of poverty and malnutrition, falling indices of productivity and living standards, and we are governed by fragile democracies threatened by the social explosion, the military coup, the violence of narcotics traffickers, and the excessive burden of our external debt. . . .

"Both capitalism and socialism, in their Latin American versions, have shown themselves incapable of extracting the majority of our countrymen from misery. . . . Even in optimal conditions, the criticism is inescapable: the Left has hoped that prosperity would arrive by decree of the centralizing state. Nonetheless, it is the Left, before anyone, that should open itself today to the lessons of our emerging civil societies, . . . abandoning the limitation of an asphyxiating bureaucratic model.

"The Right has hoped for prosperity from above, thanks to the accumulation of riches at the top and the faith that, sooner or later, the trickle would arrive to the bottom. . . . When will that drop of riches descend to today's belts of misery, to the slums, to the lost cities? Experience tells us: never, or too late."

SOURCE: Carlos Fuentes, *"La Socialización de la Política desde Abajo,"* a talk given before la Sociedad del Quinto Centenario, Madrid, 1990; *Ventana* (Nicaragua), no. 446 (November 12, 1990): 8, my translation.

be a fraudulent mercantilism. A private sector heavily skewed toward foreigners and oligopolistic in structure did not lead to efficiency and dynamism but instead to exploitation and misallocation. Moreover, even where private capital and fairly free markets were the rule, basic needs were not satisfied; and democracy and human rights were often abrogated in the name of the colonial powers or the local oligarchs. "Free trade policies of colonial governments forced on low-productivity densely settled countries such as India, Egypt, and Burma destroyed indigenous industry, thereby often worsening living standards by reducing nonagricultural employment opportunities as populations were increasing," concluded economic historians Cynthia Taft Morris and Irma Adelman.[8] Precisely because in many ways the private sector had failed at development, many countries in the 1950s and 1960s turned admiringly to the interventionist strategies of Britain's planned economy during World War II and, of course, to the Soviet Union.

Taking a longer historical view, some authors perceive a pendulum swinging between calls for a strong state (after a time when an emphasis on the market has failed) and calls for an unfettered private sector (after a period of failed state-led strategies).[9] The fact is that neither the interventionist state nor the minimalist state has guaranteed rapid development. In much of South Asia, Africa, and Latin America, *neither state nor market has lived up to the expectations of its enthusiasts.*

This observation is not meant to invite despair. It does suggest that simply criticizing third world governments is not enough—just as criticizing third world markets is not enough. We need to go beyond the usual debate over the roles of state and market in economic development—how much government, how much private sector?—and examine the reasons why neither works well and how both might work better.

A PROBLEMATIC TASK ENVIRONMENT

A useful starting point is what might be called "the environmental conditions" that make market and government institutions work less well in most developing countries than in the industrialized nations.

Consider the market first. In the most economically backward countries, the legal and institutional foundations for free and efficient markets are weak or absent. These foundations include

- a stable and credible currency
- a well-functioning legal system with well-enforced contracts and property rights
- capital markets and systems of credit and banking that enforce rules of repayment
- an infrastructure that ensures low transportation and communication costs and thereby facilitates trade
- ample market information on prices, quantities, and qualities for products and labor

Moreover, many domestic markets are thin, with few buyers or sellers and irregular demand. They are sometimes swamped by local and international economic tides. Economies of scale in key areas of the economy—for example, in irrigation and extractive industries—mean that unregulated competition can easily result in inefficiency and exploitation. Externalities and common property resources are also widespread in developing countries—and when they are present, unfettered competition will not usually be efficient.

Because the institutional foundations of free markets are so weak and because the environment often does not favor efficient competition, markets tend to malfunction or even fail to exist.

But what about governments in developing countries? Why have they, too, so often failed?

Again, in most poor countries the environment has been hostile. Conditions have not favored representative governments with efficient, publicly interested bureaucracies. Democratic traditions are fragile. Dependency on foreign capital—public, private, and foreign aid—has discouraged self-reliance and sometimes undercut national sovereignty. Ethnic, religious, regional, and tribal cleavages have often engendered political parties that represent narrow interests, which in turn give rise to political instability. Governments have tended to become employment agencies for political allies and those unable to get jobs elsewhere, which combined with these countries' poverty has resulted in ludicrously low levels of pay. Moreover, in part because of poor information, this pay is not linked to performance. Together, these factors have tended to lead to dictatorship, incompetence, apathy, and corruption in government.

In Chapter 2 I illustrate these points with the example of Bolivia. I argue that many features of Bolivia's economy—its natural resources, agriculture, infrastructure, extralegal economies, and markets for credit and agricultural products—mean that untrammeled competitive markets will fall short of economic efficiency. But I also point out some shortcomings in the functioning of the Bolivian government. Given the difficult environment of countries like Bolivia, neither market nor state functions well.

Chapter 2 stresses Bolivia's widespread poverty, particularly the regional and ethnic correlates of poverty. This latter subject generated controversy and discomfort among my Bolivian colleagues, as it undoubtedly would in other circles since the ethnic aspects of poverty within developing countries tend to be avoided or overlooked. The widespread ethnic inequalities within poor countries—whether the development strategy is state-led or market-led—is another reason to go beyond the ideological debate over the state versus the market.

THE ROLES OF GOVERNMENT DEPEND ON THE CIRCUMSTANCES

There is yet another reason that the usual debate over state versus market oversimplifies. The way economies actually work, state and

SCHUMPETER ON AVOIDING EXTREMES

In times when the state is preeminent and its shortcomings are highly
visible, economists and others seem to swoon over the charms of the
market. This is the situation in many developing countries today. But
when the market is in the ascendancy and its drawbacks are evident, the
state may be idealized. As Joseph Schumpeter pointed out long ago, both
extremes should be resisted.

Here is Schumpeter commenting on the simple advice to government
officials to leave market forces alone:

> Economists who take it upon themselves to teach such
> unpromising pupils are naturally tempted to extol the
> powers of competitive pricing. . . . Up to a point they
> are quite right, of course: everyone should know by
> now—or have Lange, Lerner, and a host of others really
> written to no purpose?—that there is nothing specifically
> capitalistic but only general economic logic about the price
> system that pure competition tends to establish in a near-
> equalitarian society and under approximately normal
> conditions. . . . But not only socialists of the old tradition
> and people who are more conspicuous for their
> enthusiasm about "welfare" and "justice" than for their
> economic competence but also professional economists
> have felt that this lesson has gone too far. And these are
> also right; for some of the exponents of free pricing fail to
> make it clear to their readers—in one or two cases
> one has the impression that it is not quite clear to
> themselves—that the rosy propositions about competitive
> pricing do not apply even in the rarefied air of pure
> theory without exceptions and qualifications; that, if they
> are to apply to actual patterns . . . this would have to be
> carefully established; and that, in particular, it will not do
> to accept "consumers' sovereignty" as a noli me tangere.

Elsewhere Schumpeter has criticized the tendency of other
economists to confide in the efficacy of government intervention along
the optimal lines advocated by economists:

> It still remains true that a large majority of economists,
> when discussing issues of public policy, automatically
> treated political authority and especially government in the
> modern representative state as a kind of deity that strives
> to realize the will of the people and the common
> good. . . . Policy is politics; and politics is a very realistic
> matter. There is no scientific sense whatever in creating
> for one's self some metaphysical entity to be called "The
> Common Good" and a not less metaphysical "state," that,
> sailing high in the clouds and exempt from and above
> human struggles and group interests, worships at the
> shrine of that Common Good. But the economists of all
> times have done precisely this.

SOURCE: Joseph A. Schumpeter, "English Economists and the State-Managed
Economy," Journal of Political Economy 57, no. 5 (October 1949): 380, emphasis in
original; and Joseph A. Schumpeter, "The Communist Manifesto in Sociology and
Economics," Journal of Political Economy 57, no. 3 (June 1949), pp. 205–6.

market blend. As economist Richard Zeckhauser argues, the clear lines between public and private activity are gone; he calls today's economies "mongrels," or "stews."[10] Indeed, thinking of a single stew may be misleading: government affects economic development in many ways and many domains. The issues concerning the proper role of the state therefore run broader and deeper than, say, the degree to which markets or governments should determine prices, or the extent to which the private sector rather than the state owns and manages productive resources—important as these commonly discussed choices are. This is why it is better to speak of the roles of the state in the plural.

What should be the roles of the state in promoting economic development? It is unlikely that the answers will be the same across countries and situations. I find it helpful to consider an analogous question from the business literature.

Suppose someone asks, "What is the best way to structure a firm or company? How should its strategy be formulated?" An important strand of business literature replies: "It depends. The proper choice of structures and strategies cannot be determined in the abstract."

Research in business shows that "it depends" among other things on the environment—that is, on the economic and political circumstances beyond the firm's control. For example, most companies have little control over the supply and demand conditions in the markets for their products or for factors of production such as labor, capital, and technology. These conditions are givens. The strategy and structure that an enterprise will find appropriate in a highly competitive, high-risk environment with a few large investments will not make sense for a firm in an oligopolistic, low-risk environment with many small investments. In other words, no one business structure or strategy is appropriate for all markets and all circumstances.

The same qualitative point holds for economic strategies and structures at the national level. The proper economic roles of government and the private sector depend in part on the environment.

As an example, consider the much-debated issue of *protectionism and import substitution*. In the 1950s and later, many developing countries were advised to erect barriers to free trade so that, protected thereby, their domestic industries could profitably produce many of the products the country imported.

Today the pendulum of opinion has swung away from this strategy. One reason is that import substitution distorted free trade and led to a misallocation of resources. Behind the protective barriers of tariffs and other restrictions, domestic industries were artificially profitable; but they often grew fat and lazy. Instead of nurturing infant industries, protectionist policies over time tended to erode a country's ability to compete internationally.

Another result, perhaps less anticipated, was that import substitution created opportunities for corruption, rent-seeking, and waste.[11] Government officials profited from licenses only they could grant, restrictions that only their good graces could relax. Producers started spending their time figuring out ways to obtain licenses and evade restrictions, rather than how to cut costs and improve quality. As economist Mancur Olson has noted, "Tariffs that are of only small significance in a comparative statics framework could still have profound quantitative importance, because they encourage, and free trade prevents, institutional sclerosis."[12]

Despite these shortcomings, judicious critics have recognized that import substitution is not intrinsically good or bad. Its costs and benefits depend on how it is carried out and on the particular circumstances—the environment—of the case at hand.

For example, in their analysis of growth patterns from 1850 to 1914, Cynthia Taft Morris and Irma Adelman show that industrial "latecomers" such as Germany, Japan, Italy, and Russia caught up by means of, among other measures, "policies for promoting import substitution. . . . Tariffs were a major weapon for initiating industrialization and for protecting grain producers." But "success with inward-oriented industrialization varied greatly," depending on particular circumstances and institutions relating to land, transport, agricultural extension, and education.[13]

Theoretical models support these findings. They suggest that the effects of import substitution will vary according to a host of factors—ranging from the size of the domestic market to the relevant elasticities of supply and demand, to the long-run prospects for an infant industry, and eventually to export.[14]

A group of younger trade theorists argue that oligopolistic market structures are widespread in international trade, and in their presence, protection may be economically efficient.[15]

When may also matter: the right strategy now may not be the right strategy twenty years hence. A strategy of export promotion may have a better chance of success if it follows a period of import substitution. This has been argued, for example, in the case of Taiwan.[16] "If the succession of 'inward-looking' and 'outward-looking' policies is examined in this light," writes economist Paul Streeten, "it is seen that some forms of import-substitution and of the creation of an indigenous technological and institutional capacity

NO RIGID RULES

In a 1958 book dealing with the proper roles of the state in development, Edward Mason suggested that rigid rules were likely to mislead.

> *Reflexion on the recent history of economic development in various parts of the world suggests that a substantial measure of government participation in the economy is compatible both with development and with stagnation. Strong doubts emerge concerning the existence of an optimum relationship between government and business—a relationship that is invariant to the stage of economic development, to the traditions of public and private management, and to the underlying social and cultural institutions of the countries in question. . . .*
>
> *What I seek to emphasize is the relativity of this role [of government in the development process]. It is clearly relevant to the stage of development of the country in question, the state of development of the surrounding world, the receptivity of the culture to private entrepreneurial activities, the administrative competence of government, the sources of development funds, and the urgency of popular demands for economic growth. . . .*
>
> *The points that have been made in this attack on the market are, generally, well taken. The market is an imperfect instrument at best, and there appears to be good reason for believing that, in early stages of development, its malfunctioning is particularly evident. Indivisibilities in factor employment are probably more serious: the opportunities for capturing external economies are larger, the relevance of information signaled by the market is less, and the market imperfections greater than at later stages of development. The inter-industry relationships and the time horizon relevant to development that can come within the scope of a planning commission are much greater than the decisions a private enterprise would normally encompass. Yet the problems of information gathering that confront the planner, not to mention administrative and political difficulties, are enormous. I do not refer merely to the lack of statistical data, although that is characteristic of all underdeveloped countries, but also to the absence of procedures of estimating those economic relations which must be known if the planner is to correct the unregulated decisions of the market. The fact of the matter seems to be that the really good arguments for planning lie in the obvious inadequacies of the market, and the really good arguments for the market rest on the deficiencies of planning. As in some other fields of activity and of discourse, the best defence is the attack. In many underdeveloped countries the planners are clearly on the attack.*

SOURCE: Edward Mason, Economic Planning in Underdeveloped Areas, *Millar Lectures no. 2* (New York: Fordham University Press, 1958): 5, 15–54.

behind protectionist barriers are the precondition for a subsequent successful liberalization phase. Yet, most contributors praise liberalization and condemn protectionism in a quite ahistorical way."[17]

It is fair to say that the early proponents of import substitution overestimated its benefits and underestimated its costs. No doubt, too, import substitution was often installed not because of its purported economic benefits for country or industry but because of the personal benefits it made available to politicians and their friends. Recent experience has taught us this much.

But a fundamental point should not be lost. Notwithstanding their defects, import substitution policies do engender benefits as well. In a particular situation, these benefits may outweigh the costs. When not engaged in rhetorical exercises, most economists recognize this point.[18] More generally, the decision to choose or reject this strategy should depend on a careful analysis of a country's environment.

This granted, several new questions arise. How should a country or a ministry go about analyzing its "environment"? Can anything be learned from any of the analyses that have been carried out in various countries and sectors? What does existing research say about the circumstances in which various roles of the state and of the private sector have led to what gains and what losses?

Unfortunately—and I think surprisingly—one finds little in the literature on economic development that illuminates, for policymaking purposes, the interrelationships between a country's environment, its public policies, and its likely success along many dimensions. Unlike the literature on business strategy, the development literature provides few models on which to build environmental analyses and few contingent generalizations about what strategies and structures work best under what environmental conditions. Dwight Perkins remarks:

> Given the amount of attention that has been lavished
> on such issues as the desirability of structural
> adjustment to ensure greater reliance on market forces,
> the need for privatization, and the like, it is surprising
> how little effort has gone into collecting empirical data
> with which one could assess the current situation in
> developing countries or measure change.[19]

One hopes that in the next decade new empirical research will shed light on what strategies and structures work how well in what environments.[20] But for now, we are in the realm of art more than science.

Economic theory, too, provides surprisingly little practical guidance. Richard Musgrave notes a perennial trade-off in determining the role of government:

> The questions of what public services should be
> provided, how they should be financed, and what role
> government should play in the macro conduct of
> economic affairs were visible to Adam Smith, and they
> still pose the basic problem.
>   So does the fact that many issues in public
> finance remain inherently controversial. To establish
> the economic case for the public sector is to delimit the
> sphere that can be left to the invisible hand and the
> rules of the market. The scope of existing externalities,
> the acceptability of a market-determined income
> distribution, the shape of the social welfare function,
> maintaining full resource utilization, the issues of
> inflation and growth, all these have powerful bearings
> on the appropriate size and activities of the public
> sector. So does the capability of public policy to apply
> appropriate corrections, with the scope of public policy
> failure matched against that of market failure. Given
> this array of problems and their linkages, ideological
> and value issues are never far away.[21]

That both markets and "nonmarkets" (governments and hierarchies) are imperfect is a theme of a growing body of theoretical research.[22] Real choices involve blends and balances between an imperfect market and an imperfect state. As economist Gordon Tullock put it,

> The injuries that externalities may inflict on individuals
> if everything is left to the market and the injuries that
> government may inflict on individuals through the
> inherent nature of its decision process are the two
> basic factors in selecting the proper institutions to deal
> with any given problem. We must always weigh the
> specific advantages and disadvantages of these two
> imperfect instrumentalities.[23]

But current economic science does not permit us to say much about this mixing and weighing—not even in the form of if-then statements. For example, take the question of public sector versus private sector production of a good or service. According to economic theory, when should we prefer one or the other? A recent review confesses ignorance:

While public production in the absence of informational problems is superior to private production (because it corrects monopoly biases or externalities, for instance), it introduces a problem of delegation of control. As the empirical debate is far from being settled, we do not think that economists have yet brought a convincing and definite analysis of the relative advantages of public and private production.[24]

Or consider the "structural adjustment" of an economy. What is known about the costs and benefits of various ways of adjusting? Here are the conclusions of one of the World Bank's leading experts:

The links between policies and objectives are complex, with large gaps in knowledge on both theoretical and empirical grounds. . . . It has to be recognized that the analytical basis for some micro policies in an adjustment program is relatively weak. The theory underlying the effects of eliminating distortions (real and financial) is not well suited to policymaking, as it quickly raises welfare issues. For example, whether removing consumer subsidies will raise overall efficiency and production is still an open question; the same is true of a devaluation.

Even on the macroeconomic front, some serious theoretical and empirical issues are still unresolved. . . . [F]or example, . . . the effects of fiscal policy on demand are ambiguous. . . . Finally, and perhaps most important, there is still much to be learned about what drives growth in developing countries and in particular about the relationship between short-run stabilization policies and long-run growth.[25]

More generally, economist Paul Samuelson concluded years ago, "There are no rules concerning the proper role of government that can be established by a priori reasoning."[26]

BEYOND THE STATE-MARKET DEBATE

Thus, the third world economic policy maker may feel abandoned. Given the imperfections of both the market and the state in countries such as Bolivia, existing research provides little empirical guidance

as to when to choose market or government. Economic theory itself
is not compelling, despite the enthusiasm of the popularizers of the
untrammeled market.

But this does not mean we must resign ourselves to current
imperfections. Moving beyond the quasi-ideological debate over
state versus market, we may pose other questions. How can the
environment for fair and efficient markets be created? How can the
state itself be made to function better? What is known about
strategies to overcome ethnic inequalities within developing
countries?

Chapters 3 to 5 look at markets, particularly those that affect
the small farmer and the urban informal sector. What might be done
to *democratize* markets—that is, to improve market institutions—not
just for sophisticates who have access to capital and foreign buyers
but also for the poor?

If policies can be found that make markets work better—and I
think they can—the benefits are many: efficiency and growth, redistribution, and political support and stability. Some would go further: if such policies cannot be found, macroeconomic stabilization
and liberalization will likely fail.

Many books might be written on this subject. From the gamut
of market-improving policies, I have chosen to focus on just one set:
information in markets. Recent advances in microeconomics provide, I think, useful insights into common problems with markets in
developing countries. By reviewing some of this theory in a non-
technical way and examining some cases of markets that worked
and didn't work because of informational problems, we can develop
guidelines for what government can do, and what the private sector
itself can do, to make markets work better.

Chapters 6 to 9 turn from improving markets to improving the
functioning of government itself. The underlying assumption of this
section of the book is that some amount of government is a given—
for example, a Ministry of Finance, public agencies in charge of
various sorts of infrastructure, and activities in education and
health. Then we ask, "In difficult environments such as Bolivia's,
what can be done to enhance the efficiency and fairness of public
institutions?" We focus on three topics—improving incentives,
combating corruption, and the decentralization of public management. These are three of many possible issues, and no claim is made
for thoroughness even there. But again, the economics of information provides interesting and important insights that help us rethink
the roles of the state.

Chapters 10 to 12 move to quite a different issue, an often

overlooked but basic issue of economic development. In a remarkably high percentage of poor countries, certain ethnic groups systematically lag in the economic and educational fields. For example, Bolivia's "Indian" population is overrepresented in every dimension of poverty. What are the roles of the state in helping backward groups? I examine some of the strategies undertaken by other developing countries to redress economic and educational inequalities among ethnic groups. At the same time, I hope to clear away some of the conceptual and emotional underbrush that has hampered discussions of this problem. The economics of information plays a central role here, too.

In the course of the book, certain themes emerge. One is the importance to economic development of *information* and *institutional development*. For example, one reason why market institutions work poorly in developing countries is that information about prices, quantities, and quality is not readily available. One reason why government bureaucracies work poorly is that information about outputs and outcomes, about laudable achievements and illicit activities, is scarce. One reason backward groups are subject to institutionalized discrimination is that "group information" is available but "individual information" is scanty. The fundamental importance of information for economic development generates, at least in my mind, a number of additional ideas. These ideas—or perhaps better put: hypotheses, guesses, and ruminations—are the subject of the final section.

Another theme of this book is that additional policy measures are needed that go beyond the remarkable structural adjustment programs undertaken by Bolivia and other developing countries. These measures also take us beyond—or rather perhaps it is better to say "below"—the important current debate over markets versus governments. They concentrate instead on ways to improve the functioning of market and government institutions under the adverse conditions actually faced by poor countries: what we might call "adjusting to reality."

2

THE SOCIOECONOMIC ENVIRONMENT CONSTRAINS MARKET AND STATE

LIKE EVERY OTHER COUNTRY, Bolivia is unique, and in this chapter we consider some of its distinguishing features. But we do so to illustrate a broader theme—namely, that the difficult socioeconomic environments in developing countries tend to have an adverse effect on their markets and government institutions. Consequently, a country's strategy for economic development must go beyond macroeconomic adjustment and beyond the debate over how much market and how much state.

POVERTY AND ITS CORRELATES

Bolivia is a country of contrasts. Its six and a half million inhabitants occupy a land twice the size of France that ranges from the Andes to the Amazon jungle, from the *altiplano* to the flatlands of the Chaco. Bolivia is a poor country. In 1986 the per capita income was $600, second lowest in the Americas (ahead of Haiti). Despite a relatively large number of doctors—about one for every 2,000 inhabitants— Bolivia is near the bottom of the Americas in life expectancy, infant mortality, calories consumed per day, and infant birth weight.

Perhaps the most salient feature of Bolivia's socioeconomic environment is that the greatest poverty resides in the indigenous Indian populations.[1] This creates special challenges for development policy.

Poverty and ethnicity have interacted throughout Bolivia's

history. One need not subscribe to the old racist theses of Alcides
Arguedas and Gabriel René Moreno, or to contemporary conspiracy
theories of internal colonialism such as Fausto Reinaga's, to observe
that remarkable economic, educational, and nutritional inequalities
separate the 70 percent of the population who are indigenous peoples from the 30 percent classified as mestizos and whites.[2] Most of
the indigenous peoples are Aymara- or Quechua-speaking and live
in the rural highlands. Most are poor. The rates of infant mortality in
these areas are among the highest in the world.[3] Of every thousand
campesinos who start elementary school, only eleven finish second-
ary school. Only 2 to 6 percent of the small farmers, most of whom
are Indians, receive any formal credit. The ratio of urban to rural
salaries was 15 to 1 in 1975. Both labor markets and social interaction
are de facto exclusionary along ethnic lines. In terms of living conditions as well as education, the language groups in Bolivia differ
markedly, as Table 2-1 shows.

Over the past three decades, there have been improvements.
Life expectancy has risen, and infant mortality has declined. Indigenous groups participate more in the monetized economy. Census
data document an increasing bilingualism, perhaps a sign of growing integration. Moreover, internal migration to the richer agricul-

TABLE 2-1

Language Spoken and Standards of Living in Bolivia
(percentage)

	Spanish Only	Spanish/ Native Language	Native Language Only
Education			
No education	10	12	96
Only basic education	34	46	3
Intermediate or technical education	41	34	<1
University education	13	7	<1
Services			
Electricity	70	61	16
Piped water	69	60	21
Sanitary facility	66	33	5
Sewer	27	23	1

SOURCE: Based on World Bank, *Bolivia Poverty Report*, Report no. 8643-BO (Washington, D.C.,
3 October 1990), which takes data from Instituto Nacional de Estadísticas, *Encuesta Nacional de
Vivienda y Población* (1988). The percentages under each column are not given, but p. 13 of the
report says that 51 percent of the whole country consists of "households speaking native language"
(36 percent of the urban households, 68 percent of the rural ones). The report notes that the ENPV
has been criticized "for not reflecting the Bolivian reality" (p. 6). The ENPV's preface says that
"remote and isolated" areas of the country were not visited, so it may be "too optimistic" (p. 7).

tural lands of eastern Bolivia has probably led to less ethnic separatism.

Still, what in the sociology of Latin America has come to be called "the indigenous problem" is nowhere more pronounced than in Bolivia. Abject poverty and ethnicity coincide to a remarkable degree—a fact that tends to be ignored in national plans and international aid documents. Ethnic inequalities are uncomfortable realities. They have implications for economic development, social justice, and political stability. In Bolivia, as in many other poor countries, group inequalities are the first reality of underdevelopment.

THE MOTOR OF GROWTH: EXTRACTIVE INDUSTRIES

Beginning with Potosí's fabulous mountain of silver in the sixteenth century, Bolivia's extractive industries have been the driving force of its economy. Tin has been a mainstay for much of this century, but few people today are optimistic about its future. Nonetheless, the government's economic plans call for great increases in mining investments and exports over the next decade. Gold prospects in particular appear good. In recent decades Bolivia has become a petroleum producer, and hydrocarbons today account for more than half the country's exports and half of its public revenues. Historically, 80 to 90 percent of Bolivia's exports have come from these extractive industries, which is one of the world's highest indices of export concentration in mining, metals, and hydrocarbons.

Various forms of mining differ in their economics. Although small-scale mining and cooperatives have a role in Bolivia,[4] most new investment will be in large, capital-intensive, high-risk activities. Similarly, the economics of the hydrocarbons sector is skewed in the direction of large projects, lots of capital and risk, and little job creation. These are not the characteristics that give rise to markets with small firms participating under conditions of perfect competition. Instead, the conditions in Bolivia, as in other developing countries, have tended to favor large, oligopolistic firms that are heavily dependent on foreign capital, technology, and management. These same conditions have also generated powerful labor unions with their own forms of monopoly power.

The history of Bolivia's mining sector exhibits in exaggerated form the excesses of monopoly capital and powerful unions. For most Bolivians, the sins of the capitalists justified the nationalization of the mines in the 1950s. The private sector had failed. But after nationalization, new problems emerged in the state-owned enterprises COMIBOL (mining) and YPFB (petroleum). Investment was meager, especially in mining. Management was haphazard. Union unrest did not abate. As a result, economic inefficiency spread throughout the mining and energy sectors. By the 1980s most people had reached a new verdict: the public sector had failed.

The roles of the state and the private sector in these extractive industries have yet to be settled. With the collapse of the international tin market in 1985–1986, the government closed long-uneconomical mines, dismissed almost three-quarters of the miners in COMIBOL, and began to encourage private investment in mining. In the hydrocarbon sector, Bolivia's constitution mandates state control. Nonetheless, recent laws have opened up concessions and created new contracting arrangements in order to lure private investment. At the same time that the government hoped to attract foreign investment in both mining and energy, the hydrocarbon sector was scheduled to receive 38 percent of all public investments from 1990 to 1995.

Even if the private sector takes on more of the exploration and production, the state will have important tasks: negotiating with foreign companies (for concessions, equity-sharing, management contracts, service and work contracts, production-sharing arrangements, and so forth); negotiating with foreign customers (especially in the case of the vital natural gas exports to Argentina and Brazil); setting tax policies; and regulating these industries.

So the private and public sectors will both have roles to play. But neither the market nor the state tends to live up to its theoretical promise in a sector characterized by high capital intensity, lumpy investments, high risk, low job creation, politicized unions, and past abuses by both public and private management. Strategies for the future should not, therefore, debate the general merits of privatization or nationalization. Instead, they must explore ways to improve both private and public performance.

HIGHLAND AGRICULTURE

Bolivia's highlands are occupied by large numbers of poor farmers and herdsmen eking out an existence on small plots of land. Almost all are indigenous peoples. Most small farmers barely subsist. "In fact," concludes one study, "if the labor opportunity cost is taken into account, their income would be negative."[5] Property rights are in many cases unclear. In Oruro, only 31 percent of the farmers have definite title to their farms. The national figure is 56.5 percent. Despite the recent effort put into large irrigation projects, the results have been unsatisfactory. Without range management, productivity remains low and environmental degradation continues unabated.

The highlands present a paradox. On one hand, Bolivia's agricultural productivity is low and declining. On the other hand, research "indicates that the highland region is potentially one of the richest, most productive grasslands in the world, rivaling or exceeding the best natural range in the western United States."[6] According to the experts, the *altiplano* should be able to support four times the present production of range vegetation.

Would highland agriculture obtain better results under different modes of organization? Under the Incas, the rangelands were carefully protected. The penalty for cutting grass without permission was death.

> The elaborate system of irrigation and the organization
> of collective work for the transport of rocks, planting,
> and harvesting were dismantled and fell into disuse,
> so that after having been one of the most advanced
> technologies known to the world under the Incas,
> Bolivian agriculture became, and has remained to this
> day, backward, primitive, subsistence farming.[7]

Economic theory suggests that irrigation schemes and range management are not ideally suited to an unregulated private market. But it is also true that Bolivia's recent experience with state intervention in highland agriculture has not been good—certainly, it has produced nothing that approaches Incan efficiency. In most developing countries, government institutions in rural areas are weak. Studies in Bolivia show that public institutions in agriculture suffer from bloated employment, politicization, low pay, and virtually no connection between pay and performance.[8]

Overcentralization has crippled rural development:

> Bolivia's public administration structure extends to the
> local community as a colonial power would govern its
> subjects. The canton is the smallest formal
> administrative unit of the state. Its boundaries do not
> necessarily correspond to those of local communities.
> The *corregidor* is the lowest state representative at the
> canton level. He does not represent local citizens or
> community organizations; he represents the executive
> branch of government. Yet, the *corregidor* has authority

over local organizations and structures just as in colonial times. This persistent colonial structure of government oscillates between benevolent paternalism and outright dictatorship, depending on the changes at the head of government. . . .

The limitations that this history places on the rural and agricultural sectors are more severe than they seem. Without being able to establish formal units of government at the local level, agricultural and rural sectors cannot take actions to build or maintain farm-to-market roads or construct conservation or drainage infrastructure. The rural population cannot legally tax itself to provide this kind of infrastructure or rural services. It cannot infringe upon private land for access or hire staff, or enter into any kind of contract. Thus, it is limited [to] two kinds of actions: negotiating with the central government and organizing on an informal basis, using social pressures on its members.[9]

Given these problems, what should be done? Leaving irrigation and range management entirely to the market runs afoul of economies of scale, commons problems, and ecological difficulties. But neither do we have confidence that Bolivia's state apparatus is benevolent or efficient. Neither the market nor the government functions well.

TRANSPORTATION

One of the defining features of the Bolivian economy is the difficulty of moving goods from one place to another.

Bolivia is landlocked and has only about 1,800 kilometers of paved roads. Even where there are roads, travel is hard. The Andean range is at its broadest in Bolivia. Rural areas are sparsely populated, and distances between cities are large. In the north, rivers and flooding present serious problems for transportation. Building roads is expensive, since construction technologies are capital intensive in most regions and corruption is widespread. Road maintenance has historically been poor.

As a result, Bolivia spends about twice as much on transportation to produce every dollar of national income as the average developing country. A World Bank study in 1987 estimated that road users in Bolivia spent $700 to $900 million per year on vehicle operating costs.[10] This was equivalent to 18 to 23 percent of the gross domestic product. The corresponding figure in many developing countries is only 10 to 12 percent. The value added in commercial transport in Bolivia made up only 8 percent of GDP.[11]

High transportation costs are a primary obstacle to efficient domestic markets and to exports. Consider rail transport. In May 1986 the cost per ton per kilometer of moving goods from Santa Cruz to the Argentine border was 2.59 times higher than the cost of shipping the same goods from the border to Rosario, Argentina. Similarly, the cost of transporting goods from Santa Cruz to the border with Brazil was 1.72 times greater than the cost of shipping them from the border to Sao Paulo.[12] It reportedly costs as much to transport a carton of beer from Cochabamba to Iquique (a Chilean free port) as it costs to ship a carton of beer from Germany to Iquique.

In most countries, road construction and maintenance are funded by the government. These matters cannot be left to the market alone, although the private sector can participate. Yet in Bolivia, as in many other developing countries, government-funded road construction is a favorite haunt of corruption. Similarly with railroads: in environments like Bolivia's, neither the market nor the government alone is guaranteed to provide efficient results.

EXTRALEGAL ECONOMIES

What are the proper roles of the state when much of the economy is outside the purview of the law? We can distinguish three extralegal economies: cocaine, contraband, and the informal sector. The first two are public problems. The third may be an opportunity.

Cocaine is a unique and complicated industry. Part of the industry is legal, indeed highly valued, and part is illegal, indeed highly criminal. Perhaps a tenth of the production of coca in Bolivia goes to traditional uses—coca chewing by indigenous peoples. These uses verge on the sacred, according to anthropologist Catherine Allen. "The ritual maintenance of this bond between people and land is a constant process, carried on in the daily routine as well as in the more intensified context of religious rites. Coca is the major vehicle for this ritual 'work.' "[13] The medical and pharmacological effects of coca chewing are apparently not well understood. Long-term coca chewing does not seem to be bad for the health, but it does not seem to be good for it, either. Many past efforts to eradicate coca chewing have failed. Because of its intimate connection to Bolivian culture, some coca production will continue—and will continue to be legal.

The other nine-tenths of Bolivia's coca crop goes through various stages of transformation toward the production of cocaine. At various stages, the production process requires large quantities of so-called precursor chemicals. It also requires transportation: from the Chapare region (where about two-thirds of Bolivia's coca is grown) to the jungles of the Beni and other northern and western districts (where the cocaine laboratories are located), and then sometimes on to Brazil, Colombia, and elsewhere for processing (but less than formerly), and then to centers for reexport. Most of Bolivia's cocaine eventually reaches the United States: an increasing proportion, perhaps a fifth, goes to Europe. Bolivian sources estimate that about 78 metric tons of cocaine were produced in Bolivia in 1989, up from 72 metric tons in 1988.[14] U.S. estimates are higher: about 54,000 hectares of coca under cultivation yielding perhaps 121 metric tons of cocaine HCL, up from about 50,000 hectares and 105 metric tons in 1988. The combined effects of seizures of cocaine and acreage reduction programs were estimated to be equivalent to less than 10 percent of production.

The industry is vertically integrated to an extent. Virtually all of the 40,000-plus coca growers are peasants, mostly indigenous peoples. Alternative crops are less profitable—by at least 10 percent, usually much more—and they require much more care by the farmer, whereas coca is a hearty shrub that grows without fertilizer, pesticides, or horticulture. Several thousand people process the leaf into coca paste, and many hundreds are wholesale paste buyers. Several hundred laboratories process the paste into base and cocaine HCL. Some thirty criminal organizations are involved in this trafficking, of which twenty-five have laboratories and five only buy and sell.

In 1987 the value of Bolivia's official exports was about $600 million and imports about $930 million. Estimates of the annual income generated by cocaine—the income that remains in the country—were close to $400 million.[15]

The cocaine industry is said to be less efficient, less organized, and less profitable in Bolivia than in Colombia. There is also less violence and more buying and selling on credit, which may make the industry easier to disrupt. Alarmingly, in the wake of Colombia's upheavals in the late 1980s, many laboratories moved to Bolivia, and hundreds of Colombian criminals did, too.

Producer prices for coca in the Chapare show marked seasonal and other variations. Since international demand does not exhibit such fluctuations, the observed variability must be related mostly to supply. But the price variations seem too large—over months and, in the same month, among the three Chapare trafficking centers of Sinahota, Ivirgarzama, and Eteramazama.[16]

So, we find what by Bolivian standards is a rich industry and by any standards one with highly idiosyncratic features.

The crop is legal—as already mentioned, coca is a cherished cultural commodity—but its transformation is illegal. Coca growing in some areas is legal, in others illegal. Peasants are paid not to grow coca, but the use of herbicides in crop eradication is forbidden by the country's constitution.

As we have seen, transportation is a key constraint to Bolivian commerce. But in the case of cocaine, bulky and now illegal precursors must be brought to the Chapare and to remote jungle locations. Various stages of processed cocaine must be moved by air and on land on paths and bad roads. Exporting must be done by small plane or boat, in difficult terrain. Much buying and selling is done on credit. All these difficult steps have taken place in Bolivia, a country where study after study of agriculture has documented the constraints of infrastructure, entrepreneurship, and rural credit. Moreover, peasants who were supposed by scholars to be irrevocably tied to their Andean plots have migrated mightily to the jungly coca-growing regions.

A remarkable success in agricultural development has occurred in Bolivia. Unfortunately, it involves an illicit export.

Contraband has been less studied. According to economist Samuel Doria Medina, from 1980 to 1983 contraband imports may have amounted to 38 percent of registered imports.[17] With the laundering of narcodollars, the percentage is probably much higher now.

The political economy of cocaine and contraband is complicated. Clearly, both "industries" play a huge though undocumented role in Bolivia's impoverished economy. They also create externalities of many kinds. They spawn corruption and intimidation. The government's enforcement efforts, including those spurred by the United States and other governments, have their own costs, both direct and indirect. Without addressing these various dimensions in detail, we note that neither the ideology of privatization nor that of state-led growth do justice to the complexities.

The term "informal sector" refers to small *comerciantes* and producers of goods and services who remain unregistered as businesses in government records. They do not pay social security or most taxes—although they may be subject to *sentaje* charges and collections by police and government officials. The informal sector is large in many poor countries. Self-employed microentrepreneurs who work alone or with a family member account for 33 percent of the labor force in La Paz, 41 percent in Cochabamba, and 33 percent in Santa Cruz. In La Paz, it is estimated that 80 percent of all households have one or more members in such an enterprise.[18] According to the Bolivian Chamber of Industry, some 92 percent of businesses have three employees or fewer. Not all of these people are in the informal sector, but that admittedly ambiguous term is said to apply to 60 to 65 percent of the economically active population.[19]

This sector is informal in part to evade government regulations and taxes, in part because its participants are not eligible for government benefits such as property rights and credit. Although some see these sidewalk capitalists as a dynamic element in the economy, others perceive a sector that is mostly inefficient and redundant. The proper roles for government here are not obvious.

MALFUNCTIONING MARKETS FOR CREDIT AND AGRICULTURE

Free-market reforms throughout the world give priority to "getting prices right" for credit and for agricultural commodities. No doubt these changes are important ingredients of economic development. But evidence in Bolivia and elsewhere shows that reforming interest rates and prices has a disappointing outcome if the markets for credit and agricultural products do not work well for small farmers and small businesses.

For a variety of reasons, small borrowers find credit to be expensive and difficult to obtain. They lack collateral. Lending has certain fixed transaction costs, so that as a percentage of the amount loaned, small loans are more expensive to the lender. Small borrowers are often unfamiliar with or unskilled in the paper work required for bank loans. And they may live in areas with few official sources of credit.

As a consequence, the formal credit market does not usually serve small borrowers very well. Therefore they often rely on informal sources of credit willing to meet them where they live and to accept higher risks—at a price, of course: interest rates in informal credit markets often run 50 percent and more. Since few projects are viable at such high interest rates, small borrowers cannot take advantage of their opportunities—and economic growth is stunted.

Agricultural markets suffer deficiencies as well. Farmers may be unaware of prices in regional capitals and thus may market their goods at the wrong times and may be exploited by transporters and middlemen. Grades and standards are often underdeveloped, which erodes the incentive to produce better quality. This problem has a particularly harmful effect on products that compete against imports or are exportable. Inefficient storage systems lead to peak markets and price instability. The fear of exploitation and corruption discourages cooperation among farmers and weakens the vertical chains of marketing. But if farmers insist on marketing their own produce, they sacrifice economies of scale and specialization.

Bolivia's free-market reforms are threatened by imperfections in credit and product markets. In such conditions, as experience shows, the hoped-for supply responses from liberalized product prices may come too slowly, if at all.[20] Consequently, the small farmer, small business person, and participant in the informal sector may reap few benefits from economic stabilization and liberalization.

What can the state do to rectify these market failures? In some countries, the government has taken over credit markets and agricultural marketing. The results have not been encouraging, as we shall see in subsequent chapters. Witness, for example, the abysmal performance of the government-run Bolivian Agricultural Bank. State development banks and marketing boards have been victimized by nonmarket failures: poor incentives for officials, monopoly power over borrowers and farmers that is corruptly used, politicization, favoritism, and pilfering.

Once again, simplistic recommendations that the market be allowed to work or that the government be allowed to take over are unlikely to be helpful.

IMPLICATIONS FOR THE ROLES OF THE STATE

We have been analyzing some of the features of Bolivia's socioeconomic environment. Although Bolivia is unique, its experience helps broaden our understanding of the proper roles of the state. Clearly, in a socioeconomic environment like Bolivia's, extreme arguments for an untrammeled market are inappropriate. Macroeconomic stabilization and liberalization are certainly welcome, but they are not likely to be sufficient to promote economic efficiency and justice. The leading sectors of the economy—in this case, the extractive industries (mining and hydrocarbons), highland agriculture, transportation, extralegal activities, small-scale credit, and many agricultural markets—will function inefficiently if left entirely to the play of market forces.

But plainly this does not mean the government should take these sectors over. The Bolivian environment has not been conducive to efficient state action either. The problem is that in circumstances like Bolivia's, many markets do not work well and many parts of government do not work well.

Consequently, economic strategies must move beyond the question of the proper extent of market and state activities. They must address the question of how the government can work with the private sector to improve or overcome the underlying conditions that render markets inefficient. And policy makers must determine how the government itself can be reformed in ways that will render its nonmarket failures—especially, poor incentives, corruption, and overcentralization—less likely and less serious.

As in most developing countries, poverty is a central issue in Bolivia. Freer markets and improved public services will benefit the poor in the long run. But the ethnic correlates of poverty raise vital questions about the role of the state. What can public policies do to overcome ethnic inequalities in education, income, and employment?

These are some of the central questions in Bolivia. Are they not applicable in many other countries?

3

INFORMATION AND MARKET INSTITUTIONS

IN NOVEMBER 1988 I asked the head of the agricultural section of the U.S. Agency for International Development in Bolivia what he thought was the foremost policy problem facing Bolivian agriculture.

"Grades and standards," he replied without hesitation. "They don't exist. Without them domestic markets don't work, and exports are almost impossible."

This is a strong response, and some people may find it a surprising one. But in many countries agricultural markets do not fulfill their promise because the institutions for measuring, certifying, and rewarding quality are weak.

Markets often malfunction in Bolivia and other underdeveloped countries. The causes of market failure are many. All sorts of markets, from agriculture to credit, from labor to housing, require certain foundations, without which these markets function inefficiently and unfairly. Moreover, these foundations depend for their existence on collective action, such as might be undertaken or encouraged by the government. These foundations include:

- a common currency not savaged by hyperinflation
- a rule of law that enforces contracts and prevents theft
- a clear system of property rights
- a financial system that includes not only macroeconomic interventions by the state but also credit and the enforcement of loan repayment
- systems of market information

Although each of these foundations is important and they are often interrelated, we will focus on the last—that is, on information about the *quality* of goods and services, labor and housing, risks and portfolios, or whatever happens to be traded. When market institutions do a bad job of distinguishing, certifying, and rewarding variations in quality, markets will malfunction or even fail to exist. These shortcomings are particularly notable in markets available to the poor farmer and the informal sector: the markets for agricultural products and for credit.

In this chapter we introduce the problem of quality in markets with several examples. Then we examine some standard results on the efficiency of competitive markets and show how things change when information is incomplete, imperfect, and asymmetric. By examining information problems in markets, we can begin to understand the seemingly bizarre or contradictory market behavior observed in developing countries.

Most important, we develop a framework to help policy makers think about ways to make markets work better. In Chapter 4 we apply this framework to two case studies, one of success in making markets work, the other of failure. In Chapter 5, we return to the framework for policy analysis and consider several generalizations.

INFORMATION AND MARKETS

When I lived in Karachi, Pakistan, for two years in the mid-1970s, its urban milk market was working poorly. Upon studying the wholesale food market, my colleagues at the University of Karachi and I learned that quality was a problem.

The quality of milk varied from seller to seller, and information about quality was asymmetric: the sellers knew more than the buyers. The consumer knew that a common practice of sellers was to add water to the milk, but the consumer could not easily judge whether and how much a particular vendor had watered his milk down on a given day. A consumer might visit the main market in Karachi and purchase milk from any of a large number of small vendors, each of whom sat in the shade with large covered vats of milk. The consumer could test the milk's freshness by lifting the lid of a vat and taking a whiff, but the market contained no institutions to certify that the milk had such-and-such an amount of butterfat. There were no grades, no brand names, no minimum levels of quality. There was only one market price for milk.

The sellers knew whether and how much they had watered down the milk. Unfortunately, consumers could not simply ask the sellers about the amount of water in the milk because the consumers knew that the sellers at various points in the marketing chain had an incentive to mislead about this dimension of quality in order to make a higher profit.[1] In the absence of better information about quality, Karachi's milk market functioned poorly, leading to suboptimal levels of milk production and consumption.

Similar problems were overcome in India, as explained in Chapter 4, with the aid of information about an effective way to gauge the quality of milk at each stage of marketing. A simple, inexpensive, hand-operated machine was developed for testing the fat content of the milk. Farmers could now be sure of receiving prices congruent with the quality of their cows' milk and would not have an incentive to water down their milk. At each stage of the marketing chain, consumers could readily ascertain whether the milk had been watered down. Brand names were used at the final, consumer stage. The market for milk worked more efficiently, and the quantity and quality of milk in India soared.

Better market institutions for providing information about quality can help to make markets work. But what do we mean by "quality"?

Quality refers to a variable attribute of a good or service, a laborer, or a risky investment that makes it more or less desirable for a particular purpose in a particular setting.[2] Thus, when we speak of the quality of shrimp we refer to their type, size, freshness, and cleanliness. We may distinguish various dimensions of the quality of a worker for a particular job, and across jobs these dimensions of quality will vary. We may metaphorically speak of the quality of potential debtors in reference to the likelihood of their repaying a loan. Both economic theory and abundant experience show that markets malfunction or fail to exist when they do not effectively distinguish, certify, and reward variations in quality. Fortunately, theory and experience also offer guidance about ways to make markets work better in these domains.

The aspect of quality that we are discussing should not be confused with other issues related to "quality." We are not saying, as some writers have, that developing countries should strive to produce goods and services of the highest possible quality.[3] This may be true in certain cases. Usually, however, the highest possible quality is not an appropriate objective for a producer, or a consumer, or a developing nation.[4] Nor are we concerned with the design of an optimal quality control system. Statisticians and systems analysts

---

ISRAELI ORANGES

Soon after Israel became a state, the international market for citrus fruit soared, making exports highly attractive. But exports grew more rapidly than did the institutions for quality control and measurement. The market for oranges began to break down:

> The citrus grower is paid for the fruit he markets on the basis of the average price which the produce obtains in foreign markets. In other words, when the citrus grower raises fruit of a certain size and type, he receives the average price obtained by fruit of that size irrespective of the quality of his wares (as an individual producer). . . . Hence there is very strong incentive for every citrus grower to export as large a quantity of fruit as possible, irrespective of its quality (since even if the fruit sent by the individual citrus grower is of low quality, the remuneration he receives will hardly be affected, and each citrus grower is only a very small factor in determining the price of the entire consignment).

The grower was paid according to the average quality in the market and not according to his own efforts and achievements. Bad oranges were as profitable as good ones. Growers therefore took less care with making sure their oranges were ripe, unblemished, and properly sorted. The average quality of Israeli oranges plummeted, threatening its export market.

This market imperfection was soon ameliorated. The Israeli government and the country's orange growers worked together to measure quality at the various stages of marketing. Coupled with a grading and permit system, the result was a highly successful export market.

SOURCE: Centre for Policy Studies, Quality Control in a Developing Economy: A Case Study of Israel (Jerusalem: Israel Program for Scientific Translations, 1970): 109–10.

---

have long studied ways to ensure that a given level of quality is met within certain tolerance limits. Techniques of acceptance sampling and process control address such questions as "What sample size does one need so that one is 95 percent sure that not more than X percent of the production is defective?" More recently, interest has grown in quality groups and other organizational means of ensuring and improving quality.[5] New research examines the extent to which these means can be utilized in various kinds of organizations, economies, and cultures.[6] Again these are important issues, but they are tangential to our concerns in this chapter.

Rather, we are interested in what happens when markets reward or do not reward variations in quality—and how market institutions can be made to work better.

STUDYING AGRICULTURAL MARKETS

We will explore these ideas in the context of a *locus classicus* of competitive theory, agricultural markets. The baseline for the study of agricultural markets in developing countries has been the simple model of perfect competition. As a recent World Bank report states,

> Farm sectors comprise highly competitive
> businessmen, producing a relatively homogeneous
> commodity for sale in a market with numerous, price
> and quality conscious consumers. In other words,
> agriculture would appear to be the ideal industry in
> which to realize a textbook-perfect competitive market
> to the benefit of both producers and consumers.[7]

For simplicity's sake the basic textbook model makes many assumptions:[8]

- The largest firm makes up a small fraction of the industry's sales or purchases.
- Participants in the market act independently and impersonally.
- Entry to the market is free.
- The commodity traded is homogeneous and fungible.
- The time and conditions of a sale are determined only by the participants in the transaction.
- Participants are economically motivated.

A final assumption is of particular interest to us:

- All participants in the market have complete knowledge of offers to buy and sell.

Economists use the textbook model to study the behavior of markets. They examine how successfully price movements can be modeled as a function of competitive supply and demand. If price movements do not follow the competitive model, it is a sign of an inefficient market. If they do, the market is efficient. Economists also use the textbook model normatively. A well-functioning agricultural market *should* allow free entry and exit, free movement of prices, and so forth.[9] The basic idea is this: if the market is competitive, it will be efficient, and government interventions will only lead to inefficiencies.

Consider, for example, the application of textbook economics to agricultural traders and middlemen. In most developing countries, middlemen have a bad name. Many farmers, consumers, and government officials would scorn the hypothesis that agricultural markets function like the efficient, competitive markets of elementary economics. Typical is the view that middlemen rip off farmers with low prices, gouge consumers with high prices, and restrict trade.[10] Some scholars have endorsed the idea that the poor farmer, in the words of Paul A. Baran, easily "slips into complete dependency on 'his' merchant or moneylender. It hardly needs to be added that the profits collected by the latter assume exorbitant proportions."[11] Such beliefs have been used to justify governmental intervention in food marketing.[12]

Most economists who study agricultural markets, however, tend to view traders and middlemen more approvingly. Using the textbook model, economists deem a market competitive and therefore efficient if the profits earned by middlemen and other marketers are not "too large." Marketing margins have received considerable attention in the empirical analysis of agricultural markets in developing countries. Studies have shown that the profits earned by agricultural middlemen are not "exorbitant."[13] Their margins seem justified, given the costs and risks incurred.[14]

Moreover, few barriers to entry exist. Traders seem to compete with one another. Indeed, to some observers the problem is too many middlemen and traders, too much competition:

> The most striking feature of this socioeconomic
> stratum is its *size*. No one who has ever set foot in
> China of old, in Southeast Asia, in the Near East, or in
> pre-war Eastern Europe can have failed to notice the
> staggering multitude of merchants, dealers, peddlers,
> trading-stand operators, and people with nondescript
> occupations crowding the streets, squares, and
> coffeehouses of their cities.[15]

To some observers, the fact that many able people have been drawn into marketing activities of many kinds has siphoned off potential entrepreneurs. "While southern Asia does not lack a class of entrepreneurs," wrote Edward Mason in 1955, "business enterprise tends to be concentrated in the distributive trades, exporting and importing, real estate speculation and money lending."[16] Whatever ill effects this may have on developing nations, a lack of competition in marketing does not seem to be one of them.

Thus, concerning agricultural traders and middlemen we perceive a contradiction between ordinary opinion in developing countries and the views of most economists. Does the usual finding of relatively small profit margins and relatively free entry mean that the common picture of exploitative middlemen is wrong?

Not always. Exploitation, at best a difficult word to define, may occur even when apparent margins are small. Asymmetric information can be the key to understanding the apparent contradiction.

First a humble example: *cheating on weights and measures*. Uma Lele provides a fascinating example from Ethiopia's Chilalo Agricultural Development Unit project in the late 1960s and early 1970s:

> Most price exploitation that has been observed in Ethiopian markets is covert, through false weights and measures, rather than overt. . . . There probably could not be a better testimonial to the importance of introducing correct weights and measures than the resistance received from traders to CADU's program of making available standard weights and measures at its trade centers. Cultivators in the program could use the facilities even if they were selling their produce to the private trades and not to the trade centers. The plan was tried on an experimental basis in four village markets and the primary market at Asella. . . . [L]ocal merchants resented it vehemently; and at times they were violent.[17]

Economists studying such traders might well document "reasonable" profit margins calculated in terms of the illicitly measured volume handled.

It is not uncommon in underdeveloped countries for *farmers to be ill-informed* about market prices. For example, a study in Malawi in 1972 showed that three-quarters of maize farmers did not know the price of maize that could be obtained through the legal outlets: "half of all the male growers surveyed had no idea of the current maize price and were unwilling even to hazard a guess."[18] Such ignorance opens farmers to exploitation. When no widely known market price exists, each transaction is attended by bargaining, which imposes costs and in general reduces the amount of trade from the economically optimal level.

"More generally," writes Joseph Stiglitz,

> while peasants may, in many respects, be rational, responding to market forces, they are not fully informed about the consequences either of their actions, or of the institutions through which they operate. Indeed, how could we expect them to be,

A MYSTERIOUS AUCTION

There is another way that evidence of "small margins" can mislead: when fraud and cheating are present. In the mid-1970s, several colleagues and I studied Karachi's wholesale fruit and vegetable markets, and we documented what looked like small and reasonable margins for traders. Auctioneers received produce from farmers and sold it to retailers for a commission of about 2 percent. The auctioneers weighed and sorted the produce, paid for its movement from truck or camel cart to auction stand, and occasionally provided credit. At first glance, then, there was no evidence of exploitation.

But problems surfaced when we searched for the right numbers to use in the calculation of profits. Many vegetables and some fruits were sold through open bidding. Others, including mangoes, were sold via an exotic form of sealed bids. The auctioneer would open a crate of mangoes and let the retailers and hawkers examine the goods. Then he would go to each prospective bidder in turn. The bidder would shake the auctioneer's hand, and the auctioneer would cover the handshake with a kerchief. By squeezing various combinations of fingers at various knuckles, the bidder would signal his price to the auctioneer. Then the auctioneer would move on to the next bidder. After the process was complete—it took a couple of minutes to get twenty or so bids—the auctioneer would designate a winner. No one would learn the winning price. The auctioneer's assistant wrote that down in a well-guarded record book.

We were fascinated by the existence of two forms of auctioning—open and sealed bid—in the space of a hundred meters in a single marketplace. Could both be efficient? Under what circumstances? For several weeks we gathered data and tried to develop theoretical economic models that could answer these questions. In the process, I became friends with the mango auctioneer. The purpose of the closed bidding system started to become clearer. Closed bids tended to be used on goods that were produced by farmers near Karachi; the open auction was used when goods were trucked in from afar. If the local farmer came to the Karachi market to ascertain the going price for mangoes, he would have a hard time finding out; winning bids were not made public. The auctioneer confessed to me that he routinely passed on to the growers lower prices than those he had actually received. Even if a grower came to the market, it would be difficult for him to discover the truth.

The mango seller confided that this was his way of making extra profits. He was exploiting the growers of mangoes. Did this mean such exploitation did not occur with the commodities sold via open auction? Not necessarily, he explained.

"You don't have to be secretive with the goods that are sold in the open auction, such as potatoes or coriander," he said. Both of those crops were shipped in from hundreds of kilometers away, and their growers would never come to the Karachi market. "The auctioneer in those cases can easily lie to the farmers about the prices their goods fetched."

Even when profit margins are low according to available records, therefore, exploitation may nonetheless be taking place.

when we, who have devoted our lives to studying
these questions, are ourselves uncertain?[19]

INFORMATION AS REMEDY

When information is an obstacle to fair and efficient markets, information may also be part of the solution. The Chilalo project in
Ethiopia transformed the local agricultural economy in part because
it employed standardized weights and measures. In the Karachi
fruit and vegetable market mentioned in the box on the facing page,
fraud and cheating would have been reduced if credible information
about market prices had been available.

Many economists have pointed out the importance of standard
measures and the dissemination of price information. Indeed, they
have emphasized government's leading role in these informational
domains. For example, in a textbook on agricultural marketing,
Harold F. Breimyer stated: "No government service to marketing
has been so recognized as proper or even essential to good marketing as the providing of market information."[20] Bruce F. Johnston
and Peter Kilby have argued that "a paucity of information about
prices" is one of the "inherent characteristics of an underdeveloped
economy." Consequently, government has an "important role in
perfecting the working of markets," including the dissemination of
information and the enforcement of "standards, weights and measures. . . . Supervised uniform weights and measures, engineering standards, soil surveys and similar provision of exact knowledge
about products and factors of production is an essential prerequisite
for the application of more advanced techniques as well as for the
improvement in the functioning of markets."[21]

Information is necessary to make incentives effective. "There
is no substitute," wrote the Nobel prize–winning economist Theodore W. Schultz in 1964, "for a system of product and factor prices as
a means of providing farmers, regardless of the size of farms, with
essential economic information."[22] But clearly, "getting prices
right" will not have this effect unless the prices are known and
linked to the quality of the products being marketed.

PRIVATE AND PUBLIC ACTIONS

Economic theory suggests that information is exactly the sort of
good for which atomistic markets perform badly. Put another way,

ZAMBIAN PRICE SURVEYS

When private firms cannot be encouraged to inform the public of their prices, perhaps the government can do the informing. An example from Zambia is interesting.

In the early 1980s Zambia was embroiled in what was then called its worst economic crisis since independence. The International Monetary Fund was asked to help, and in December 1982 substantial economic reform was undertaken. Prices of most consumer goods were decontrolled. By mid-1983, inflation had more than doubled. The prices of staples, particularly mealie meal (corn flour), rose faster than the rate of inflation. This led to popular unrest.

By mid-1984 elected officials in Zambia's one-party system were openly criticizing the government for not doing more about prices. Consumers as well as politicians laid the blame on "exploitation by unscrupulous traders and speculators."

Within the administration, the mounting pressure was felt most acutely within the Prices and Incomes Commission. One official described the situation to me this way:

> *We are supposed to formulate a price and income policy here, but in the current context it is difficult to pinpoint what that means. The public and the politicians expect us to act as police on prices. But now that prices are decontrolled, we don't have the legal mandate to do it even if we had the political power.*
>
> *So, we asked ourselves what we could do, realizing the public's expectations. We decided we would collect and publish information on the prices charged for the same goods by different stores.*
>
> *At present this is all we think we can do, convey market intelligence to consumers. This may help to prevent exploitation.*

markets often do not work well unless, through collective action or public policy, the right amounts and kinds of information are supplied and demanded. Although market forces can be utilized to induce the optimal provision of information, market forces alone are unlikely to lead to the best informational results.

When John Kenneth Galbraith and several colleagues studied the marketing system of Puerto Rico in the early 1950s, they learned that sales outlets engaged in relatively little price competition, even under what seemed to be competitive conditions. Galbraith—who, incidentally, was originally appointed to the Harvard faculty as an agricultural economist—and his coauthors emphasized that providing price information to consumers was a key to enhancing the efficiency of the urban food market. "It will not be easy to alter the

> *Therefore, the Prices and Incomes Commission carried out a price survey in Lusaka on August 8, 1984. Fifty-eight retail outlets, including marketplaces, were visited. Data were collected on the availability and the price of more than twenty basic commodities. The results attracted widespread attention. For example, only five of thirty-two shops that "wanted to sell bread" actually had any in stock, and fewer than a quarter of the shops wanting to sell milk were carrying it. Prices varied widely, even for "identical" commodities.[23]*
>
> *Commission chairman L. S. Chivuno appeared on television and radio and was interviewed in the press. The commission paid for a full-page advertisement in the Zambia Daily Mail that gave all the statistics and named particular stores at both ends of the price range. Commissioner Chivuno decried the 300 percent price differentials on some items. But his main point was simply that "if this kind of information is carried out at given intervals, the information conveyed will assist consumers in being better informed about where prices seem generally to be most attractive and where goods are available."*
>
> *From this example several points emerge. First, governments may intervene in price policies, not to set prices but rather to provide information about them. Second, traders themselves, who seemed miffed by the commission's surveys, may as a group benefit from the information in the long run. As economist William O. Jones noted in a survey of African markets, traders often are poorly informed about prices.[24] The operations of Zambian retailers may become more efficient as they learn more about market conditions. Third, price variation is not evil. Even at a given point in time in virtually all competitive markets, considerable price variations can exist—and can be theoretically explained.[25] Furthermore, price variations certainly reflect quality differentials. Part of the variation observed in Lusaka's prices for tomatoes and ordinary ground meat reflected the freshness, size, and quality of the products sold in different retail outlets.*

prevailing *attitude* toward the desirability and feasibility of price advertising in foods. No opportunity should be overlooked for encouraging it. Nothing is more likely to alter the 'tone' of competitive behavior than aggressive publicizing of lower prices."[26]

We might restate Galbraith's point as follows: even when the conditions of apparently perfect competition were met, this did not result in an efficient market because information was insufficient and asymmetrically held.

The Zambian initiative mentioned in the box above did not include information about the quality of the commodities of different sellers. Nor was quality included in the path-breaking studies of African markets directed by William O. Jones and summarized in his book, *Marketing Staple Food Crops in Tropical Africa*. This omission is perhaps understandable, since to have gathered such information would have required much more time and effort. But this omission of the quality dimension has a parallel in the theoretical study of agricultural (and other) markets in developing countries, where quality has been given too little attention.

The textbook model of competition is part of the problem. The standard model includes only quantity and price; the only information that matters concerns those two variables. (Thus, if information is mentioned at all, one speaks in terms of the need for standard weights and measures and for data on prices.) In the textbook model, goods are homogeneous. Price signals only tell a producer to supply more or less, not better or worse. For some purposes, these are convenient simplifications.

But introducing quality yields a rich harvest in insight and policy relevance. By including quality in the analysis of markets, we can fathom certain otherwise baffling institutions in primitive and bazaar economies. Many other market institutions—such as brand names, guarantees, contingent contracts, and standard grades—are hard to understand using textbook economics but can be analyzed as responses to adverse selection, moral hazard, and related problems. We can generate new hypotheses about "exploitative" traders, despite "low" margins.

More relevant to our practical focus—by including the quality variable we can generate new ways of assessing public and private policies toward market regimes.

QUALITY IN THE EMERGENCE OF A NATIONAL ECONOMY

Consider a simple story of the emergence of quality as a *problem* for the marketplace. "In agriculture," Barrington Moore, Jr., concluded, "economic development means the extension of market relationships over a much wider area than before, and the replacement of subsistence farming more and more by production for the market."[27] Economic development transforms primitive local economies. A more-than-local market develops from exogenous changes in production and transportation technologies and a growth in demand. Regional and national markets emerge. Commodities that used to be traded with one's fellow villager or neighbor are now transported to distant points. Credit markets expand— indeed, are created. National labor markets reallocate some people from their traditional villages to other regions and more specialized jobs. As the market expands, specialization takes place. But the division of labor among producers cannot proceed efficiently unless market institutions expand and improve. Experience shows that markets grow more rapidly than the rate of economic growth.[28] And this expansion creates new requirements for *information*—not only about aggregate quantities and average prices but also about quality. Increasing specialization requires increasingly specialized information.

Alas, institutions that provide, certify, and reward such information are often slow to develop. Without the right public and private policies, market institutions will lag behind, thereby braking economic growth.[29]

I mentioned that quality *emerges* as a problem; it was not much of an issue in what we might stylize as the primitive economy. Consider credit. Who is a good risk? Put another way, what is the "quality" of a prospective borrower in terms of his or her future capability and willingness to repay? In the primitive economy, the lender knows the borrower well. They are neighbors. The lender may also have powerful means to induce the borrower to repay, such as one relative has over another or the landlord has over the tenant or the owner of the only agricultural supply shop has over the farmer. The lender will have little trouble distinguishing the riskiness of one potential debtor from another. There is no informational problem about quality here.

Now, look at the situation in what we might call the transitional economy. Here, the economy expands because of exogenous changes in the technologies of production and transportation. A credit market of more than local scope is created, and it has advantages: economies of scale, greater competition, and the ability to spread risk over larger domains. But along with these advantages comes a disadvantage: evaluating the quality of potential loan recipients becomes more difficult. Little information on potential debtors is available to the transitional economy's lending market. Credit ratings do not yet exist, and it may be difficult to define or verify the collateral of loan applicants. Moreover, the means to enforce repayment may be limited.

As a result, what at first looks like a clear improvement in efficiency—an expanded and partly modernized credit market—may only benefit a small subset of the economically relevant population: those with readily visible collateral. Because the "quality" of potential debtors is not readily apparent, the size of the credit market will be limited. Credit will not be allocated to those who could use it best.[30] Until the market can develop better means to distinguish quality, the first result of the transition from the primitive to the underdeveloped credit market may be inefficient and regressive. Why? Because market institutions have not developed as fast as the market for credit.

Other markets in developing countries encounter related problems. In the process of development, many markets expand faster than the institutions needed to discern and enforce quality distinctions. The primitive economy evolved its own institutions to deal with problems of poor information about quality. The most pervasive were (and are) *reciprocity* and multiplex relationships. Suppose that you always trade with me and I always trade with you and we have many transactions in common. Over time we become adept at making judgments about the qualities of each other's goods—judgments that are difficult or impossible to make at the time of each transaction. Even though it restricts competition, we value our long-term trading relationship in part because it overcomes the problem of judging quality.

Anthropologists and others have recently used similar reasoning to explain a variety of institutions in primitive and bazaar economies. Legal scholar Richard A. Posner, for one, writes,

> With regard to trade in the ordinary sense—trade of
> unlike articles between strangers—in primitive society,
> transaction costs are presumably high because of the
> costs of information regarding the reliability of the
> seller, the quality of the product, and trading
> alternatives (that is, the market price). However,
> institutions have arisen which reduce these transaction
> costs.[31]

The institutions that substitute for good information about quality include gift-exchange, "customary" prices rather than prices determined by negotiation, "the transformation of an arm's-length contract relationship into an intimate status relationship," and "a buyer's deliberately overpaying a seller in order to induce the seller to deal fairly with him in the future. The overpayment increases the cost to the seller of a breach of trust that would induce the buyer to withdraw his patronage."[32] The "breach of trust" here means the misrepresentation of a product's quality.

Anthropologist Clifford Geertz writes that "the search for information—laborious, uncertain, complex, and irregular—is the central experience of life in the bazaar."[33]

> In the bazaar information is poor, scarce,
> maldistributed, inefficiently communicated, and

intensely valued. Neither the rich concreteness of
reliable knowledge that the ritualized character of
nonmarket economies makes possible, nor the
elaborate mechanisms for information generation and
transfer upon which industrial ones depend, are found
in the bazaar: neither ceremonial distribution nor
advertising: neither prescribed exchange partners nor
product standardization. The level of ignorance about
everything from product quality and going prices to
market possibilities and production costs is very high,
and much of the way in which the bazaar functions
can be interpreted as an attempt to reduce such
ignorance for someone, to increase it for someone, or
to defend someone against it.[34]

Geertz emphasizes "clientelization" (or repeated purchases) and
"intensive rather than extensive bargaining" as the key institutional
responses to informational problems.

As the market expands, the institutional responses of the
primitive and bazaar economies brake economic efficiency and may
even no longer be viable. Until institutions develop to certify and
reward quality, a market will not live up to its potential as an
efficient allocator of goods and services.

Indeed, the ability to develop such institutions is a key factor in
economic development. Douglass C. North argues that the transition from common property to private property depends on the
technology for measuring quality.

The costs of measuring the dimensions of the inputs
and the outputs will dictate the various property rights
structures for the diverse sectors of the economy,
which therefore will be dependent on the state of the
technology of measurement. . . . The existence of
exclusive property rights implies the ability to measure
the dimensions—quantity and quality—of the good or
service exchanged. Common property resources have
persisted where the costs of measuring the dimensions
of the resources have outweighed the benefits.[35]

Although pursuing these lines would take us too far afield, we
see a common pattern. In the transition away from a primitive
economy that we call "development," the market's growth outstrips
the ability of institutions to measure and reward quality distinctions.
As a consequence, the market malfunctions.

For one thing, the initial expansion and development of the

market disproportionately benefits the most advantaged. This can occur because local monopolies, extra-economic coercion, and other forms of market power gather strength at this stage, as both capitalist and Marxist commentators have observed. But it also happens for reasons we are now able to appreciate. The people who benefit disproportionately often have an *informational* advantage. They enjoy a head start in access to (or ability to process) information and knowledge and access to the means of certifying and guaranteeing quality. Thus, both the efficiency and equity of markets is hampered because informational institutions are underdeveloped.

ECONOMIC THINKING ABOUT QUALITY IN MARKETS

Economic theorists have investigated the characteristics of markets with imperfect information about quality. In 1970 George Akerlof posited a simple model in which producers were paid a price based on the average quality of all goods in the market, not on the quality of their particular offering. This could happen, for example, when sellers knew the quality of their wares but buyers could discern only the average level of quality in the entire market. In this example of a market with asymmetric information, some producers would respond by withholding high-quality goods from the market. The average quality of goods offered would therefore decline—and so would the going price. This in turn would induce other producers to withdraw their relatively high-quality goods from the market. In this fashion the market could disappear. The bad would increasingly drive out the good: a phenomenon called adverse selection.

Akerlof argued that this admittedly extreme model captured an important feature of markets.

> There are many markets in which buyers use some market statistic to judge the quality of prospective purchases: in this case there is incentive for sellers to market poor quality merchandise, since the returns for good quality accrue mainly to the entire group whose statistic is affected rather than to the individual seller. As a result there tends to be a reduction in the average quality of goods and also in the size of the market.[36]

In most realistic cases the market will not disappear. Producers may not have full control over their levels of quality, or certain minimal levels of quality may be obtainable at virtually no cost—this is often the case for agricultural products. It is safe to conclude, however, that a market with asymmetric information about quality will have lower levels of both quality and quantity than are socially optimal. Theoretical analyses using more realistic assumptions about the information and the responses of sellers and buyers confirm that when information about quality is asymmetric, markets tend to be inefficient. Michael Rothschild and Joseph Stiglitz showed that imperfect information can lead to inefficient market equilibria—or even no equilibria at all. "We began this research with the hope of showing that even a small amount of imperfect information could have a significant effect on competitive markets. Our results were more striking than we had hoped."[37] Another article "indicates that Akerlof's original result on breakdowns in the trading of high quality goods is quite robust. . . . [and] that allowing partial information does not improve matters."[38]

Economic research has shown that when prices function partly to provide information about quality, the usual conclusions of economic theory about the optimality of competitive markets no longer hold. This phenomenon has been examined in financial, labor, insurance, and commodity markets.[39] Akerlof's pioneering article explicitly connected the problem of quality in markets with the proposition that "business in underdeveloped countries is difficult." He used his model to discuss the costs of dishonesty, the importance of merchants in many developing nations, and extortionate credit markets.

Too few studies have followed his lead and examined the importance of information and market institutions in development.[40] In particular, too few case studies have examined quality, information, and markets in the third world. Most important from a practical point of view, there has been little work on the public and private policies that might improve market institutions.

Akerlof himself made a brief mention of the possibility of market-improving policy measures:

> It should be perceived that in these markets social and private returns differ, and therefore, in some cases, government intervention may increase the welfare of all parties. Or private institutions may arise to take advantage of the potential increases in welfare which accrue to all parties. By nature, however, these institutions are nonatomistic, and therefore concentrations of power—with ill consequences of their own—can develop.[41]

But his hint remains a general one. We need to go further. How do informational problems manifest themselves in under-developed economies? What government interventions or private institutions might make markets work better? What new problems do these suggestions themselves present, and how might they be met?

KEY ELEMENTS OF THE PROBLEM

Before we can address these questions, we need to define the problem more precisely.

1. *Quality varies, partly as a function of the producers' efforts.* The opportunity cost of being in the market has to increase with quality; supplying additional increments of quality must somehow depend on the seller's costly efforts.

2. *Information about quality is asymmetric.* Akerlof's model supposed that each seller has complete knowledge about the quality of his or her product, but the buyers know only the average quality of all products on the market. A more general formulation would posit that participants in the market have differential levels of knowledge or differential costs associated with increments in effective knowledge.[42] (Sometimes buyers may know more than sellers.)

3. *The parties have an incentive to mislead one another.* The seller will profit from inducing the buyer to think his product's quality is higher than it is. Understanding this, the uncertain buyer cannot overcome asymmetric information simply by asking each seller about quality. If, on the other hand, the seller has no incentive to mislead or is required to tell the truth, then problems of adverse selection and moral hazard will decrease.

In these conditions the comforting conclusions of textbook economics no longer hold. Prices may be set competitively and yet not clear the market. Even with free entry and many sellers and buyers—two of the classic conditions for perfect competition—the market will send inefficient signals. In the words of Keith Leffler, "When quality is variable and the costs of measuring complex products are not zero, casually applied supply and demand analysis will likely lead to incorrect predictions."[43] As Joseph Stiglitz and Andrew Weiss put it, when quality matters, "the Law of Supply and Demand is not in fact a law, nor should it be viewed as an assumption needed for competitive analysis. It is rather a result generated by the underlying assumptions that prices have neither sorting nor incentive effects."[44]

Under such circumstances, relying on the untrammeled market may not be a wise strategy. Market institutions themselves need revamping.

A FRAMEWORK FOR POLICY ANALYSIS

There are a large number of possible remedial measures. The three-by-three matrix of Table 3-1 may be useful to organize them.

The columns of the matrix correspond to the three possible policy makers—the sellers, the buyers, and "third parties." The last category includes but is not limited to the government. The rows of the matrix correspond to the three defining conditions of the problem: varying quality, asymmetric information, and incentives to mislead. Different actors can therefore address different aspects of the problem of quality in markets.

In Chapter 5 we will go through this framework cell by cell, with examples and some references to relevant literature. For now we review the main ideas.

Let us begin with the first key feature of the problem, the fact that *quality varies*. Here we ask, "What can sellers, buyers, or third parties such as the government do to reduce the variation in quality across sellers?"

One idea is to regulate or control production processes or the selling of final products directly so that variations in quality are diminished. An example of sellers doing such a thing is the Bolivian Medical Association, which establishes standards for the production and certification of various kinds of physicians. But this strategy has its costs: it reduces consumer choice by restricting the range of available quality, provides a greater opportunity for monopoly power to gain a foothold and be abused, and requires monitoring and enforcement.

The second key feature of the problem is *asymmetric information*. The question here is: What can be done to overcome the fact that some parties have more information than others?

TABLE 3-1

Quality and Markets: A Matrix of Problems and Policy Solutions

Problem	Policy Solutions		
	What Sellers Can Do	**What Buyers Can Do**	**What Government Policy Makers and Other Third Parties Can Do**
Quality varies across sellers	Form producers' groups with quality standards	(No policies required)	Regulate quality of products, processes Facilitate the formation of producer and consumer groups Regulate producer and consumer groups
Information is imperfect and asymmetric	Provide buyers with information about products, processes (e.g., through advertising, labeling, samples) Create brand names whose products share quality characteristics	Gather information Use consultants, information services	Improve the informational infrastructure (e.g., communications [hardware]; the development and dissemination of standards [software]; laws and policies) Measure quality
Sellers have incentives to mislead	Offer contingent contracts (e.g., warranties) Invest in reputation for quality Merge with the buyer (integrate forward)	Threaten retaliation Become a repeat customer Link the purchase of one product with the purchase of others from the same supplier Merge with the seller (integrate backward)	Put into effect and enforce contingent contracts Require high-quality sellers to stay in the market Offer arbitration (e.g., to settle a price dispute) Set prices for different qualities of goods Nationalize production or distribution

In our archetypal case where sellers know the quality of their products but buyers do not, sellers themselves can take certain actions. They can send signals to consumers about their product (or in some cases about the processes used to produce that product). But these signals will not be effective unless sellers overcome two additional problems, which I call *identifiability* and *credibility*. First, the seller's particular product must be identifiable over many transactions, and so a brand name, plus quality control, may be called for. Second, the seller's message must be credible, and to establish credibility the seller may have to resort to devices ranging from free samples to the third-party enforcement of truthful labeling and advertising.

Buyers, too, can take steps to obtain information. They can act individually or as a group, or through hired help such as consultants or information services, to find out more about products, processes, or producers.

Third parties such as the government can help to make information more symmetric. They can provide the means for both parties to make quick and credible measurements of quality. They can do the measuring themselves, offering the service or making it mandatory; the entities measured may be products, production processes, or producers. Third parties can create the infrastructure for information transfers, including hardware (such as public communications), software (such as education and consumer training), and practices such as the enforcement of truth in advertising and the enforcement of contingent contracts.

The third key feature is the *incentive to mislead*. Sellers may reduce these incentives through contingent contracts, such as guarantees and warranties. Sellers may also invest in their reputations for quality across many products and transactions.

The incentive to mislead may also be overcome if buyers and sellers combine through forward (or backward) integration in the market. Each of these steps carries its own costs and risks.

The government may help overcome the sellers' incentives to mislead in ways ranging from mild intervention to draconian takeovers. The government may require contingent contracts, as for example in liability laws regarding product safety. It may regulate the market in a number of ways—it overcomes adverse selection in health insurance, for example, by requiring all citizens to be part of the scheme. The government may nationalize the industry, in a sort of grand forward or backward integration, which (at least in theory) may remove the incentives to mislead by making both sellers and buyers part of the government. The possible costs of such steps are many, not the least of which are the managerial inefficiencies of monopolistic control.

We will develop these points in Chapter 5. Let us first examine two real cases involving quality problems in markets. In the process, we will apply the ideas of the framework for policy analysis and get a feel for its practical uses and limitations.

4

INFORMATION
AND MARKETS:
TWO EXAMPLES

HOW MIGHT THE IDEAS of Chapter 3 help us on practical problems? This chapter presents two brief case studies that use those
ideas to examine the success of public policy and private action in
improving the functioning of India's market for milk. Then we look
at the much less successful example of the Pakistani shrimp industry. In both cases, information and the development of market institutions prove crucial.

QUALITY AND THE MILK MARKET
IN INDIA

In a country of many vegetarians milk and milk products play a
crucial role in nutrition. But milk markets present problems. Milk
production is seasonally variable in India, whereas both the demand
for milk and the needs of small producers for income are stable. Milk
is perishable and requires a sophisticated infrastructure for its transport and processing. These problems affect quality.

Milk varies in quality for several reasons:

■ Milk spoils. Bacteria grow rapidly. Without
refrigeration, milk can be stored only for short periods
and transported over short distances.

■ Better cows produce better milk with higher content of
butterfat and nonfat solids. Better cows can be had by

obtaining more prolific breeds or by producing them
through artificial insemination, by feeding cows
higher-quality fodder, by providing improved
veterinary services, and by better farm management.

■   Milk can be cut with water, which creates a higher
volume but lowers the percentage of butterfat and
nonfat solids.

In India, milk is marketed in stages. The small village producer
sells the milk to a local purchaser, who then transports the milk to a
town, where it is sold to a processor. The processor turns the milk
into a variety of products, including pasteurized milk for household
use. These products are distributed through the retail market. At
each stage milk may be mishandled or diluted by the incompetent or
unscrupulous: adverse incentives lurk.

In the early 1960s, India's milk market was in trouble. With the
expansion of the urban milk market had come incentives to move
cows from rural areas into the cities. Urban cattle colonies had
several advantages. Problems of milk storage and transportation
were reduced. Moreover, the processor could keep a closer watch on
the quality of the milk purchased.

But cities were not desirable places to raise cows. Feed had to
be imported. Space was limited. Consequently, only the highest-
yielding cows were worth importing into the city, which meant
those with newborn calves. Once lactation was well-established,
the calves were allowed to die because it did not pay to rear them in
the city. The dam itself was slaughtered after a couple of lactations
because it was not economical to return the animal to the rural
milkshed for freshening. Thus, about half of the dams brought to the
city were slaughtered prematurely. In largely Hindu India, these
practices had religious as well as economic costs.

In this fashion the dynamics of urban milk production began to
deplete the stock of high-quality cattle. The costs of producing milk
in the city rose. Urban processors responded by diluting the quality
of the milk. Although the expansion of urban cattle colonies had
"solved" some problems of quality, it exacerbated others.

Foreign aid played an ironic role. In the 1960s the European
Community generously donated large quantities of surplus pow-
dered milk, which was distributed at low prices to consumers. In
response, the price of Indian milk dropped, and processors had yet
another incentive to dilute its quality.

By 1970 milk consumption in India had fallen to 105 grams per
capita, down from 126 grams in 1960 and 139 grams in 1950. The

poor were particularly hard hit. Many small farmers and landless rural inhabitants depended on milk production. These two groups owned 53 percent of India's "animals in milk" and produced 51 percent of the nation's milk supply. The declining market for milk threatened to render even more tenuous the livelihoods of these poor farmers.

OPERATION FLOOD

To help remedy the situation, the National Dairy Development Board (NDDB) launched Operation Flood. This program aimed to improve dairy production and marketing in seventeen nucleus milkshed districts and four major cities.

The NDDB modeled its efforts on a successful cooperative in Kaira district, Gujarat. Called AMUL, this cooperative had many attractive features.[1] We will focus on several that were particularly relevant to the milk market's problems of quality:

First, the NDDB established objective criteria for determining the quality of milk. More important, an inexpensive and credible technology for measuring that quality was made available to both buyers and sellers. Each village cooperative society received a hand-operated machine for testing the butterfat content of milk. The cooperative collected milk from local farmers twice a day. The milk was tested for fat content by the cooperative's officials, who were well-respected villagers. Twelve hours later, the cooperative official returned and paid the farmer in cash, depending on the quality and quantity of the milk. The fat tester was also used at later stages in the marketing of milk. Incentives were restored to produce and market milk of appropriate levels of quality.[2]

Second, the NDDB took direct steps to improve and standardize the quality of milk its members marketed. Participating farmers were provided with an integrated package of services. These included artificial insemination, better cattle feed, veterinary services, and technical assistance.

Third, quality was also improved through technical improvements in transportation and marketing. The NDDB subsidized the states and the local cooperatives in creating modern, decentralized processing plants. The NDDB instituted refrigerated transportation. Milk was picked up twice a day by district union trucks and taken to simple feeder-balancing dairy plants or chilling centers that served contiguous milkshed areas. Spoilage was thereby reduced. Since the processing plants were capable of producing milk powder, butter, and cheese, they could be used to remove liquid milk from the market in periods of excess supply. In this way, the NDDB uprooted many of the incentives for urban cattle colonies, whose demise in the long run would lead to improved quality.

Fourth, the NDDB promoted its own brand names to distinguish its products. Its ice cream was considered to be of unprecedented quality in India.

The results were impressive. Milk production and consumption rose sharply. The quality of the milk and other products was improved. By 1979 the NDDB had approximately doubled the incomes of the one million rural families. On average, the NDDB paid 15 percent more for their milk than the traditional traders, and the milk reached consumers at prices 9 percent lower.[3]

The NDDB was widely considered to be one of India's great successes in rural development. In villages where the NDDB was active, outside observers reported that peasants said they needed "something like the dairy" to solve the community's other economic problems. The NDDB was lionized in a cover story in the Indian equivalent of *Business Week*. It even reached the silver screen: a feature film melodramatically depicted the fight waged by a zealous NDDB cooperative against a vicious village milk trader.

In the 1980s some controversy arose about who had benefited from this success. Some said that the rich gained the most. Others argued that grain production went down as milk production went up, with uncertain net social benefits. But a careful study of a sample of villages that did and did not participate in Operation Flood estimated 17 percent higher production in the former group, with all but the very poorest (who had no cows) benefiting directly. Furthermore, there were no adverse effects on grain production.[4]

The reasons for the NDDB's success were many. It enjoyed high-level political support, had access to considerable amounts of untied resources from foreign assistance and the government budget, was under the leadership of an extraordinary chief executive, and the ideology of cooperatives went over well with the public.[5]

ANALYZING SUCCESS

The NDDB also dealt well with problems of quality. The matrix of policies in Table 3-1 can be used to analyze its success.

The NDDB is a third party. It acted to *reduce quality variations* across sellers by upgrading the technology of milk production. It helped improve the cows, the inputs going into the cows, and the infrastructure through which milk was processed and delivered.

These steps would have been much less valuable had not the

NDDB also acted on a second front, *making information symmetric in the market*. The key was the butterfat tester. By providing cheap and credible information about quality, it immediately minimized the problem of adverse selection. The NDDB also put out its own brand name, which enabled consumers to buy its superior products with confidence. In the case of processed milk products, the NDDB successfully sold its high-quality goods for well above the usual market prices. Eventually, the private sector competing with NDDB raised its prices as well.[6]

The NDDB overcame some of the *incentives for sellers to mislead* buyers through vertical integration. Its farmers were linked vertically to cooperatives, transportation, processing plants, and the retail brand names, all under the aegis of the NDDB. Since co-op members bought the milk from other co-op members, presumably the incentives to mislead were reduced.[7] Integrating forward into processing in rural areas helped remove the incentives for urban cattle colonies. A study of beneficiaries showed that "the primary motive for joining seems to be the prospect of better milk marketing."[8]

QUALITY AND THE PAKISTANI SHRIMP INDUSTRY

Let us turn to a second case that enjoyed less success and see how the framework of Table 3-1 helps us understand why.

Again we begin our account with a market in trouble. In 1974 the Pakistani shrimp industry was reeling. In a year export earnings from shrimp had fallen from Rs 45 million to Rs 16 million. By October 1974 the situation had become drastic. Faced with a declining export market, Karachi's shrimp processors refused to buy all of the local catch. Fishermen rioted. The government reacted by ordering the processors to buy all the shrimp that was landed and imposing a minimum price of Rs 7 per pound. Eight of the sixteen processors responded by shutting down their plants. Three of the processors who remained open refused to buy their share of shrimp. The government countered by jailing them. The market broke down.

One reason for the dramatic drop in exports was a scandal involving the quality of Pakistani shrimp. An unscrupulous individual who had purchased a shrimp-processing plant had sold the Japanese a large consignment that contained many rotten shrimp and shrimp that were smaller than their alleged sizes. Like all

Pakistan's shrimp exports, this shipment had been inspected and approved by the provincial government's Marine Fisheries Department. When the consignment reached Japan and the fraud was recognized, the Japanese government lodged an official protest with the Pakistani embassy in Tokyo. For a year the Japanese bought virtually no shrimp from Pakistan.

As it happened, the offending entrepreneur escaped. He sold his plant and disappeared.

These were the headlines of the shrimp crisis, but behind the scenes lurked other problems. Pakistani shrimp customarily fetched lower prices than biologically identical shrimp from India and Indonesia.[9] It was said that the Pakistani shrimp "was of lower quality."

"Quality" has several dimensions here. Several genera of shrimp are sold on the world markets: white and brown are the common names of the two most commercially important, and white shrimp fetch higher prices. The size of the shrimp also matters. In 1975, the largest white shrimp (10/15 count, meaning between 10 and 15 shrimp per kilogram) fetched about $5 per kilogram on the international market, whereas much smaller white shrimp (71/90 count) went for about $1 per kilogram. Even among shrimp of the same genus and size, quality depends on freshness and cleanliness. And if a producer is known for systematically overstating the size of his shrimp—calling 31/40 count what are really 41/50 count, for example—this will also affect his reputation for quality.

The export market recognized only one price for frozen Pakistani shrimp of a given genus and size. Thus, the price that a Pakistani shrimp processor received for his shrimp depended on the average quality of all Pakistani exports of that genus and size, not on the quality of his own product. Already one can see the potential for adverse incentives. But before discussing the export market, let us look at some of the problems in Pakistan's internal market for shrimp.

Shrimp production and marketing included several stages, at each of which quality could be affected. In 1975, roughly a thousand trawlers plied the waters of Pakistan, with an average of ten to twelve fishermen per boat. There was evidence of overfishing: the total catch of shrimp had not shown appreciable growth over the previous half dozen years even though the number of trawlers had approximately doubled. Moreover, an increasing proportion of the shrimp caught were smaller and therefore less valuable.[10] Too few baby shrimp were being allowed to grow into the bigger shrimp that might be worth five times as much per kilogram.

The first stage of shrimp marketing presented several other problems. The central figures in the shrimp auction were the twenty-three middlemen called mole holders. When a trawler returned with its catch, its skipper informed his regular mole holder. The shrimp were conveyed by basket from the trawler to the auctioning area. White and brown shrimp were sorted. Then, with the fishermen excluded from the process, the mole holders auctioned the shrimp to the processors. From the sale price the mole holders deducted 6¼ percent—3 percent went to the mole holder and 3¼ percent went to the Fishermen's Cooperative Society, an organization dedicated to the sale of equipment and ice, the care of fishermen's widows, and such.

Near the harbor where the shrimp auction took place were the processing plants. Most of the shrimp was frozen; some was canned. On bare concrete floors inside the plants, squatting women selected shrimp from conveyer belts and tossed them into buckets corresponding to different sizes. Then the shrimp were washed, quick-frozen, and put into plastic packages.

Shrimp were shipped from docks near the fish harbor. Because of the torrid daytime temperatures, the shrimp were loaded at night. This, however, created problems for the quality inspector of the Marine Fisheries Department, as Karachi harbor was poorly lit.

This is a brief description of the industry as it was in 1974 when the crisis erupted. Pakistan's fourth largest source of export earnings was threatened, and policy makers felt compelled to act. But what should they do? Although many issues were involved, for our purposes we focus on problems of quality.

Quality problems occurred in two stages of the marketing process. First was the fish harbor auction. Shrimp were sold in large lots, unsorted except by genus. Because the quality dimensions of size and freshness were not measured and rewarded, fishermen had inappropriate incentives. They would continue to catch too many baby shrimp. It was not worthwhile to travel longer distances to catch larger shrimp when they could catch many small ones near shore. Nor did they pay enough attention to the freshness of the shrimp, which could have been improved by deheading at sea and more careful icing.

Second, problems developed in the export market. Because processors were paid according to the average quality of all Pakistani exports and not according to the quality of their own material, they had incentives to cut corners regarding freshness and cleanliness and to cheat on counts. As a result Pakistan's produce was discounted on the world market.

Both markets can be analyzed by returning to the matrix of policies presented in Table 3-1.

THE DOMESTIC MARKET

Too many baby shrimp were being caught. One possible remedy would have been to sort the shrimp by size before the auction. This would have restructured incentives in the right direction and could have been done by the sellers, the buyers, or a third party.

But sorting is costly. The key questions for analysis are: How much sorting is optimal at the fish harbor? And who should pay for it? Complete sizing before auction might take too much time. If so, a compromise might be feasible, such as sorting the shrimp into small, medium, and large sizes. Or since small shrimp were the problem, they might be separated from the rest. Both buyers and sellers should benefit in the long run from sorting before auction.

If so, why did such sorting not take place? One reason may be that the mole holders were responsible for sorting and auctioning. If they were to bear the costs of additional sorting, the additional expense might not be covered by their 3 percent commission on a more valuable base. An arrangement might be made for the fishermen and the processors to pay for additional sorting charges.

Another reason was also at work, which reflected a deep problem in the marketplace. The processors were engaged in collusive price-setting. Each Monday they would meet to set an artificially low base purchase price. As a result, the processors made greater profits at the expense of the fishermen. My investigations into financial records provided by one forthcoming shrimp processor revealed profit rates in excess of 100 percent.

In 1981 the mole holders organization wrote to the government recommending that "the mole holders auction the fish and shrimp in the open market in order to fetch the highest possible rates," something that was not currently done because "the factory owners make a kind of pool to lower the rate to the detriment of poor fishermen." The practice of having only one price may have facilitated collusion. If so, then better grading policies will not be advocated by the sellers, and antitrust measures may be necessary. Still, we might expect that the government could improve the functioning of this market by encouraging pre-auction grading.

The top row of Table 3-1 asks us to look for policies that might *reduce quality variations* in the market. A significant problem is the overfishing of baby shrimp, which produces a lower quantity and quality of shrimp. To reduce overfishing, the government could require minimum mesh sizes, prohibit fishing during the spawning season, and restrict fishing near river mouths where spawning takes place. Analytically, these steps would be akin to regulating the "production process" as opposed to the quality of the product itself (the appendix to Chapter 5 discusses this distinction).

As it happened, the Pakistani government did nothing regarding mesh sizes, apparently believing that with the large capital stock of existing nets and the problems of enforcement, restrictive rules would be unenforceable. The government did attempt to prohibit fishing in certain seasons and waters. In 1978 the federal Ministry of Food, Agriculture, and Cooperatives declared that May and June would be a closed season for shrimp fishing. It was during this time that most spawning occurred. In Pakistan the federal government has jurisdiction over waters from 23 to 200 miles offshore. However, the provincial government did not follow suit—perhaps to protect the poor artisanal fishermen who worked in primitive launches along the coast—and fishing remained legal close to shore. Consequently, the ban did not work.[11]

A second problem in the domestic market was the freshness of shrimp. Since fresher shrimp did not bring a higher price on the local market, adverse incentives again rose up. One possible remedy would have been to grade the shrimp at auction by freshness as well as size. Alternatively, measures might have been undertaken to regulate the catching of shrimp. Fishermen might be trained in the importance and techniques of deheading shrimp and icing them at sea. Such steps might be required, with fines for violators. If ice could not be obtained, the role of the Fishermen's Cooperative Society might be reexamined.

The third row of Table 3-1 suggests that we try to *overcome the seller's incentives* to foist off lower-quality shrimp on the buyers. Vertical integration is one possibility. Fishermen would make arrangements with the processors directly. Prices would be determined after the final sorting in each processing plant.[12]

THE EXPORT MARKET

The export market also malfunctioned because quality was not adequately gauged and rewarded. A shipment of bad shrimp had disastrously eroded the country's reputation and revenues. Further instances of poor quality continued to hamper the Pakistani shrimp industry. In 1980 the U.S. Food and Drug Administration

(FDA) blacklisted Pakistani shrimp, citing decomposition, filth, and evidence of salmonella. The country's shrimp was banned from the U.S. market until the Pakistani government took action to improve quality.

What might be done to overcome these problems?

Consider the sellers. In the upper left-hand cell of Table 3-1, we see that sellers might consider forming a producers' group to *reduce variations in quality* among sellers. In the early 1980s an effort was made to toughen up the shrimp processors association. Membership was to be mandatory, with group-enforced penalties and policing. But Pakistani laws concerning trade associations had a loophole. "If the exporter is engaged in more than one trade or industry and becomes a member, it shall not be compulsory for such exporter to become a member of any other association." Many exporters were involved in several industries and for some reason did not participate in the shrimp processors association. "One big change since 1976," said a senior official of the Marine Fisheries Department in 1982, "has been that the traditional shrimp plant owners have lost interest. Now entrepreneurs are renting the factories."

Apparently many of them did not want to participate in a collective, long-term effort to raise the industry's standards. One processor described the situation in an article in a Karachi newspaper:

> The motives behind the creation and membership of
> various Trade Associations . . . is to promote the
> concerned trade and industry and to instill discipline
> amongst its membership, so that no member indulges
> in any kind of malpractice. But in the event of non-
> existence of mandatory membership, of specific Trade
> Association, those exporters who are not members of
> their specific Trade Association could ignore such
> Association and the concerned Association just can not
> do anything about it.[13]

Sellers might also try to *overcome informational asymmetries* by improving the information available to international buyers. In 1976 a Japanese delegation came to Pakistan to inspect the shrimp-processing plants. The visitors gave the Pakistani material as a whole a mediocre grade. According to one processor, the Japanese told him that his shrimp were of better quality but that they could not give him "your deserving price." Perhaps the Japanese did not have confidence that what was higher quality today would be higher quality a month from now. (An option might be to station a Japanese inspector at the plant.) Brand names were tried for some processors in the 1970s but somehow (or nevertheless) did not result in different prices for different processors' goods.

Again using the policy matrix of Table 3-1 to guide us, we might ask what the sellers could do to *overcome the incentives to mislead* the importers. One idea is a contingent contract. Indeed, such an institution was already being used (and abused) in 1975. Upon making their purchase, American importers paid Pakistani processors 80 percent of the listed price. If the shipment was found to be of good quality when it reached the U.S. market, the processor would be paid an additional 15 percent. The remaining 5 percent was apparently kept by the importer.

While studying the books of the remarkably forthcoming shrimp processor mentioned above, I found that the supplementary 15 percent was hardly ever paid. "Was your quality that bad?" I asked.

"Not at all, " replied the candid processor. "The payments are made, but to my brother in London. I do not report them here."

In this way, the payments did not appear on the company's books—nor on its Pakistani tax returns. A contingent contract designed to guarantee good quality had been twisted to serve other purposes.[14]

The sellers and the buyers might consider market integration. A Japanese importer, for example, might undertake a joint venture with a Pakistani processor. As of 1982, however, no such step had been taken.

The buyers had few other alternatives. The Japanese reaction of not buying for a year and later sending a delegation to inspect the plants might be placed under the categories of "retaliation" and "gather information" in the second column of Table 3-1. The FDA's action, too, might be usefully classified as a retaliatory step on behalf of the buyers.

What role might third parties such as the government play in improving the export market?

It took the FDA's ban to galvanize the federal Ministry of Agriculture. It did not have control over the Marine Fisheries Department, a provincial body. But the ministry's Live Stock Division had an animal quarantine station in Karachi. The ministry decided to have this station approve the quality of all shrimp exports.

Unfortunately, this move presented several difficulties. The officers of the animal quarantine station had been trained to assess beef and mutton, not shrimp. Their office was located far from the fish harbor, too far apparently for its officers to be willing to travel in order to investigate the shrimp. Consequently, according to various reports, unscrupulous processors would drive half an hour to the station, pay a bribe, and receive a livestock certificate attesting that "the animal has been properly slaughtered."

Eventually the federal ministry realized that the animal quarantine station was not the answer. At a meeting in Karachi in June 1980, a major governmental effort in quality control was planned. These policies fell in the top right-hand cell of Table 3-1: regulating quality. The production process would be regulated. Twelve government inspectors would be placed at the twenty-eight freezing and canning plants for shrimp and fish. They would also make periodic trips to fishing settlements along the Sind and Baluchistan coasts. Quality would be checked at the fish harbor as well. Eight inspectors would be placed there to check the freshness of the landed shrimp and fish. Finally, quality control at the export stage would be upgraded. In particular, the Marine Fisheries Department's laboratory for quality testing would be resurrected.

The focal point of these actions was the dimension of quality raised by the FDA: freshness.[15] Notice that the government's planned measures would have little impact on undersizing in the export market. The policy response was direct regulation and inspection. The government did not undertake other possible measures, such as changing rules and laws to strengthen the shrimp processors association, imposing penalties and liabilities for substandard products, encouraging brand names, improving information, fostering vertical integration, or even getting into the shrimp business itself. The Fishermen's Cooperative Society played virtually no role in overcoming quality problems.

As it happened, the government's initiatives were slow to materialize. The plans formulated at the June 1980 meeting did not become a detailed project until November 1981, and the project was not funded until March 1982. At that time (shortly before my last visit to Pakistan), one could not say that quality problems in the shrimp market had been solved.

But the point of this analysis is not to evaluate the actors in the Pakistani shrimp story. Like most analyses of real markets in developing countries, a case like this one clearly shows the futility of extreme and general advice to let the market work (at one extreme) or to have the government take over the industry (at the other). It suggests the value of an analysis of the problems of quality in markets and of the possible ways these problems might be addressed. This case also illustrates the difficulties that may impede—and indeed may ensue from—policies to overcome adverse selection. As the appendix to Chapter 5 explores in more detail, each of the possible remedies for problems of quality and markets carries its own costs and risks. These will need to be appraised for each particular problem.

5

ACTIONS BY BUYERS, SELLERS, AND GOVERNMENTS

INFORMATION PROBLEMS plague all sorts of markets in developing countries. We have been focusing on agricultural markets, in part because they are often taken as the prototype of perfect competition. But related issues arise in markets for credit, labor, insurance and education; and they are especially severe among the poor in developing countries, where information is scarce and market institutions weak.

As a brief example, consider credit for so-called microenterprises. The term has many meanings but here let us apply it to small businesses with fewer than five employees, sometimes referred to as the informal sector. Recent studies in Bolivia and many other developing countries reveal three important facts.

First, as a source of jobs and incomes in times of economic difficulty, the informal sector is large and growing in importance. As we saw in Chapter 2, an estimated 80 percent of the population of La Paz has at least one family member working in the informal sector.

Second, although in my view it remains debatable whether many microenterprises are technically efficient, their resilience indicates that the entrepreneurial spirit is not absent in supposedly backward economies. Some evidence suggests that today's hawkers and microentrepreneurs become tomorrow's middle class. The informal sector may be the breeding ground of indigenous enterprise.

Third, the most important obstacles facing microenterprises are a lack of property rights and a lack of credit. Although it has been argued that poor management and bookkeeping skills also constrain small businesses in developing countries, in the informal sector these are usually not crucial.

By property rights, I mean first of all the legal right to exist. Studies show that it is time-consuming and expensive to obtain the licenses and permits necessary to exist as a small business—much less to import inputs and export products. If a small firm is unable or unwilling to bear these costs, it remains at the edge of the law or may even be classified as an illegal enterprise. This has some advantages, for example, when taxes are evaded. But it also entails costs, such as being unable to take advantage of contracts and, in Bolivia, being unable to receive bank loans. Therefore, the reform of laws and regulations is the first step toward empowering the informal sector.[1]

Even when small enterprises are legal, the credit market often does not serve them well. Our discussion of quality in markets helps us understand why.

Consider potential loan recipients from the perspective of a profit-maximizing bank. Suppose there are fixed costs to making a loan that do not depend on the size of the loan. A bank will then make a higher profit per peso loaned for larger loans. Apart from transactions costs, though, there is another reason why banks prefer large loans. The bank loses money if the loan is not repaid. It reduces this risk in two ways: by screening loan applicants and by obtaining guarantees for the loans, such as collateral. Small borrowers often do not have credible collateral, whereas those who obtain large loans frequently do (houses, factories, farms, and so forth).

Loan applicants therefore have different *qualities:* the cost per peso loaned, collateral, and the availability of information useful for screening bad risks. We can think of potential borrowers as having a distribution of riskiness akin to the distribution of quality of Israeli oranges or the quality of Pakistani shrimp. Each enterprise has an incentive to appear creditworthy and to promise to repay; and because the bank understands this, the bank cannot believe everything an applicant tells it. Once again we have a situation of variable quality, asymmetric information, and the incentive to mislead.

Solutions to the credit problem for small businesses may therefore profit from our framework for policy analysis in Table 3-1. Without going through the table in detail, let us mention three possibilities that have proved successful in other countries. Each can be understood in terms of our previous work.

First, *form credit groups.* In some successful credit programs, recipients in groups of five to ten guarantee each other's loans. This practice has several benefits. In forming the groups, the members, recognizing their joint responsibility, screen each other, lowering the bank's screening costs. Moreover, by transacting one loan instead of five to ten, the bank saves on the fixed costs of lending. Finally, members can enforce each other's repayment in ways that neither the bank nor the legal system can cheaply duplicate.[2]

Second, *use information brokers.* Some successful credit programs have relied on community agencies to perform credit screening (and other functions such as monitoring progress, providing some technical assistance, and helping with loan collection). From the perspective of this chapter, one virtue of this mechanism is that it utilizes the community agency's comparative advantage in information about local conditions and recipients.

Third, *use small loans for short periods of time.* In effect, the idea is to encourage "repeat buying" (in this case, repeat borrowing), which tends to overcome the problem of incentives to mislead.

EXTENSIONS

We have been discussing one aspect of markets in developing countries, namely, the ways that varying quality and poor information can make those markets malfunction. The discussion is not just important for capitalist economies. Marketing is also important under socialism. "There is a tendency among economists of capitalist countries," wrote the Romanian professor Mihail C. Demetrescu, "to underestimate the usefulness of marketing within the socialist countries." He went on: "Marketing is a set of ideologically and morally neutral management principles and techniques aimed at facilitating this flow of goods and services from producer to consumer. Marketing can therefore be used by any political or economic system."[3]

We expect an inefficient market when "the flow of goods and services" takes place under conditions of varying quality, asymmetric information between the parties of the transaction, and an economic incentive for one party to mislead the other about quality.

Information is a key. Most developing countries are not well endowed with information or information processing, even in their agricultural markets. Consider this recent appraisal of the situation in Cameroon:

> There remains, however, a nearly absolute absence of
> regular information at the intermediate (farm and
> village) market level. . . . As Cameroon restructures
> its economy to place more emphasis on the private
> sector, the need for appropriate and timely data

becomes critical. It will be especially important that the
Government has information to support (and evaluate)
the private sector, monitor and control its import tax
programs, and detect and adjust to emerging problems
(such as food emergencies, for example). The
importance of such information to both public and
private sector decision makers cannot be
overemphasized. Cameroon should move immediately
to strengthen existing data collection and
dissemination systems and to extend the system to
include farm and village markets.[4]

We have focused on agricultural markets, but not because they
provide the clearest evidence of informational problems. Indeed, if
one would expect the untrammeled competitive market to work
anywhere in an underdeveloped economy, it would be in agriculture; at least, this seems a popular view these days. A common cry to
governments is to leave agricultural markets alone, or something
close to that: let the prices reflect international and domestic scarcity
values; let the traders trade and the farmers farm and the consumers
consume. Any deviation from laissez faire in agricultural marketing
invites inefficiencies.

This advice has been justified in several ways. Agricultural
growth in Bolivia and many other developing countries has been
disappointing over the past decade. Large-scale government intervention, such as marketing boards and price fixing, have led to
corruption and loss.[5] At the microeconomic level, studies have concluded that agricultural middlemen do not report exorbitant profits
and that entry into the agricultural market seems unrestricted—two
classic conditions of competitive markets. And in the background is
the reassuring result of textbook economics: competitive markets are
optimal.

But the competitive Indian milk market was not working well.
Information about quality was imperfect, and incentives were therefore distorted. At various stages of the marketing process, sellers
could cut the milk with water, raising the volume but reducing the
quality; and buyers had a hard time telling if and to what extent this
had occurred. The quality and quantity of milk consumed was low,
especially given the country's nutritional needs and the millions of
poor rural people whose livelihoods depended on their milk
animals.

With a number of shrewd interventions, India's National
Dairy Development Board helped the market work better. I have
already discussed one of these interventions: the dissemination of a

cheap and credible mechanism for measuring the butterfat content of milk. Henceforth, both buyers and sellers could test the milk's quality, which removed the incentive to cut the milk, which in turn helped the market take off.

The competitive Pakistani shrimp market did not work well either, and again a culprit was poor information and the resulting distortions of incentives. Because the local auction did not reward fishermen for catching larger shrimp, they caught too many smaller shrimp, and both the catches and the revenues were less than optimal. The export market did not possess institutions to gauge and reward the quality of the shrimp of individual Pakistani processors. This allowed undersizing and other abuses such as the export of decomposed, filthy, and salmonella-infested shrimp to the United States, with the result that Pakistani shrimp exports were blacklisted by the U.S. Department of Agriculture.

These two cases are not isolated instances. Because of poor information in many market institutions, around the globe we witness arrangements typical of primitive or bazaar economies: reciprocal clientized buyer-seller relationships instead of competition for one's products; business and trade within the family instead of in open markets; even the virtual destruction of markets for cash crops as peasants return to subsistence activities.

Because of poor information, the trading sectors in many developing countries are much larger than necessary. Entrepreneurial talent is tied up in transacting rather than producing. As in the bazaar studied by Clifford Geertz, because of poor and asymmetric information,

> searching for information one lacks and protecting the information one has is the name of the game. Capital, skill, and industriousness play, along with luck and privilege, as important a role in the bazaar as they do in any economic system. They do so less by increasing efficiency or improving products than by securing for their possessor an advantaged place in an enormously complicated, poorly articulated, and extremely noisy communications network.[6]

In contrast to a market in which information is widely available, much of the activity of these traders can be seen as privately profitable but socially wasteful. The profits they earn can be linked to the Marxian idea of an economic surplus, even if one does not go so far as Paul Baran's condemnation of the mercantile class as "a parasitic stratum."[7] Putting it another way, the efficiency of a market

PART OF A MARKETING PROJECT THAT WORKED

A recent internal review of the World Bank's experience with agricultural marketing was extremely negative. The Operations Evaluation Department examined the results of the 402 agricultural projects funded by the Bank from 1974 to 1986. Only about half had marketing components, and only half of these "succeeded" in meeting their marketing objectives.

> Notable omissions include the lack of any measures for providing a framework within which markets could operate more efficiently—commercial legal code, regulation or inspection. . . . The marketing skills needed to exploit a specialized market niche were not recognized. Incentives for improving the product quality were invariably overlooked. The implicit assumption seems to have been that "if it is produced, it will get sold". . . . It is striking how little attention seems to have been given to the government's role in providing standardized weights and measures, defining and policing nationally recognized quality grades, collecting and disseminating timely price information, or encouraging competition.

The study recommends that governments consider a range of activities "to make the market more competitive and transparent. These include encouraging competition, ensuring a free flow of market information, defining and maintaining quality standards, and strengthening the legal system to uphold the enforceability of contracts and the guarantee of property rights."

But one Bank-funded project stood out in the minds of the evaluators. The state of Bihar in India had implemented a transparent auction system that works. Farmers and middlemen display their wares on the auction floor. Then, the project performance audit report says, wholesalers inspect the goods and place their bids in a locked box.

> Since competition of wholesale traders is keen, prices offered are usually highly satisfactory to the sellers. Reaching fair prices is further assisted by excellent market intelligence: price ranges for all commodities are noted on blackboards next to the market entrance, offering interested sellers immediately an idea about the market situation.

Bidders cannot renege on their offers—as often happened before—and "there are no discussions about correct weights and measurements, since for the first time the relatively 'weak' sellers have the possibility, in case of real or imagined unfairness, to appeal" to a committee of farmers and traders who administer the market.

The report cites studies by Indian researchers that document the cost-effectiveness of marketing improvements on agricultural production. The Bank report concludes—almost plaintively, as if trying to remind people down the hall as much as readers around the globe—that "marketing services add value in the same sense that fertilizer or irrigation investments do."

SOURCE: World Bank, Operations Evaluation Department, Agricultural Marketing: The World Bank's Experience, 1974–85 (Washington, D.C., July 1990): 2, 3, 5, 49, 43, 44.

is not guaranteed by the presence of pure competition, in the sense of many traders and apparently small profit margins.

Writing with hardly a mention of Marx, Harold M. Riley and Michael T. Weber evaluated economic studies of marketing in developing countries. Some of their observations are worth quoting at length:

> Many of the studies done by economists and agricultural economists are based upon conceptual perspectives of market organization dominated by the perfectly competitive theoretical model of economics. And much of the research has been concerned with issues involving the testing for conditions of structure, conduct and performance predicted by the purely competitive model. . . .
>
> A major problem with the research framework developed in most of the diagnostic assessments is the lack of concern for the dynamic impacts which marketing services can have both on production and consumption. . . . Relatively little effort has been made to better understand how the effectiveness of marketing services influences supply and demand functions, especially for small scale farmers and low income consumers. . . .
>
> The most important marketing problems related to achieving the desired structural transformation are in the design and promotion of new technologies and new institutional arrangements which may be unprofitable or unavailable to individual market participants, but if adopted by all participants, could yield substantial system improvements.[8]

Among the "new technologies and new institutional arrangements" with significant "dynamic impacts both on production and consumption" are the host of informational improvements we have been discussing.

What many people would call exploitation by traders can be real, even when competition is abundant. Two factors explain this situation.

First, many studies underestimate traders' margins because they do not take into account cheating on weights and cheating on market prices—as we saw above with examples from Africa and Karachi's market for fruits and vegetables.

Second, "exploitation" may refer to the traders' propensity to

MARKET EFFICIENCY IN AFRICA AND ASIA

Raisuddin Ahmed and Narendra Rustagi of the International Food Policy Research Institute studied agricultural marketing in five African and four Asian countries. They found the Asian markets to be much more efficient.

In general, African farmers receive only about 35 to 60 percent of the terminal market price of their goods, whereas Asian farmers receive from 75 to 90 percent. In other words, the marketing process in Africa sucks off about twice as much from farmers as it does in Asia. Moreover, in Africa regional prices within each country often differ by a factor of two or three, whereas regional variations rarely exceed 70 percent in Asian countries. Regional differences in Africa are well above the marketing margin (the producer-consumer price spread), but in Asia the two are close. This indicates a lack of spatial market integration in Africa. In addition, seasonal variations in prices are wider in Africa than in Asia.

The authors strove to explain these differences. Taxes are higher in Africa. Transportation is more difficult, in part because of sparser populations (15 to 30 people per square kilometer in Africa compared with 500 to 750 in Asia) and in part because of worse roads (0.01 to 0.11 kilometers of developed road networks per square kilometer of land area in Africa compared with 0.30 to 0.45 kilometers in Asia, and only about 10 percent of roads are paved in Africa compared with about 35 percent in Asia). Other marketing costs are higher in Africa, too. Furthermore, "wage rates are generally two to five times higher in Africa, even though average labor productivity is lower." The table summarizes the authors' findings from Kenya, Malawi, Bangladesh, and Indonesia (where better data were available).

The authors believe that public policies have influenced these differences in market efficiency. Government intervention has hurt Africa in two ways—in what it has done and in what it has not done. Africa's thin markets, which tend to be unstable markets, have given rise to public parastatals and marketing boards, price controls, and other interventions, which have "contributed to the large marketing margin and price spreads (implying disincentives to both producers and consumers) in Africa."

give and take different prices, to take advantage of the other party's ignorance, to make money through sharp deals rather than by large volumes of transactions at fixed prices. When information is scarce, traders can earn noncompetitive rents even in the presence of large numbers of buyers and sellers. Their intensive wheeling and dealing—which can in part be understood as a search for information—and the lack of fixed prices and fixed lots may appear to their trading partners as evidence of exploitation.

The economics of imperfect information may help explain the widespread accusation that middlemen in developing countries are exploiters. Consider this passage from a theoretical article:

	Marketing costs as a share of final price*			Share of factor as % of Africa/Asia difference
	Africa	Asia	Difference	
Taxes	3.9	0.6	3.3	9.4
Transport and associated costs	27.5	13.8	13.7	39.1
Profit	12.6	4.0	8.6	24.5
Transaction costs (residual)	11.0	1.6	9.4	27.0
Total	55.0	20.0	35.0	100

* Percentage points of the difference between the prices paid by final consumers and those received by primary producers; thus, the African farmers in this sample received only 45 percent of the final price, compared with 80 percent for the Asian farmers.

But African governments have not done as well as their Asian peers in promoting competitive markets through public policy. "In the selected Asian countries private trade is not only allowed to operate side by side with public trade but is encouraged through various market development activities," which include "development of market places, dissemination of price and production information, introduction of standard grades and weights, maintenance of law and order in transport channels and markets, provision of credit to traders, initiation of agricultural processing and specific storage facilities, and provision of electricity to rural markets."

African governments, the authors say, should allow private trade "to work freely. Market development policies improving legal and physical facilities and flow of information should be another component of this transition."

SOURCE: Raisuddin Ahmed and Narendra Rustagi, "Marketing and Price Incentives in African and Asian Countries: A Comparison," in Dieter Elz, ed., Agricultural Marketing Strategy and Pricing Policy (Washington, D.C.: World Bank, 1987), 113, 114, 116, 115.

Competition is usually thought to be in the consumers' interest; although we would not disagree with this general presumption, there is another side to this that must be borne in mind: with costly search, competition may take the form of attempting to find better ways of exploiting the small but finite degree of monopoly power associated with costly search and information. (More successful firms may not be more efficient firms, but more efficient discriminators.)[9]

Traders discriminate among customers—according to how well informed they are—as well as among qualities of products.

When information is imperfect, government intervention *may* make everyone better off. ("May" is emphasized because market interventions have their own costs, as emphasized in the appendix to this chapter and in Chapters 6 to 8.) As we have seen, sellers themselves can undertake actions to make things better; so can buyers. However, remedial measures by sellers and buyers often require the support of third parties such as the government. For example, contingent contracts need outside enforcement; and attempts to inform buyers about quality may founder without governmental rules concerning truth in labeling and advertising.

Moreover, information can be a public good, precisely the sort of good that competitive markets do not provide efficiently—at least, not without an institutional framework and incentives supported by the state.

Thus, government intervention in competitive markets is often essential for markets to work well. As we contemplate the variety of possible measures summarized in Table 3-1, it is worthwhile to distinguish between "direct" and "indirect" public policies.

Direct policies include those that set and regulate quality standards for products or processes, impose mandatory inspection and grading, establish requirements for contingent contracts such as warranties, force sellers to stay in the market to avoid adverse selection, and promote nationalization (or forced vertical integration).

Indirect policies include those that help producers' groups set quality standards and enforce them; encourage optional inspection and grading; disseminate technologies for measuring quality; collect and distribute data about prices, quantities, and qualities; enable buyers and sellers to design contingent contracts (perhaps even providing them with technical assistance in doing so); and facilitate vertical integration by private firms.

Which policies a government should pursue of course depends on a number of political and normative judgments, as well as on the specific circumstances. Still, we can hazard some guesses. Direct measures would seem to carry the greater risks of monopoly and misuse. Direct measures insert the state into decisions about appropriate levels of quality, quantity, and prices, and sometimes even into the management of productive activities.

In contrast, indirect measures work through private sellers and buyers. They provide the ingredients that will enable the private sector to solve its own problems. Among the most essential ingredients for efficient markets is information—and the infrastructure needed for information to flow more cheaply and reliably. Also important is a well-functioning legal system that facilitates binding contracts. All of these state actions enable buyers and sellers to undertake contracts, integrate vertically, or form producers' or sellers' organizations. Apart from promoting efficiency, these "indirect measures" have a certain gentleness about them.

This chapter reminds us to go beyond the state-versus-market debate, in agriculture and elsewhere. Often the state can work with private sector buyers and sellers to create more efficient markets. Indeed, the state must help lay the legal and informational foundations for markets. The state should not be thought of as a replacement for the private sector, but as a complement to it.

APPENDIX:
IMPROVING MARKET INFORMATION—
A FRAMEWORK FOR POLICY ANALYSIS

Table 3-1 arrays possible policy measures in a three-by-three matrix. The three columns refer to the possible policy makers: the sellers, the buyers, and third parties (including, but not confined to, the government). The three rows correspond to the three key features of the problem of quality and markets: quality varies, information is imperfect and asymmetric, and sellers have incentives to mislead buyers about the quality of their products. Let us examine the possible policies in somewhat more detail.

POLICIES BY SELLERS

Reduce Quality Variations across Sellers. Sellers can try to combine forces and impose group quality standards. The idea is to reduce the quality differences among sellers so that adverse selection does not begin. Professional groups are one example.

These policies have several costs. First, restricting the range of quality limits consumer choice. Second, a sellers' group may use its monopolistic powers in ways that work against efficiency—for example, by restricting entry and competition. Third, collective action is difficult to organize and hard to enforce. The temptation is present for free-riding members to enjoy the benefits of the group's quality standards but to produce substandard goods themselves.

Improve Information, Including Its Symmetry. Suppose sellers know more about their products than buyers do. One way to overcome this informational asymmetry is for the sellers to provide the buyers with information. For example, they could publish data on products, allow inspections, provide informative labels, permit buyers to have trial periods, and advertise. If the quality of the product itself is hard for consumers to judge, sellers may provide information about their production processes. The quality of, say, a training program may be hard to gauge when it comes to its effect on productivity. Consequently, the sellers of training programs may provide information about the training process, such as handbooks or details about the faculty.

Sellers may give free samples or discounts to encourage buyers to gain more information about the products. This step will be effective in the repeat buying of relatively small ticket items, the quality of which the buyer cannot judge at the time of purchase but can upon using the product.[10]

Apart from the costs of such informational undertakings, sellers face two problems: *identifiability* and *credibility*. If buyers cannot differentiate between the products of various sellers, it will not make sense for sellers to advertise. A brand name is one way to become identifiable.[11] The buyer may also wonder whether and to what extent to believe what the seller says. Since the seller wants the buyer to overestimate the quality, why should the buyer put faith in labels or advertisements? At times, credibility problems cannot be resolved without the help of third parties. For example, communications may become credible if the government promulgates and enforces laws regarding false labeling and advertising. Indeed, it is possible to imagine a situation in which each seller would be advertising falsely and yet would vote in favor of third-party intervention to penalize false advertising.[12]

Overcome Incentives to Mislead.   It is useful to separate three types of actions here: contingent contracts, investing in a reputation for quality, and forward integration.

The seller may try to share the buyer's risk concerning quality. The seller may offer the buyer a *contingent contract*. A warranty is an example. The seller who provides a warranty aligns his incentives with the buyers: both now care about how well the product performs after the sale. The usual rule of caveat emptor is replaced at least in part by caveat venditor.

Contingent contracts can take many forms, including full liability, deductibles, replacements, and repairs. Such arrangements face implementation problems. First, if buyers are to judge the quality or can, through their use of the product, affect later evaluations of the product's quality, they may have incentives to lie or not to take proper care. In effect, the incentives to mislead may be partly reversed. Second, it may be administratively difficult to enforce contingent contracts. Who will make sure that a guarantee is honored? Again, we should note the possible importance of third-party intervention—in this case the government's enforcement of liability laws and seller-buyer contracts.

Note that merely offering a guarantee or other sort of contingent contract can send a signal of quality to buyers. Thus, contingent contracts not only make it possible to share risks, they also have an informational function.[13]

Not all contingent contracts are written down or need to be. In this regard *reputation* may play a role.[14] The seller may acquire a reputation for fair dealing, a kind of informal warranty. Or the reputation may be for above-average and relatively invariant quality. The problem of unreliable quality is severe in many developing countries. Even the weights of basic goods may be misstated. Consider this example from Malaysia:

> In September 1977, the Consumers' Association weighed loaves of bread from nine Penang bakeries. Each fell short of the government standard. A fuss was made at the Department of Weights and Measures, and the bakeries agreed to conform. In February 1979, 10 samples were tested. Nine were below weight. Nine brands of rice sold in "39-pound" bags also were caught short. And of 11 brands of soy sauce, six bottles held half of what the labels claimed.
>
> The association tested various teas and discovered that some contained dyes, some were only tea dust and some were loaded with ash. It tested a dozen brands of ground coffee and found that each had less than the required 50% coffee content. One had just 4.6%.[15]

Part of the success of multinational companies may be attributed to reputation and quality signaling. A multinational corporation may have a competitive advantage in signaling quality—not necessarily the highest level of quality, but a consistent level. For informational reasons, then, consumers may prefer the goods and services of a multinational company.

Creating a reputation for quality can be expensive. Small sellers may try to group together and form a kind of collective brand. But they may encounter the problems described above for forming producers' associations.

The incentive to mislead buyers can also be reduced through *forward integration*. The seller and the buyer merge; a vertically integrated company is formed. In theory, the seller no longer has an incentive to deceive the buyer, since both are members of the same organization.[16]

Another example of combining buyers and sellers is seen in firms that do business with relatives. Family firms and trade among family members or close friends are prevalent in developing countries in part because they tend to mitigate incentives to mislead. This is also the case for trade within clans or ethnic groups.

Forward integration has its costs as well as its benefits. The forces of competition may be weakened. Moreover, in practice the integrated buyer and seller may not turn out to share interests or information. Finally, economies of specialization may be sacrificed through vertical integration.[17]

POLICIES FOR BUYERS

Buyers can do little directly to reduce variations in quality among sellers. Thus the top middle cell of Table 3-1 is empty. But buyers have some recourse.

Improve Information, Including Its Symmetry.   Individually or in groups, buyers can screen or invest in information. They can examine products, look into the processes through which those products were created, and examine the trustworthiness of particular sellers. Through education and training they can increase their capabilities to process relevant data about quality. Information can be purchased. So can the services of information processors such as consultants, evaluators, and so forth. Buyers may even use each other as sources of information about the utility of particular goods and services.

Each of these steps entails costs. An individual buyer may well find it uneconomical to carry out a thorough investigation for every transaction. As markets expand, we expect institutions to arise that will provide buyers with credible information about quality at a lower cost. Examples of such informational intermediaries are newsletters, consumer services, testers, consultants—and experienced relatives.

Reduce Sellers' Incentives to Mislead.   Retaliation is one possibility. If sellers know that buyers will get back at them through boycotts or even violence, sellers may be less likely to misrepresent quality. But it may be difficult in advance for buyers credibly to threaten retaliation, and obviously reprisals carry several sorts of costs.

A more likely possibility is repeat buying. This practice recalls the institutional relationships and reciprocity of the primitive economy. If the seller understands that the buyer will be a regular customer unless deceived about quality, the seller may well forgo opportunities for short-run profits made possible by deceit. A problem for the buyer is to convince the seller that repeat buying is likely—easier for small and frequent purchases than for large and infrequent ones. (The credibility problem may then run the other way: buyers may have to invest in *their* reputations.)

In this regard, buying on credit may seem a useful instrument. The seller may be more wary of misleading the credit buyer, for if misrepresentation occurs, the credit buyer may not pay up. Nonetheless, studies show that credit buying can actually reduce the buyer's leverage regarding quality. As Galbraith and his colleagues found,

> Consumers will serve both themselves and the
> marketing system to the extent that they are
> (1) conscious of quality and (2) conscious of prices in
> their purchases of consumer goods. As long as credit
> plays an important part in determining the buying
> habits of Puerto Ricans, there is certain to be
> considerable indifference as to sources of supply, and
> the benefits of greater price and quality consciousness
> will not be fully realized.[18]

Furthermore, buyers may integrate backward into the market. Some management texts refer to the choice between making and buying. "Making" means the purchaser creates or absorbs his own productive capacity in order to provide the needed good or service. The advantage of making as opposed to buying is, at least in theory, that it overcomes both asymmetric information and the incentive to mislead. In practice, however, backward integration encounters the same costs and risks mentioned above for the option of forward integration.

POLICIES BY THIRD PARTIES

"Third parties" refers to others besides the buyers and the sellers. In most but not all policy contexts, the relevant third party is an agency of the government.

Reduce Quality Variations across Sellers.   Government action can attempt to raise quality levels and reduce the variation among sellers. It is useful here and below to separate direct and indirect policies, as mentioned above.

Direct actions include the regulation of product quality. The government sets standards that firms are expected to meet. The government can work through incentives and penalties, or it may mandate certain production processes or product specifications.

Minimum quality standards are desirable under some circumstances but not others. In general, minimum standards will be more advantageous in markets that exhibit the following tendencies: consumers are quite sensitive to quality variation; consumers exhibit a low elasticity of demand; suppliers have relatively low marginal costs for providing additional increments of quality; and consumers place a low value on low-quality goods. Minimum standards make sense only under conditions of imperfect information. If one assumes that consumers can readily discern quality levels before purchasing, then minimum quality standards lead to a loss of consumer welfare.[19]

Indirect actions instead create an environment in which sellers and buyers can solve the problem of quality variation themselves. For example, the state may facilitate the formation of producers' associations. It might encourage producers to initiate them, create laws that make possible mandatory membership rules, enforce penalties for transgressions, and publicize agreements.

Improve Information, Including Its Symmetry. The government may enjoy two important advantages with regard to the production and diffusion of information: credibility and economies of scale. Often these advantages justify direct action on the part of the government in supplying and certifying information. The state may gather and publish data on qualities, prices, and quantities—and, as in the Zambian example, on particular sellers. The state may offer voluntary tests of quality at the request of either party; or it may make such testing mandatory. For example, the grading of beef carcasses by the U.S. Department of Agriculture is available to any buyer or seller who wishes to pay for it. In 1979 the cost was $18.20 per hour, or about $0.30 per carcass. About 56 percent of commercial production was voluntarily graded by the USDA.[20] In contrast, the grading of tobacco by the USDA is mandatory.[21]

When grading is done, it may take several forms. It may be binary—above or below a certain minimum standard of quality. It may be categorical—in one of several quality classifications, such as the USDA's eight grades for beef carcasses. Or it may be virtually continuous—as in the percentage of butterfat in milk.

The government may also undertake indirect measures that might be called "the information infrastructure." Here we can distinguish among hardware, software, and the legal infrastructure.

"Hardware" refers to the communications infrastructure and other technologies, such as computers, that facilitate the movement and processing of information. In many developing countries the economic returns to telephone services and other communications investments have been systematically underestimated because the informational "externalities" for economic activities have been omitted. Hardware also includes devices to measure product quality: recall from Chapter 4 the butterfat gauge distributed by India's National Dairy Development Board.

"Software" includes the development and dissemination of standards and technologies of measurement. Weights and measures are one example. Consumer training courses are a narrow example, but one might include the gamut of policies designed to raise the citizenry's information-processing capabilities.

The legal infrastructure includes all the laws and policies that facilitate the flow of information. Examples include laws, regulations, and pricing policies relevant to warranties, freedom of press and expression, and advertising.

Reduce Incentives to Mislead.   As noted above, third parties such as the government may propagate laws and regulations that facilitate warranties and other forms of contingent contracts. It has been said that making contracts requires the right to be sued. This is only credible if the legal system works well. In general, the rules of the game governing commerce—and the enforcement of those rules—affect the incentives of the more informed parties to mislead the less informed.

Sometimes price setting is a solution. For example, suppose a seller and a buyer bargain over an item that both know is more valuable to the buyer. Suppose the quality of the item is not well known and information about quality can be acquired by either the seller or the buyer, but only at a cost. If quality uncertainty is great and information is expensive, the parties may find themselves in an inefficient situation: both are unwilling to negotiate without the information, but if they spend the money to get the information they spend more than the product is worth. Despite certain gains from trade and symmetric (though imperfect) information, they may not be able to agree on an appropriate price. Both could benefit by agreeing to a price set by an impartial third party, perhaps a private arbitrator or perhaps the government.

The government may act to stop adverse selection. For example, insurance markets may not be able to charge premiums that reflect the true "quality" (riskiness) of each client. The less risky clients may therefore exit the market, leaving behind riskier clients and initiating a spiral of higher premiums, more exiting, and eventually a malfunctioning insurance market. The government may require all citizens to be part of the insurance scheme.

We saw above that backward and forward integration can be viewed as an attempt to change the incentive to mislead. The government analogy here is the nationalization of an industry, a sort of grand forward or backward integration that makes both sellers and buyers part of the government. Another alternative is to nationalize the marketing process. The possible costs of such steps are many, including the managerial inefficiencies of monopolistic control. Tanzania represents an extreme case, but one that has resonance in other countries:

> The initial purpose of the parastatal was to function as a countervailing force to private middlemen, but after their establishment they were soon given monopoly control over major crops. The structure, organization, and operations of the various marketing parastatals varied. However, the general tendency has been to expand their role from purely marketing into production, extension services, financing, licensing, grading, processing, exporting, and importing the primary product. By 1973, there were 12 statutory bodies concerned directly or exclusively with marketing of agricultural commodities. The rapid increase in the number of parastatals coupled with the low level of skilled and experienced manpower available in the country resulted in understaffing of key posts and weak management.[22]

6

MAKING GOVERNMENT INSTITUTIONS WORK BETTER

ESPECIALLY IN DEVELOPING countries, neither markets nor governments work as well as we might hope. In deciding what the roles of state and market should be, economist Gordon Tullock reminds us that

> We must always weigh the specific advantages and disadvantages of these two imperfect instrumentalities. The choice is one between two instrumentalities both of which have considerable error, noise, and inefficiency inherent in them. We choose between two imperfect instrumentalities and thus must face much the same situation as the mechanical engineer who must choose the power for a new ship. Since no engine is perfect, he chooses the one that, for the particular use concerned, is least inefficient. We will be doing the same.[1]

Tullock is right about the imperfections, but the metaphor of engines is too discrete. He implies the choice is either state or market, whereas in practice the choice is among blends of both. Moreover, thinking of the problem as state versus market may lead us to overlook ways to improve both of these "imperfect instrumentalities." In Chapters 3–5, we considered how improving information and institutions might help markets work better. Now we turn to the state.

Today's free-market reforms are limiting the role of the state in economic development. Nonetheless, even after structural adjustment, government institutions continue to play crucial roles. Consider the example of Bolivia's New Economic Policy. As we saw in Chapters 1 and 2, even after the shift toward the market, government interventions are still important—and will remain so.

- Most activities in mining and hydrocarbons are marked by economies of scale and large-scale foreign participation. Therefore, government regulation (if not direct government management) will be essential in these industries, which historically have accounted for more than four-fifths of Bolivia's official exports.

- Bolivia's highland agriculture—including its grazing lands, irrigation, and the natural environment in general—is characterized by commons problems. The unregulated private market is not likely to deal with such problems efficiently, and again government involvement will be important.

- Transportation and other investments in infrastructure are crucial for the efficiency of domestic and export markets in Bolivia. In most countries of the world, infrastructural investments are in one form or another carried out by the government.

- Poverty will continue to be a grave problem, perhaps the most challenging one facing public leaders. Although nongovernmental organizations can play many roles in combating poverty, every country in the world assigns the government a leading part, particularly in education and public health programs.

Like it or not, the state will play a major, though revised, role in these domains. For reasons well understood in classical welfare economics, governments will tend to be involved in, if not to run, industries characterized by economies of scale in nonrenewable resources and by issues involving commons problems and environmental management, the infrastructure, and human resources such as education and health.

Nonetheless, in Bolivia, as in most other developing countries, such government involvement has often foundered. Chapter 2 suggested three related culprits: government agencies have unclear objectives, poor measures of success, and weak incentives linking pay to performance; corruption, waste, and abuse plague public organizations; and the state apparatus is too centralized.

This list is by no means complete. It focuses on economics and administration instead of politics, for example; and it leaves out issues such as popular participation, civic associations, public order, the legislature, and the judiciary. The problems of the state in developing countries could fill libraries—and they have.[2]

Although our focus is much more circumscribed, we deal with some fundamental questions. Our focus is practical. How can governments deal better with the chronic problems of public sector incentives, corruption, and overcentralization?

A DIFFICULT ENVIRONMENT

Let us begin by considering some basic ingredients for a well-functioning bureaucracy, be it public or private.

For an organization to work well, presumably its leaders and members should understand the organization's *objectives*, should be able to *measure* their success in achieving those objectives, should have well-defined *tasks* to perform that contribute to those objectives, should have *means to carry out and coordinate* those tasks in a timely fashion, and should have clear *lines of authority*. To reiterate, a successful organization is successful in five areas: objectives, measures, technologies, incentives, and authority.

In the private sector, we can exaggerate and posit that these five conditions are easily fulfilled. The private firm's objective is maximizing profit. Profit is measured through a single metric, money—there is, at least in theory, a transparent bottom line. The organization is built around a production technology and associated tasks whose costs and profitability are measurable. Managers are able to hire and fire, promote, raise wages, and install other incentives in order to make sure tasks are carried out and coordinated properly. Because a company has private owners, it is clear who has authority and who does not.

In reality, of course, this oversimplifies. A private firm has multiple objectives, its production processes are difficult to monitor, and managers have trouble rearranging its internal structure of incentives. But it is probably fair to say this: most private firms are better situated along these five dimensions than are most public sector organizations (see Table 6-1). Contrast the public bureaucracy:

■   *Objectives* are multiple and vague. What are the goals of
    a Ministry of Education? Of a Foreign Ministry? Even
    of a Ministry of Industry and Commerce?

■   *Measures* of performance often are untimely,

incomplete, and inaccurate. Sometimes, measures for the most important objectives are simply unavailable.

■ *Production technologies* for providing public services may be poorly understood, ineffectual, and in some cases nonexistent. Tasks to be performed may be unclear.

■ *Motivation and coordination* may be difficult because of fixed civil service rules, an inability to hire and fire, standard operating procedures, and fractionated authority.

■ *Authority* is often fractionated, with different levels of government, different bureaucracies, politicians, and the legislature all having the ability to influence.

It would be nice if by a stroke of the pen we could magically change these attributes of public sector organizations. Unfortunately, many of these characteristics are ingrained. The goals of governmental activities tend to be vague, multiple, and value-laden. Similarly, it is often inherently difficult to measure outcomes or outputs in the public domain—or, therefore, to link pay with performance. And many of the constraints on the authority of public managers, such as civil service rules, have their origins in a laudable attempt to depoliticize the public service.

Because it is so *difficult to measure performance* in public sector activities, we observe a combination of vague objectives, poor outcome measures, poorly understood technologies and tasks, weak incentives, and fractionated lines of authority. *Information* therefore comes front and center. As in our analysis of market institutions,

TABLE 6-1

Contrasts between Public and Private Institutions

Organizational Dimension	Private	Public
Objectives	Clear, unique	Vague, multiple
Measures	Bottom line exists	Soft bottom line
Production technology	Known, measurable	Often poorly understood, hard to gauge
Powers of management to motivate, hire, and coordinate	Extensive: can alter rules and incentives; can hire and fire	Often minimal: hard to change rules and incentives; hard to fire
Lines of authority	Clear, unique	Multiple, fractionated

information again turns out to be crucial to understanding what is going wrong and what might be done to make things better. The problem is not just more information, but information that is relevant, timely, transparent, inexpensive, and resistant to fiddling and fraud. Such information will be difficult to obtain. But experience in other developing countries suggests that improvements are possible.

Chapter 7 examines the problem of incentives in the public sector. Confronted with economic crises, many countries have been forced to let public sector wages slip below levels that can attract and retain talent. Moreover, the connections between pay and performance have eroded. The results are widespread incompetence and corruption, which in many countries now threaten the basic functions of government. Although the problems are intrinsically difficult, there are interesting possibilities for the governments of countries such as Bolivia to consider. Many involve better information about the achievement of government objectives.

Chapter 8 turns to the not unrelated problem of corruption. Bribery, fraud, extortion, kickbacks, embezzlement, and other forms of corruption are widespread in the developing world. By undermining citizens' and officials' incentives to work hard and productively, corruption leads to retarded economies, predatory elites, and in some cases political instability.

Many people think that corruption is primarily caused by cultural factors, or that it is the particular sin of certain countries, peoples, or races. Instead, we analyze corruption in economic terms. Government officials have a *motive* for corruption when they cannot live on what they are paid, when the payoffs for being corrupt are large, and when the chances of their being caught and punished are small. They have an *opportunity* when they have a monopoly in relation to the public, plus discretion, minus accountability. So anticorruption strategies must change incentives in the public sector, both the positive and negative ones. Corruption is reduced by leavening government's monopoly powers, constraining official discretion, and increasing public accountability. Information once again proves a key to doing better.

In Chapter 9, we briefly turn to several aspects of governmental reorganization. We do not spend much time on administrative reform as usually practiced. In addition to the reforms discussed under the heading of corruption control, we analyze the integration and centralization of public services. We find that in deciding how to organize public institutions, once again information proves a central variable.

IMPROVING INCENTIVES IN THE PUBLIC SECTOR

FREE-MARKET REFORMS emphasize incentives. "Getting prices right" is a watchword—and properly so. But the reforms, in their understandable focus on freeing the dynamism of the private sector, have tended to overlook a whole domain of incentives: the public sector. I call this phenomenon "incentive myopia."

Among the prices that need to be right are wages, which are prices for effort and ability applied in defined directions. When it comes to public sector wages, many poor countries such as Bolivia have the prices radically wrong. I believe that distorted incentives in the public sector threaten free-market reforms and the provision of basic services. It is no exaggeration in many developing countries to speak of a crisis in public sector incentives.

The crisis has two parts, *levels* and *linkages*. Wage levels have fallen far too low to attract and keep needed talent. The linkages between financial rewards and performance have become so weak as to eliminate economic incentives. As we shall see, many poor countries have cut and compressed public sector salaries to a degree unimaginable in the industrialized West. Among the predictable results are widespread incompetence and corruption in government.

Bolivia's situation follows a common pattern. A poor country faces an extraordinary budget deficit engendered by years of overly ambitious, inefficient public policies and expanding public employment (especially at lower levels), and now exacerbated by external economic adversities. Because of heavy debt, the country cannot readily borrow to cover its deficit. The budgetary shortfall leads among other things to drastic reductions in real wages in the public sector and to the compression of salary scales. As a consequence, the incentives facing public employees erode, and this results in a brain drain, inefficiency, moonlighting, demoralization, and corruption. As these phenomena become generalized, government starts to break down. More foreign technical assistance is "required," adding to both debt and dependence. The business of government moves further away from development, toward predation.

I first became acutely aware of the incentive crisis in late 1985. Ronald MacLean Abaroa had just become the first democratically elected mayor of La Paz, Bolivia, in forty years. He invited me to assist the new administration with its economic strategy.

La Paz was virtually bankrupt. From 1978 to the middle of 1984, the city's own revenues—the taxes, fees, and so forth that it collects—had fallen in real terms by a factor of eight. By 1984, the budget deficit was fabulous: the city's own revenues covered only 24 percent of its expenditures. Moreover, laws passed in 1985 stipulated that the central government would no longer provide budget support to municipalities. At the time, the state-owned Bolivian mining company COMIBOL was shutting down its money-losing mines and dismissing almost three-quarters of its workers. Around city hall, gallows humorists quipped that if the city government were a tin mine, it would have been the first one closed.

The city's financial crisis coincided with a collapse of economic incentives. The municipal work force had grown from 4,065 employees in 1982 to 5,300 in 1985. With a larger work force, declining resources, and hyperinflation, real wages had collapsed by as much as a factor of four. Salary scales became compressed to the point where in 1984 a director earned only 1.4 times as much as a manual laborer. (See Table 7-1.)

Technical staff such as engineers were in 1985 earning the equivalent of only $30 per month—this in a city in which the cost of living in the modern sector was perhaps two-thirds of that in the United States. The mayor earned $100 a month. Not surprisingly, high-level talent had been leaving the city government. This exodus, according to informed opinion, was largely responsible for the breakdown in the quality and timeliness of public services. The collapse in pay and incentives had also stimulated unprecedented corruption.

Mayor MacLean quickly perceived the low levels of pay and the lack of linkages between pay and performance. But he also could not fail to note the city's budget deficit, which seemed to rule out higher pay and better incentives.

OTHER EXAMPLES

Consider a few other examples of the crisis in public sector incentives.

EQUATORIAL GUINEA

In 1986 I took up a two-year assignment in this tiny, impoverished African nation. Again, macroeconomic woes coincided with a dramatic erosion in public sector incentives.

In 1985 the government deficit amounted to about 12 percent of revenues. Heavy foreign debt, worth about four and a half times annual exports, meant that Equatorial Guinea could not rely on additional borrowing to finance the deficit. Spending would have to be cut. The country's creditors suggested the public payroll as a prime candidate.

But what was there to cut? Public sector wages constituted only 20 percent of current government spending. Equatorial Guinea's neighbors spent proportionally more. The corresponding percentages were 61 percent in the Central African Republic (1983), 43 percent in Cameroon (1982), and 22 percent in oil-rich Gabon (1983). Salaries were meager. As a multiple of per capita income, the average salary in the central government was lower than in any developing country analyzed in a major review by the International

TABLE 7-1

Real Average Salaries for Various Categories of Municipal Employees in La Paz, Bolivia (director's salary in 1978 = 100)

Salary	September 1978	December 1980	November 1984	October 1985
Director	100	96	40	24
Professional	69	63	30	21
Worker	13	21	29	5
Ratio (director: worker)	7.7:1	4.6:1	1.4:1	4.8:1

SOURCE: Author's reworking of data provided by Mabel Cruz, Planning Department, La Paz.

Monetary Fund.[1] The average government salary, even if spent
entirely on food, would not cover the cost of a basic basket of food
for a family of four in the capital, Malabo, and the continental
region's main town, Bata.

Simultaneously, under the auspices of the United Nations
Development Programme, a five-year plan was being prepared for
discussion with aid donors. The document noted a vacuum of
skilled people in government, which in the plan's eyes would continue to justify the presence of high-priced technical assistants from
abroad. They (and I) earned from forty to eighty times the salaries of
our Equatoguinean counterparts, not to mention elaborate fringe
benefits. The five-year plan lamented that many trained Equato-
guineans were residing in Spain, Gabon, and elsewhere and not
working to rebuild their nation. But the document was myopic about
a major reason why: the crisis in public sector incentives.

In 1985 the wages and salaries of the central administration
came to 1,291 million Communauté Financière Africaine francs
(CFAFs). I carried out a few calculations and discovered, to my aston-
ishment, that in the same year the wages and salaries of the very
much smaller number of foreign technical assistants financed
through aid and loans totaled CFAF 3,369 million. In other words,
foreigners working on foreign aid projects—this excludes diplo-
mats and representatives of international agencies—were
earning 2.6 times as much as the government's entire payroll. The
five-year plan designed by foreign experts would lead to even
greater and more expensive dependency[2]—in part because of
incentive myopia.[3]

NEPAL

An appraisal of Nepal's "demoralized, unproductive civil service"
laid the blame in large part on a crisis in public sector incentives.

> The most severe work-related constraint on morale is
> the lack of discriminating financial incentives and a
> basic pay scale that does not provide for even
> minimum subsistence for most civil servants,
> combined with a ponderous system of promotions that
> offers little hope for improvement on the basis of
> superior performance. The result of these two
> conditions is an invitation to moonlighting and
> corruption that, according to rumor, few can resist.[4]

AN INCENTIVE CRISIS IN GHANA

From 1975 to 1982 public employment in Ghana grew 14 percent per year. During the same period, the government's payroll for personal emoluments fell in real terms by 15 percent per year. By 1985 the real salary of a permanent secretary was only about one-eighth of what it was in 1977. Fringe benefits eroded less, and by the mid-1980s fringes accounted for more than half of the compensation of public servants; but the fringes came nowhere near making up for the collapse in real wages.

Salary scales became so compressed that by 1985 the ratio between the highest and lowest salaries in the civil service was only 2.3 to 1. After taxes this ratio was only 1.5 to 1.

The links between rewards and productivity eroded in other ways. The merit system disintegrated because of promotions based on seniority or favoritism and not on evaluations of performance. This pernicious phenomenon—what one might call the breakdown of meritocracy—is widespread in the developing countries.

Yet the government did not have the economic wherewithal to be able to raise pay or improve incentives. In 1983, for example, the budget deficit was 48 percent of the government's total revenues and grants.

SOURCE: *Author's field research in Ghana, June 1986. See also Robert Klitgaard,* Elitism and Meritocracy in Developing Countries *(Baltimore, Md.: Johns Hopkins University Press, 1986).*

JAMAICA

From 1972 to 1982, while Jamaica's consumer price index rose more than 450 percent, salaries in the three highest professional grades of the public service increased only 40 to 80 percent. This erosion led to a

> large exodus of skilled and experienced professionals from the civil service and, frequently, from the country itself. This emigration translated into high vacancy levels in key ministerial posts. For instance, one line agency reported a 57% vacancy rate in these posts, and an average of 47% of top positions in core agencies were vacant. Often the remaining positions were filled with marginally qualified staff.[5]

UGANDA

In September 1988 the real wage of a permanent secretary was 3 percent of what it was in January 1975. The corresponding declines were less but still striking for lower grades in the civil service: for example, to 4.8 percent of the 1975 figure for a new recruit in the entry grade of the administrative class, 11 percent for a new clerical officer, and 26.6 percent for the lowest grade (such as a messenger or cleaner). The highest monthly wage in September 1988 was that of a permanent secretary, about $43. This amount was estimated to be sufficient to buy enough green bananas to feed a family of four two meals a day for nineteen days.

This collapse of public pay has had many negative results. Officials scramble to survive by means of "internal adjustment." For example, they manipulate "undeserved or premature promotions"—a practice that "undermines not only the meaning of working hard but the very concept of a civil service as a career service where staff are recruited and promoted on the basis of merit." There has been a "massive withdrawal of working hours." "Fraudulent practices" have flourished.[6]

WORLD BANK STUDIES

The World Bank has begun to take note of public sector incentives. Arturo Israel, when he was head of the Bank's Public Sector Management and Private Sector Development Division, argued that "the World Bank's experience suggests that distortions in wages and salaries are probably among the most costly obstacles to institutional development"—in particular, paying high-quality people in the public sector too little.[7]

A World Bank review of public pay and employment problems in West Africa concluded:

> In many countries the level of real public sector salaries . . . has eroded substantially over time. The result is remuneration that is too low either to sustain lower echelon workers above the poverty level or to attract and retain skilled manpower.
>
> Compressed salaries and deteriorating working conditions have made it difficult to attract and retain high level professionals in the civil service and to keep those who remain honest and hardworking.
>
> Indeed, overstaffed bureaucracies afflicted by eroding salary scales, pervasive demoralization, corruption, moonlighting, and chronic absenteeism are often unable to carry out the essential economic policy and management tasks that are a key part of emergency economic recovery programs.[8]

An internal World Bank study bluntly criticized shortcomings in technical assistance in West Africa:[9]

> Difficulties in getting highly qualified nationals to work in the public service (low salaries, unsatisfactory working conditions, etc. . . .) increase the demand for short-term TA [technical assistance], while impeding the process of long-term institution building. . . . Government's *working environment for local professionals is not attractive and is deteriorating* in most WAN [West African] countries, prolonging dependence on foreign aid.

Consequently, the task force concluded, the Bank should do more. "We are not doing enough to improve *inadequate environment* (low salaries, unclear responsibilities, no career prospects, etc. . . .) in which trained people will have to work. This results in trained staff going to other jobs, thereby prolonging the dependence on foreign TA or reducing the performance of projects" (p. 6, emphasis in original). The World Bank should help forge "simpler and more performance-oriented government institutions," especially with respect to salaries and career prospects (p. 8).

The calls to action are welcome. Unfortunately, as Barbara Nunberg's review pointed out, the Bank's internal "studies stop short, however, of providing an operational guide for dealing with pay and employment issues."[10] Meanwhile, the International Monetary Fund (IMF) "appears generally to have prescribed wholesale wage reduction without significant attention to the detailed mechanisms by which this reduction might take place."[11]

A CONCEPTUAL APPROACH

How much should a public employee be paid? Elementary economic theory suggests "the social value of his or her long-run marginal product." In other words, society should compensate the employee at the margin for the long-run social benefits his or her efforts produce. In theory the level of such compensation will depend on a host of factors such as the characteristics of the particular employee and the rest of the public and private labor force, opportunities in the private sector, and the social evaluation of various public goods and services.

This is the elementary theory. Things are less simple when the connections are uncertain between what an employee does and the social outcomes. For example, information about those connections may be prohibitively expensive for the employer to obtain. The employer may design proxies for both effort and outcomes, but using these proxies introduces uncertainty and error, and therefore risk. An employee whose pay is linked to results will still work harder, but when uncertainty is a factor he will also face greater risks than when working for a fixed wage, since his pay will now be a function of risks he cannot control. To examine this trade-off, economists have developed the *principal-agent model*, which we will consider in Chapter 8. With this model, one can analyze, under various assumptions, the optimal mix of a base wage and an incentive payment based on results. The answer is that the assumptions matter. But only in the strangest cases is it right to pay the worker a straight wage. Some part of his remuneration should depend on the outcomes achieved.

The elementary theory also leaves out the complications of unemployment and labor sorting. Some economists argue that pay-for-performance schemes such as profit sharing reduce aggregate unemployment.[12] In another vein, the so-called new labor theory emphasizes that incentive schemes affect the employees' choices of occupation and employer. In the parlance, different payment schemes have sorting as well as incentive effects. This phenomenon has wreaked havoc with empirical estimates of the effects of linking pay and performance (and, more simply, of raising pay).

Nonetheless, voluminous research supports the idea of elementary theory that pay should be linked to performance. The literature on the relationships between pay and productivity in the United States, Europe, and Japan has been reviewed at length recently.[13] Although the linkage schemes vary and methodological problems, as always, plague empirical estimation, a good rule of thumb is that linking pay to performance induces a 20 percent increase in productivity, other things being equal. Here is another rule of thumb: Incentive and bonus payments should not exceed 25 to 30 percent of the base pay. Research also indicates, though less robustly, that pay-for-performance schemes work better when employees participate in defining the objectives and performance measures.

Where should the money for public employees come from? Elementary economics responds, "Citizens will pay for public services through nondistorting taxes and user charges." If the present generation is unable to finance public projects that also benefit future generations, the country should borrow. In a perfectly functioning capital market, creditors will be happy to fund projects whose social benefits outweigh their costs.

Conceptually, then, the crisis of public sector incentives is this. Many public employees—in particular, the skilled—are now being paid far less than what their long-run marginal value products *would be* with appropriate incentive systems. Compensation is not well-linked to socially useful outcomes. Consequently, public employees produce many fewer social benefits than they would with better incentives. Moreover, they turn to the creation of public bads like corruption. Because many poor countries face grave financial situations, they can use neither tax revenues nor borrowing to rectify this situation.

Conceptually, the solution is to evaluate the long-run social marginal products of effective performance and link to them at least part of the compensation of government employees. This change would increase social benefits. The government would cover the costs of improving incentives through increased taxes, user charges, and borrowing. But practical problems intrude:

I.   *Microeconomic problems of measuring and rewarding marginal products.* Even in the private sector it is hard to measure and reward productivity. For a variety of well-known reasons it is even more problematic in the public sector. How can one gauge long-run social benefits? Over the past thirty years social cost-benefit analysis has emerged to try to do so, but it remains a highly imperfect science.[14] Overlaying a further degree of difficulty are the problems of measuring the marginal products of particular individuals and teams within a project or ministry.[15]

Even where a marginal product can be roughly gauged, many governments find it hard to reward. Ideology, populism, and bureaucratic forces often work against raising salaries for those who produce more. Some people argue that certain cultures constrain performance-based compensation.[16] Even in advanced countries one encounters resistance to merit pay: the inevitably incomplete and imperfect measures of performance will, it is argued, result in injustices and in adverse incentives. "The basis for most of the problems with merit pay plans," observed one personnel expert, "is that the great majority of the people think their own job performance is above average. Even a well-designed merit pay plan cannot give positive feedback to the majority."[17]

Another theme of the personnel literature is that professionalism, socialization, and idealism are sometimes substitutes for financial incentives. Or to put the point another way, relying strictly on performance-based pay—if it were feasible—would cost something in terms of the self-image and morale of professionals and dedicated public servants.

These problems and competing considerations are real. The current breakdown in incentives demands that we try to do better in measuring and rewarding marginal products. But it is also true that in implementing new schemes we need to be attentive to measurement problems and the various sources of resistance and deviation. Below we will look at some efforts to measure and reward productivity that have borne fruit, and we will consider how to adapt them in other settings.

2.   *Macroeconomic disequilibrium.* Over the past thirty years, many governments in poor countries have taken on too many tasks and too many employees. The current budget crisis and need to cut public spending are in large part the result of overexpansion. No doubt, too, some government employees will do more good for their countries by working instead in the private sector. These are political judgments, not defended here, with which readers may disagree.

Nonetheless, I insist that the *extent* of the recent collapse of public sector incentives goes far beyond a wholesome correction. As described above, the radical cuts in real earnings and the incredible compression of salary scales are clearly dysfunctional. The need for adjustment reflects external disequilibriums and not just the correction of domestic mistakes or a lack of tax effort. There is a case for structural adjustment loans and grants to improve public sector incentives.

To summarize: we need to do better in measuring and rewarding productivity, and we need to devise means of raising the revenues to cover the costs. For good and bad reasons, neither will be easy.[18]

INCOMPLETE SOLUTIONS

Unfortunately, neither of these two objectives is well served by some current responses to problems of public sector pay and employment.

Unsatisfactory Answer I.   Exhort civil servants to increase "professionalism" and "discipline." In theory, professionalism is a way to overcome problems of poor measures and poor financial rewards. Well-indoctrinated professionals can be exhorted to act in the public interest. And indeed it is remarkable, given the obstacles facing public sector organizations, how much public-interested work actually does get done. Despite all the problems, most teachers do teach, most customs officials are honest, and most government health workers work hard in the interest of their patients. Still, in Bolivia and elsewhere experience shows that there are limits to a reliance on professionalism. When pay erodes—and when budgets are cut and meritocracies subverted—exhorting professionals to do their best proves in many cases to be ineffectual, and understandably so. The fact is that salary erosion tends to have professionalism as one of its victims.[19]

A separable type of exhortation calls for discipline. The key here is not professional discretion as a solution to problems of information and incentives, but the use of rules and orders. The official must be at a certain place at a certain time, performing certain tasks. Under socioeconomic conditions such as those in Bolivia's, this approach, too, often fails. Simple rules are inadequate for highly variable professional tasks, and calls for more discipline eventually sound hollow in the absence of information and incentives.

Unsatisfactory Answer 2.   Cut public payrolls. If this means lower pay, of course it exacerbates the incentive crisis. Sometimes reformers call for cuts in the numbers of employees but increases in pay levels. As it turns out, in the short run employment cuts often do not result in higher pay for those who remain. Among other things, severance pay tends to eat up the anticipated savings.[20]

Reducing public employment is politically perilous. Among the problems facing former Panamanian president Nicolás Ardito-Barletta in 1985 was the need to cut public employment by perhaps a fifth. The politically powerful public unions struck at the first whiff of a rif (reduction in force). This marked the beginning of the end for the president's economic adjustment program. Today almost all the public employees are still at their jobs, while Ardito-Barletta is not.

Apart from payrolls and politics, what are the economic effects of firing government employees? Few studies show how to absorb redundant public officials in the debilitated private sectors of poor nations undergoing economic crises. If employment cuts are required as conditions for structural adjustment aid, it would seem desirable to know much more and do much more about the human costs of transition.[21]

Nonetheless, there is a way to cut the public payroll by perhaps 10 percent: by ridding public payrolls of "ghosts," those who draw pay but do not exist. (In Panama these fictitious employees are called *botellas*, "bottles.") A methodology for "ghostbusting" is outlined later in this chapter.

Unsatisfactory Answer 3. Allow corruption to act as a correction for low wages. It has occasionally been asked, mostly by Westerners, whether bureaucratic corruption should not be welcomed. Don't bribes introduce market-like valuations of public services? If I am willing to pay you a tip for processing my customs declaration more rapidly, is that not a good indicator of the marginal product of your extra effort? And don't corrupt payments in effect substitute for higher salary scales, making the crisis in public incentives less severe than it appears?

Corruption can be socially useful if it enables inefficient or unjust rules to be circumvented. But as we shall see in Chapter 8, many studies and common experience in poor countries show that most corruption is socially harmful. Even the seemingly innocent case of illicit tips often degenerates into sandbagging and inefficiency. In general the bribe price is inefficient for several reasons. First, it reflects the marginal value to the briber of the monopolistically supplied public service, a price that will not be socially efficient because it is monopolistic. Second, the transaction may generate a host of social costs and injustices, ranging from distorted policies to public bads to distribution of goods that favor the rich and powerful.

Third, bribes reinforce perverse incentives in government and in the private sector. Corruption does result in a higher net salary for the corrupt official. What happens, though, is that officials and clients seeking corrupt payments distort the public service provided and turn the supposedly beneficent monopoly of government into a rapacious, inefficient, and unjust exploiter. As we shall see in Chapter 8, the real economic harm of corruption is the perversion of incentives. Ignoring this phenomenon is another sort of incentive myopia that has plagued the study of economic development.

Unsatisfactory Answer 4. Grant a wholesale pay increase. Higher pay is necessary to attract able people, and for some officials it may eliminate the necessity of being corrupt. Nonetheless, wholesale pay increases retain the current distorted structure of incentives (or nonincentives). What is required is to link rewards to productivity, not just to raise everyone's level of rewards (even if it were feasible). Milton Esman and John D. Montgomery's recent analysis of Nepal has general relevance:

> Bureaucratic egalitarianism in Nepal has worked to
> reduce the level of rewards and recognition to the
> lowest common denominator. Across-the-board pay

increases that would bring salary scales in HMG [His Majesty's Government] to the level of the private sector would be financially unfeasible and administratively unwise. They would not reward performance or even eliminate corruption (rich people are not more honest than poor people). What is needed is a method for providing pay incentives and bonuses (1) associated with development projects for which HMG wants to attract and reward the best talent, and (2) available on an equitable basis to civil servants engaged in other important work when their performance merits it.[22]

As public administration professor Ledivina Cariño recommended for the Philippines: "Provide inducements to do good—reward faithful, innovative service not by general system-wide increases in salary scales—that is a humanitarian gesture, not a reward—but by providing merit increases and promotions to deserving people. Across-the-board salary increases confirm the notion that government pay is independent of performance."[23]

SUGGESTIONS FOR IMPROVING INCENTIVES

Reforming public sector incentives should work if several steps are followed:

1. Measuring and rewarding performance
    a. Specifying and attempting an economic valuation of the social objectives of public programs
    b. Generating measures of and information about how well those objectives are being achieved
    c. Linking part of the compensation of public officials to the achievement of those objectives
    d. Implementing improved incentives in possibly hostile political, bureaucratic, and cultural contexts
2. Raising resources to pay for improved incentives

But for the good and bad reasons we have discussed, at every step in this process theoretically optimal answers are not in the cards. Workable responses will involve simplifications and compromises, even some distortions, especially in poor countries. The second-best nature of the situation has several implications. As we have seen, some but not all of an employee's compensation should depend on imperfectly measured achievements. Aggressive experimentation should be the thrust, rather than final answers derived from a priori theorizing. Learning-by-doing will be the rule, and mistakes will inevitably obtrude and require correction.

It proves easier to improve incentives in the "economic sector" (public works, revenue raising, agriculture) than in the "social sector" (education, health care). But it is not impossible even in the latter.[24] Necessarily simplified systems of objectives, measurements, and rewards must of course be watched carefully and corrected over time, as employees may discover unhealthy ways of achieving performance targets. It is also true that incentive schemes can be subverted, either through corruption and favoritism or, eventually, by making "performance bonuses" automatic.

Problems abound. But many developing countries now face crises that demand improved pay and incentives. Moreover, there are success stories. We should be inspired by the possibilities of improvement, not paralyzed by the theoretical and practical difficulties that we must always keep in mind.

I was inspired by the achievements of Mayor MacLean in La Paz. Among other changes, he shifted the incentives of city employees and taxpayers. In early 1986, his administration created new incentives for the revenue-raising departments. Employees were given a share of additional revenues generated. Paying city taxes and fees was rendered less costly and more automatic. As a short-term measure to correct property tax values that had been hopelessly eroded by hyperinflation, taxpayers were asked to value their own homes. The incentive for truthfulness was the veiled threat that the city might expropriate houses for the value that citizens assigned them!

These incentives proved powerful. Within less than two years the city's own revenues rose by a factor of about ten in real terms. Corruption was said to have been greatly reduced. (Computerization, strong penalties for corruption, simplification of rules, and Bolivia's control of inflation were also important factors in this success.) In 1987 the formerly bankrupt municipality found itself able to make a $1 million loan to the federal government to help settle a teachers' strike.

The experiences of other countries also contain lessons, not in the way of foolproof ideas to copy but as stimuli to experimentation and study. Let us now shift tone and proffer some practical advice to policy makers about how incentive myopia might be overcome. Table 7-2 provides a summary framework.

TABLE 7-2

Improving Public Sector Incentives:
A Framework for Policy Analysis

1. Measuring and rewarding performance

    a. Specifying and attempting an economic valuation of the social objectives of public programs
        1. Involve employees in defining goals and in defining quality.
        2. Carry out studies of the social benefits of services provided (and their improvement).

    b. Generating measures of and information about how well those objectives are being achieved
        1. Involve employees in defining measures.
        2. Use employees as measuring instruments.
        3. Understand the organization's "technology" better by carefully defining key tasks with employees' help.
        4. Involve clients and citizens in providing information.
        5. Empower clients (mechanisms for feedback, vouchers, inform clients about services and outcomes).
        6. Remember the principle of the sample.

    c. Linking part of the compensation of public officials to the achievement of those objectives
        1. Experiment and learn from experience.
        2. Resist incentive master plans.
        3. Begin with the easiest cases (economic sectors, revenue-raising agencies).
        4. Team incentives are often more feasible than individual incentives.
        5. Incentives include money but also more.

    d. Implementing improved incentives in possibly hostile political, bureaucratic, and cultural contexts
        1. Cultivate political support.
        2. Publicize the crisis of public sector incentives.
        3. Use experiments evaluated by all after a fixed time period.

2. Raising resources to pay for improved incentives

    a. Cut public employment.
        1. Freeze hiring.
        2. Reduce staff through attribution and, if possible, by firing redundant workers.
        3. Bust ghosts (fictitious workers).

    b. Cultivate the support of donors and lenders (link incentive reforms to their strategies and interests).

    c. Institute user charges (and share them with employees).

    d. Challenge technical assistance by foreigners (base their pay on performance, competition with locals, and incentive funds for locals based on salaries of foreign advisers).

    e. Privatize creatively.

MEASURING AND REWARDING
MARGINAL PRODUCTS

Incentives depend on information being available, and information depends on knowing what is interesting to measure—that is, what the public organization's objectives are. In recent years, interesting progress has been made with methods for involving employees in specifying public sector objectives. For example, the United Nations has developed a systematic workshop lasting several days that enables officials to begin to define the mission of their agency, measure success, and consider the first steps toward organizational change.

In a lecture in the People's Republic of China, Herbert Simon provided wisdom on the relationship of goal-setting to incentives.

> Even when the value of an organization's product is difficult to measure, the very attempt to define goals and to define quality will help management to guide the organization and raise its standards. . . . Neither whips nor money rewards will permit an organization to achieve its goals unless most of the members, from top managers to unskilled employees, think of what they are doing in terms of the accomplishment of its goals. . . . [Incentives are one means of] inducing subordinate managers and employees to make their decisions in terms of the goals of the whole organization . . . and every ingenuity must be used to find ways to measure their success in accomplishing those goals.[25]

Involve line employees in the specification of objectives, the definition of performance measures, and the structure of incentives. Without employee involvement, one is likely to get the wrong answers and, even if the right ones are obtained, employees are likely to resist change.[26]

Use employees as measuring instruments. Sometimes performance cannot be quantitatively calibrated but can be roughly assessed by groups of professionals. A kind of peer review procedure can be used to rank performance. This is one way of building a quality dimension into an information system; and, at the same time, of legitimizing the process.[27]

Understand the organization's "technology" better by carefully defining key tasks. Exactly how an agency accomplishes its ends is often poorly understood. One way of understanding this is, again, to involve employees in exercises that define what needs to be done for certain results to occur. Remember that task definition is crucial. In the words of James Q. Wilson, "People matter, but organization matters also, and tasks matter most of all. The principal challenge facing public managers is to understand the importance of carefully defining the core tasks of the organization and to find both pecuniary and nonpecuniary incentives that will induce operators to perform those tasks as defined."[28]

Include information from clients. Both exceptionally good performance and corruption can be more readily discovered if clients have easily accessible channels for reporting them. Examples of useful channels include publicized addresses for such communications, telephone hot lines, suggestion boxes, client surveys, the press, ombudsmen, client oversight groups, and political organizations.

Empower clients. Especially in the provision of social and agricultural services, search for ways to give the clients some form of market power. In Mexico's successful rural education program of the early 1970s, for example, the government allowed the local population to express its satisfaction or lack thereof with the teacher assigned, and to translate that satisfaction into better or worse conditions for the teacher.[29] Voucher schemes should be considered: for example, giving clients chits for fertilizer or agricultural extension services or educational services and allowing clients to choose among alternate providers.

There is, of course, a crucial link between information and empowerment: the former is necessary for the latter. When India published comparative data on infant mortality by state, it generated tremendous popular pressure for change in some of the states. Among Indian states, Tamil Nadu ranked second from the bottom. The shock of this revelation jarred Tamil Nadu's citizens to demand—and the government to provide—a new and successful nutrition program. From this example and others, Samuel Paul concludes that "comparative studies of public services and wide dissemination of their findings can, thus, help mobilize public opinion and initiate public action. This approach promises to be a useful surrogate for competition in the public sector."[30]

Remember the principle of the sample. Incentive systems require information systems. Unfortunately, too many governments think of information in terms of a census instead of a sample. They try to check or review every decision, purchase, school, or office. Reviewing every case costs too much, creates red tape, and proves undoable; the pretense of this policy ends up being so cumbersome that few real reviews take place. (The minister signs a hundred approvals in an evening.) The principle of the sample says that we can learn a lot from a random selection of thirty to fifty cases no matter how

---

IMPLEMENTATION ANALYSIS

*Charles Wolf offers five paradigmatic questions to guide the "normative/
inventive part of implementation analysis" for public programs. Notice
how they avoid incentive myopia.*

   *1. Are there relatively simple and easily administered fixes in the
operation of markets that would enable the private sector to take over
the service now publicly provided?*

   *2. Can policies be invented that, while recognizing the need for
government intervention, nevertheless try to retain valuable
characteristics of market solutions (such as competition, tangible and
publicized performance measures, beneficiary charges, and a profit center
mode of operation)?*

   *3. Can improved measures for government output be devised, so
that "nonmarket failures" resulting from a lack of a suitable metric are
reduced?*

   *4. Can the standards or goals that currently provide the incentives
for individual and agency behavior be revised so as to be more closely
connected with the final intended output?*

   *5. Can information, feedback, and evaluation systems be improved to
reduce the risks of cooptation by a client group (and to publicize this if it
occurs)?*

SOURCE: *Adapted from Charles Wolf, Jr.,* Markets or Governments: Choosing
between Imperfect Alternatives *(Cambridge, Mass.: MIT Press, 1988): 110–11.*

---

large the universe of cases. We can discover central tendencies and
patterns (such as distortions of information) with less expense and
red tape.

   The principle of the sample means things like spot checks,
random sampling of cases that are then painstakingly reviewed, and
summoning a few officials to the central office to justify their reports
in detail. This principle has a corollary in deterrence theory. As long
as people perceive that there is a small probability of their misbe-
havior being discovered, if penalties are large enough an information system built on samples will deter the penalized behavior.

   Experiment. Reforming incentives is at once an uncertain business and a controversial one. This means that a government should
experiment. For example, over a specified time period, one might try
bonuses contingent on meeting performance targets. One possibility is along these lines: "If the customs bureau generates at least 20
percent more revenue in the next six months, then 10 percent of this
additional amount will go to customs officials as a bonus and 90
percent will go to the treasury. If the target is not met, no bonus."

   A corollary of this advice to experiment might be: Resist incentive master plans for all agencies and all time. Proceed boldly but incrementally, learning from experience and sharing results and controversies. Commissions that intend to solve the incentive crisis with a single system for all agencies all at once are likely to fail. Insisting from the outset on horizontal equity across sectors of government may short-circuit reform.

Begin with the easiest cases. Revenue-raising agencies are prime candidates for two reasons: results are specific and easy to measure, and successful incentive schemes can be self-financing. In general use simple schemes with short-run outcomes instead of complicated, multiple-objective evaluations over a long time period.

Team incentives are often more feasible than individual incentives. This may be so for cultural and ideological reasons as well as technological ones having to do with the production function. In the United States, efforts to reform incentives in the public schools have generally moved from individual incentives (which failed) to schoolwide incentives (which have enjoyed some success). Competition among teachers within the same school seems to be too threatening to the schools' egalitarian culture. Better are incentives that reward, if variably, everyone in a given school (team, office).[31]

In China the "responsibility system" for organizing agriculture takes a variety of forms, but the objective is "to tie the reward received more closely to the work performed." One important technique has been to reward groups in exchange for completing specific tasks—for example, transplanting one hectare of rice seedlings.[32] The use of group rewards instead of individual ones may be for technical reasons (interdependence among workers) as well as ideological ones.[33]

Similar issues arise in modern capitalism. Rosabeth Moss Kanter emphasizes the importance of performance-based pay in the corporation of the 1990s. She highlights the five key trade-offs in incentive systems: (1) individual versus group contributions, (2) whole agency versus units, (3) discretion of management versus automatic or target-based rewards, (4) incentives relative to base pay versus relative to the value of the contributions to the agency, and (5) a single system versus multiple systems.[34]

Incentives include money but also more. I have emphasized financial incentives because their absence is now pronounced in many poor countries. Although pay and promotions are primary, incentives also can include training, travel, special assignments, transfers, awards, favorable recognition, and simple praise.

Information itself turns out to function as a reward. If an

SUCCESS WITH INCENTIVES IN GHANA

There is good news from the Ghana Railways Corporation (GRC), Highways Authority (GHA), and Ports Authority (GPA).

With the help of the World Food Programme, in 1983 the GRC linked heavily subsidized packages of food to the achievement of measurable results for each worker and for the Corporation as a whole.

Targets for Individual Productivity in
Ghana's Program of Railway Rehabilitation

Measure	Objective (4/1985–12/1986)
Selective elimination (posts/man/day)	1
Overall examination (ties/man/day)	10
Insertion of emergency ties (ties/man/day)	5
Carrying of ties (ties/man/day)	40
Unloading of ties (ties/man/day)	80
Creosotation (ties/man/day)	10
Placing of rails on the line (rails/man/day)	1
Placing of rails at point of connection (rails/man/day)	10
Painting and sanding of bridges (square feet/man/day)	100

Workers as well as administrators also had to fulfill targets for tardiness and absenteeism to be eligible for food packages. In addition the GRC established six quantitative targets for overall achievement in railway rehabilitation, as well as four targets for rehabilitating and making available locomotives and ten targets concerning the rehabilitation and availability of rail cars.

The value of the food packages in September 1984 was estimated to be 100 to 150 percent of the minimum wage. The new incentive program was crucial in the achievement of a remarkable 149 percent of the GRC's objectives in the renovation of railway lines.

Similar programs in the GHA and the GPA enjoyed similar successes. Quantitative objectives were worked out and measured, and food packages were linked to results. The GHA achieved most of its goals of road rehabilitation, and labor turnover was dramatically reduced from its pre-project level of about 50 percent. In the GPA, from 1984 to 1986 the tonnage lifted per hour per worker increased by 23 percent in the port of Tema and by 29 percent in the port of Takoradi.

SOURCE: World Food Programme, Committee on Food Aid Policies and Programmes, "Informe Resumido de Evaluación Provisional del Proyecto Ghana 2714," WFP/CFA: 24/8-A (ODW) Add. 4, Apéndice (Rome, 5 August 1987), my translation.

information system enables employees to know something about their own attainments as well as those of the people working under and around them, it provides a powerful incentive.[35]

Cultivate political support. Some labor organizations and politicians may resist incentive reforms in the name of professionalism or populism. One must have a strategy for winning their acquiescence. Publicize the crisis in public incentives and the likelihood that without reform it will only get worse. Involve the unions and the politicians in the design of the reforms, but be firm that reforms will take place. In order to reduce resistance, select experiments that all parties can judge after a relatively short time.

RAISING REVENUES

Cut public employment by busting ghosts. How do bloated bureaucracies become less so? They freeze hiring. They use normal attrition to reduce the work force. They may consider firing redundant workers; but if this proves infeasible, at least they can eliminate the ghosts.

Phantom workers can be numerous. In Zaire in 1978, about two-thirds of the names on public payrolls were fictitious; their "salaries" constituted about 20 percent of the government's budget.[36] In a typical African country, ghosts may make up a tenth of those receiving public paychecks.

The ghostbusting methodology is briefly this: list all employees, and then coordinate the often separate records in personnel management and finance departments. The list is derived from a census of government workers. To overcome political resistance it has proved advisable to carry out the census with the muscle of the presidency and—to reduce information fiddling—to obtain the help of foreign experts. It may prove desirable to re-register all government workers. The next step is to computerize personnel management records, and make certain they are compatible with payroll records, usually held in the Ministry of Finance.

Cultivate the support of donors and lenders. In the name of fiscal austerity the IMF and other international organizations may resist any increase in the public payroll. Their financial support will be important. To convince them, one should emphasize the need for capable managers of structural adjustment and for reducing corruption. Indicate that their ideas about incentives will help to invigorate the private sector and that the reform of public sector incentives is a version of the same strategy. (One might talk of "the structural adjustment of the public sector.") Donors will be pleased with the

notion of experiments with revenue-raising agencies as the first
step, especially if pay hikes are contingent on targets being met.

Institute user charges (and share them with employees). Ideally user
charges should reflect the marginal costs of providing a (private)
good or service. Nigeria has recently experimented with low user
charges that eventually redound not to the treasury but to those
providing the service.

Challenge technical assistance by foreigners. The contracts of foreign experts should contain incentive clauses based on outcomes,
including the competence attained by their local counterparts. Long-
term advisers should be considered primarily as teachers: the justification for their great cost should be the transfer of their skills to
nationals, not carrying out a specific assignment. Consider two
experiments:

- *Competition.* Create a team of local experts and existing
  government officials to carry out the same task for
  which foreign experts and their counterparts have
  been contracted. Evaluate which group does better.
  Anticipate an Adam Smith Effect: Foreign advisers
  faced with such competition will do better work than
  their norm.

- *An incentive fund based on the salaries of foreign advisers.*
  Calculate an implicit income tax of 5 to 10 percent of
  these salaries. This amount would be provided by aid
  donors to separately budgeted projects under a new
  "Program in Public Sector Incentives." The projects
  thus funded could include such things as experiments
  with performance bonuses, ghostbusting campaigns,
  organizational exercises in specifying and measuring
  objectives, anticorruption measures, and subsidies for
  the fixed costs of repatriating nationals now working
  abroad. Why the format of a pseudo-income tax? Even
  a small implicit tax rate will generate significant
  funds.[37] And the tax metaphor provides a healthy
  reminder of how huge are the tax-free salaries of
  foreign aid workers relative to those of their local
  counterparts.

Privatize creatively. Privatizing public programs can lead to both
reduced public spending and improved incentives.[38] Without entering deeply into the issues surrounding privatization, let me suggest
once again that the choice is usually not between public and private
programs.[39] Actually one encounters a spectrum of possibilities be-

tween the government's making a good or service and the government's buying it: that is, between pure public sector production and pure private sector production. In the coming years I foresee increasing experimentation with public-private combinations and hybrids: for example, private consultants working on teams with government employees or as part of government agencies, governmental management of private firms delivering public services, informal public-private decision making and advisory bodies, various kinds of nonprofit organizations, pro bono consulting by businesses and universities, careers that allow experts to move in and out of the public service, and activities carried out competitively by both public and private organizations (such as job training and placement). Nongovernmental, nonprofit organizations will also play diverse roles.

CORRECTING INCENTIVE MYOPIA

These pieces of advice have a common theme: link rewards to results. This idea is a central tenet of what some have called the new development economics. Appropriate prices for goods and services *do* work as incentives. Deepak Lal's polemic, *The Poverty of "Development Economics"* concluded: "What the experience of developing countries does show is that, other things equal, the most important advice that economists can currently offer *is* that of Stewart and Streeten's so-called Price Mechanist: 'Get the Prices Right.' "[40] In the context of this increasing emphasis on incentives, it is curious that the corresponding problem in the public sector of developing countries has scarcely been noticed.

Perhaps this oversight is the result of a desire to cut back the role of government in poor countries. But in many cases the erosion of public sector financial incentives has been so severe as now to threaten the viability of government itself. Wages are prices, and poor countries need to get these prices right in the public sector. The links between performance and rewards for public officials must be strengthened. Improvements will take diverse forms, and will usually be tentative and incomplete. Developing countries will have much to learn from each other, and from analogous problems and their solutions in the private sector and in industrialized countries. Over the next decade correcting incentive myopia will be one of the foremost challenges for public policy and management in developing countries.

CURBING
GOVERNMENT
CORRUPTION

CORRUPTION IS A SENSITIVE subject. Many citizens in developing countries shy away from the topic because they are simply exhausted by it. They have watched their leaders posture and moralize and make half-hearted efforts against corruption, all to no avail. In February 1990, when Tanzanians debated a campaign against corruption, the public reactions expressed on the front page of the government-run newspaper were overwhelmingly skeptical. A lecturer at the party's ideological college wrote, "We have the Anti-Corruption Squad under the President's office, the Permanent Commission of Inquiry, the Leadership Code, the Control and Discipline Commission of the Party and courts of law. What else do we need?"[1] Despite it all, corruption still reigned.

At about the same time as the Tanzanian debate, an article published in Guatemala illustrated another alarmingly widespread view. "When in a society the shameless triumph," the author began, "when the abuser is admired; when principles end and only opportunism prevails; when the insolent rule and the people tolerate it; when everything becomes corrupt but the majority is quiet because their slice is waiting. . . ." After a series of such laments, she ended pessimistically: "When so many 'whens' unite, perhaps it is time to hide oneself; time to suspend the battle; time to stop being a Quixote; it is time to review our activities, reevaluate those around us, and return to ourselves."[2]

The defeatism and despair are responses to ever deeper corruption in much of the developing world. Robert Wade's remarkable

study of corruption in India describes systematic government predation. "The essential business of a state Minister," he concluded,
"is not to make policy. It is to modify the application of rules and
regulations on a particularistic basis, in return for money and/or
loyalty."[3] Jean-François Bayart's monumental study of African politics is subtitled *La politique du ventre*, the politics of the gut; corruption, he says, is now the abiding reality of the African state.[4]
The United Nations sponsored an international conference on corruption in 1989. The delegates were blunt about its extent and
seriousness.

> Corruption in government is pervasive at all levels of
> public management, including, in some countries, the
> deliberate mismanagement of national economies for
> personal gain. . . . Examples were given of pernicious
> corruption in the agricultural, manufacturing,
> industrial, financial and commercial sectors. . . .
> Corruption is pervasive and is apparently
> expanding. . . .[It] has become systematic and a way
> of life in many countries.[5]

Increasingly and around the globe, a central issue in popular upris-
ings and election campaigns is corruption and what to do about it.

In the long run, today's worldwide movement toward the free
market and toward democracy will help reduce corruption. "The
general view" among delegates at the UN conference "was that the
larger the public sector, the greater the scope for corruption."[6] As
we shall see, in the long run competition and transparency—both
associated with free markets and with democracy—are the enemies
of corruption. (In the short run, however, the liberalization of markets seems to be correlated with greater, not less, corruption; and
democratic competition has sometimes, in the short run, fostered
undisciplined rent seeking that seems to citizens even more corrupt
than the previous dictatorial regime.)

Free markets, free press, democracy, and the separation of
powers are to be joyously welcomed. But again, much of the action
in controlling corruption will lie below these macro-level changes.
More than one country has discovered that macroeconomic reforms
and elections have not immediately reduced corruption. Whatever
size and roles of the state that a country deems appropriate, it
encounters the threat of bribery, extortion, influence-peddling, kickbacks, fraud, and other illicit activities.

Fighting corruption is said by almost every new third world
government—whether elected or not—to be at the top of its agenda.

CORRUPTION AND BUSINESS IN LATIN AMERICA

"Could it be a coincidence? . . . The front pages of Latin American newspapers are full of terrible stories of corruption: millions of dollars dance, the corrupt escape, some are jailed, others are conveniently let go.

"It would appear that a war has been declared throughout the continent: President Menem talks of life sentences for the corrupt, Collor de Mello promises the punishments of hell in Brazil, and there has been no lack of demands for executions.

"But men of business are pragmatists: they have watched as one after another government parades by proclaiming a clean-up, and little has happened. If today there is more vocalizing, says this skeptical majority, it's because the sweet silver left the taste for easy money, but there is little money to capture.

"Moreover, buying favors is for some cheaper than competing for contracts or bids. The region's businesses are not only the victims of corruption, sometimes they're its instigators.

"But the costs of corruption as a system are enormous. The most visible is the fact that one has to pay a percentage—which varies from 2 to 15 percent—to achieve any movement on the part of those who decide about a deal. A general cost is the lack of transparency. For some, corruption makes in profitable to regulate, to intervene in the economy, to create agencies and committees, laws and regulations. The economic system is transformed into an entanglement of barriers that have to be lubricated with bribes. The apparatus of the state inflates itself, it becomes heavy and arbitrary, it suctions off what it can. Everything becomes particularized, there are dominions of this or that economic group associated with this or that political group. Competition is brought to a halt, and a Creole-style feudalism is crowned.

"One must recognize, of course, that we aren't the only ones. Corruption is a serious problem in the United States, Japan, and Europe. Here it is more painful because it is now a vital gear [engranaje] of the economy. And this is so because our countries combine an enormous state apparatus with an endemic poverty: the best broth for the cultivation of corruption.

"Does any hope remain that we get rid of the legion of money-eaters? In truth, yes. Incorporating the fight against corruption is part of the overall modernization of our societies.

"The fight against corruption is the other modernization, whose necessity makes itself felt at the hour of going forth to compete in the world, of attracting foreign investment. The rest of its liberalizing efforts probably depend on its success."

SOURCE: *"El Negro Mapa de la Corrupción,"* AMERICAECONOMIA, no. 42 (August 1990): 9, my translation.

Unfortunately, the literature on development provides little guidance.

A LACK OF POLICY ANALYSIS

True, new scholarly work shows that rent-seeking and "directly unproductive profit-seeking activities" can distort incentives.[7] Recent research on "influence activities" in organizations reveals other sources of distortion.[8] And empirical work shows—no surprise to people living in poor countries—that corruption causes harm.[9]

But the academic literature says little about how to reduce corruption. Typical is a study carried out under the auspices of the World Bank's Management and Development Series in 1983. The authors expend all their energies to support this simple conclusion: "Corruption has a deleterious, often devastating, effect on administrative performance and economic and political development."[10] None of the monograph's eighty-six footnotes refers to strategies for fighting corruption. After showing corruption to be a bad thing, the authors note, as though in an afterthought, that "governments may increasingly wish to consider possible measures to counteract this scourge" and then they simply list, without examples or supporting arguments, four vague and unhelpful "possible measures."[11]

Many students of development have simply been reluctant to study the subject. Of course, there are practical reasons for this: data are scarce, and countries are unlikely to welcome such scrutiny. But there is another factor: first world scholars do not want to be seen as calling third world people corrupt. Gunnar Myrdal decried this "diplomacy in research. . . . The taboo on research on corruption is, indeed, one of the most flagrant examples of this general bias . . . [which] is basically to be explained in terms of a certain condescension on the part of Westerners."[12] Not incidentally, some social scientists have argued that bribes cannot be distinguished from transactions, that to try to do so is to import Western or one's own normative assumptions. A bribe, a fee for service, a gift—analytically, it is said, they are the same. So we should not talk too much about corruption or, if we do, not be too critical of it.

But as many poor countries have slid into deeper economic trouble, the sheer fact that corruption is so widespread and so devastating to economy and society has become impossible to avoid. People in the developing countries have led the outcry. One top official was offended by the social scientists' suggestion that corruption could help development:

I think it is monstrous for these well-intentioned and
largely misguided scholars to suggest corruption as a
practical and efficient instrument for rapid
development in Asia and Africa. Once upon a time,
Westerners tried to subjugate Asia . . . by selling
opium. The current defense of Kleptocracy is a new
kind of opium by some Western intellectuals, devised
to perpetuate Asian backwardness and degradation. I
think the only people . . . pleased with the
contribution of these scholars are the Asian
Kleptocrats.[13]

Professor Ledivina Cariño of the University of the Philippines,
in a paper written before the overthrow of Ferdinand Marcos, complained that the "careful balancing of good and bad effects seems to
be a recognition that everyone knows corruption is not really beneficial but positive effects must be discovered so that one does not
condemn a country completely. Compare the outrage of American
scholars against Nixon's indiscretions and their near-approval of
more blatantly corrupt regimes in countries where they have
worked."[14]

By its nature corruption is difficult to observe. It is inherently a
secretive activity; and when it is made public, corruption occasions
shame. This last trait of bribery and related activities, one that has
been observed throughout history and across cultures, is a sign of its
immorality, as legal scholar John T. Noonan, Jr., concluded:

Bribery is universally shameful. . . . In no country do
bribetakers speak publicly of their bribes, or
bribegivers announce the bribes they pay. No
newspaper lists them. No one advertises that he can
arrange a bribe. No one is honored precisely because
he is a big briber or a big bribee. . . . Not merely the
criminal law—for the transaction could have happened
long ago and prosecution be barred by time—but an
innate fear of being considered disgusting restrains
briber and bribee from parading their exchange. . . .

Shame and hypocrisy in the use of language are
vice's tribute to virtue. Shame may be culturally
conditioned. Shame so strong and general is
acknowledgment that there is something objectionable
in the conduct that goes beyond the impolite and the
merely illegal. Shame does not conclusively establish
but it points to the moral nature of the matter.[15]

Corruption is therefore doubly difficult to discuss: it is secretive and it is sensitive. Its moral nature combines with its social destructiveness in an explosive combination.

And so corruption has left us intellectually paralyzed. The frustrated, cynical citizen asks, "What can be done if the whole system is corrupt and the people on top do not care?" The scholar may also ask, "If I look at corruption, don't I accuse a people of being morally derelict?"—and this in the academic culture is forbidden. Beyond calling for less government and more democracy—both admirable but not sufficient—the effect is of a collective shrug of the shoulders.

We will focus instead on corrupt *organizations.* Thomas C. Schelling provides this useful reminder:

> An organization, business or other, is a system of
> information, rules for decision, and incentives; its
> performance is different from the individual
> performances of the people in it. An organization can
> be negligent without any individual's being negligent.
> To expect an organization to reflect the qualities of the
> individuals who work for it or to impute to the
> individuals the qualities one sees in the organization is
> to commit what logicians call the "fallacy of
> composition." Fallacy isn't error, of course, but it can
> be treacherous.[16]

The subject of Schelling's essay is the social responsibility of business, but his insight is applicable to the problem of corruption as well. The fallacy of composition lurks here, too. It is too often assumed that organizations, or entire governments, are corrupt simply because of immoral people and therefore that nothing can be done about corruption short of generations of moral education. But let us pursue Schelling's idea. Is it not possible that organizations can alter their "systems of information, rules for decision, and incentives" to reduce corruption? How?

TYPES OF CORRUPTION

First let us say a few words about the many types of corrupt and illicit behavior. Corruption is the misuse of public office for private ends. Examples range from the monumental to the trivial. Bolivia has had experience at both extremes: in the regime of General García Meza from 1980 to 1981, which has been described as the first government "of, by, and for narcotics traffickers"; and in the many instances of small-scale corruption encountered routinely by citizens of the principal cities. Corruption can involve the misuse of important policy instruments—tariffs and credit, irrigation systems and housing policies, the enforcement of laws and rules regarding public safety, the observance of contracts, and the repayment of loans— or simple procedures. Corruption may become systematic—for example, when it infects the daily business of government like collecting taxes, passing items through customs, letting public contracts to build or supply, or carrying out police work. On occasion a corrupt act may be socially harmless, even helpful. It may allow the circumvention of a stupid rule, for example, or it may effect a kind of politically stabilizing redistribution. But as most Bolivians will attest, and as careful studies in other countries repeatedly show, most corruption is socially pernicious. When corrupt behavior is widespread, it stunts economic growth, undermines political legitimacy, and demoralizes both public officials and ordinary citizens.

Granted that corruption is generally harmful, at the heart of policy analysis is the differentiation of corrupt behaviors and the careful analysis of their extent, social costs, and particular beneficiaries. Corruption can encompass promises, threats, or both; can be initiated by the public servant or the interested client; can entail acts of omission or commission; can include illicit or licit services; can be inside or outside the public organization. The borders of corruption are hard to define and depend on local laws and customs.

Consider the problems encountered by Justice Efren Plana when he took over the Philippines' Bureau of Internal Revenue (BIR) in 1975. Positions within the bureau were being bought and sold. One job that paid $10,000 a year was going for $75,000 because of its lucrative opportunities for corruption. Plana also discovered embezzlement, fraud, counterfeiting, extortion of taxpayers, *lagay* (money to speed up paperwork), *arreglos* (side payments to reduce tax liabilities), and corrupt internal investigation and enforcement. Table 8-1 presents a summary of what Plana found.

Confronted with this botanical garden of illicit activities in an environment as corrupt as the Philippines, many people would have concluded that nothing could be done. Plana, however, launched what proved to be a successful campaign to reduce corruption. How he did so is instructive.

THE USEFULNESS OF
ECONOMIC METAPHORS

First, Judge Plana had to consider the causes of corruption. This is a topic on which much has been written from many viewpoints. Some ancients attributed official corruption to greed—the fourteenth-century Islamic scholar Abdul Rahman Ibn Khaldun blamed it on "the passion for luxurious living within the ruling group"—no doubt true but perhaps not particularly helpful. Others have ascribed corruption to particular cultures (be they dictatorial, personalistic, or gift giving)[17] or racial groups ("mulatto states" are more prone to corruption, according to Samuel Huntington; certain Orientals, according to Max Weber).[18] Still others have pointed out that corruption tends to be most prevalent when social norms are in flux or break down, and during a boom or a bust. Corruption has been blamed on too much capitalism and competition as well as on too little; on colonialism and on the withdrawal of the colonial powers; on traditional regimes and on the breakdown of traditions.[19]

TABLE 8-1

Types of Corruption in the Philippines' Bureau of Internal Revenue, 1975

External corruption	
Lagay	Speed money and payments for supposedly free paper work. Extensive, small sums. Taxpayer involved gains, but overall taxpayers lose.
Extortion	Assessors threaten taxpayers with higher rates, preying on their ignorance or their unwillingness to subject their cases to costly litigation. Fairly extensive and political dynamite. Taxpayers lose.
Arreglo	Assessors and taxpayers collude to reduce tax liabilities. Widespread, large sums. Taxpayer involved gains, but noncorrupt taxpayers lose and government loses millions in revenues.
Internal corruption	
Embezzlement	Employees make off with funds collected. Widespread, especially in provinces. Government loses millions in revenues.
Fraud	Overprinting of tax stamps and labels. Not very widespread, not very costly.
Personnel scams	Choice positions within the BIR allocated for bribes. Systematized, widespread in provinces. Contributes to BIR's culture of corruption.
Delaying remittances	Tax collectors take the float on funds received. Fairly extensive, small losses.
Corruption of internal investigations	BIR's Internal Security Division rendered ineffective, exacerbating all the Bureau's problems of corruption.

MANY, MANY CAUSES AND CONDITIONS

In this chapter, we do not analyze what might be called the ultimate causes of corruption. An example of the opposite predilection is a recent book by the Nicaraguan accountant Francisco Ramírez Torres. After observing at length that corruption's causes include the family, the school, attitudes toward work, the enterprise, the nation, and the international situation, the author arrives at the level of the individual transgressor. Here the causes of corruption include excessive consumption of alcohol, extramarital activities, speculative losses, excessive gambling, "causes related to vanity," administrative disorganization, resentment inside the business, frustration on the job, "the thirst for illicit enrichment," and five others.

This chapter oversimplifies the complex reality that Ramírez Torres describes. The reason for doing so—as in the rest of the book—is certainly not scientific completeness. It is pragmatic: to focus on certain ways that policy and management can reduce corruption.

SOURCE: *Francisco Ramírez Torres, Los Delitos Económicos en los Negocios (Managua: Talleres de Don Bosco, 1990): 22–26, 40–50.*

And then there are the thoroughgoing cynics, who do not understand why corruption needs to be explained because corruption is everywhere, even (as recent events underscore) in the most "advanced" countries. This idea leads naturally to demeaning anticorruption efforts as necessarily futile, as if one were to mount a campaign against the sun's daily setting.

When rhetoric deflates, however, several points seem important. First, corruption is a matter of degree and extent. It does and has varied over space and time. Second, experience shows that corruption can be reduced, if never eliminated. Third, most corrupt acts are not crimes of passion but crimes of calculation. Officials are not corrupt all the time, at every opportunity; and so it is reasonable to posit that an official undertakes a corrupt action when, in his judgment, its likely benefits outweigh its likely costs. The benefits and costs vary according to many factors—some of which may be influenced by public policy.

In the Philippines, Judge Plana asked why so much corruption existed inside the Bureau of Internal Revenue. He looked at the motives and opportunities facing agents within the BIR. We can appreciate this approach, I think, by using economic metaphors to analyze corruption.

First, imagine a *public agent*—such as a judge, civil servant, or politician—trading off her benefits from undertaking a corrupt act

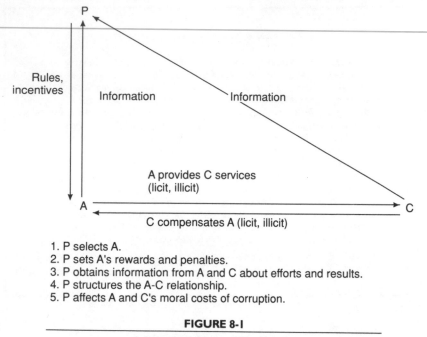

1. P selects A.
2. P sets A's rewards and penalties.
3. P obtains information from A and C about efforts and results.
4. P structures the A-C relationship.
5. P affects A and C's moral costs of corruption.

FIGURE 8-1

A Principal-Agent-Client Model

against the costs to her of doing so. (A similar analysis can be made of the person—or "client"—offering the bribe.) Second, imagine a *principal* like Justice Plana—for the moment assumed to be non-corrupt—facing another trade-off: between the social benefits of reducing the agent's corrupt activity and the social costs of taking various steps to obtain that reduction. The combination of these two metaphors is a *principal-agent-client model* (see Figure 8-1).

The public official is an agent pledged to act on behalf of the principal to produce public services. But the agent can use her position to reap private benefits in transactions with the client. These transactions may create public bads. The agent engages in them depending on their costs and benefits to her. The principal's problem is to induce the agent to create the optimal amounts of public goods and bads.

Suppose the agent is offered a bribe. The economic metaphor says that the agent faced with a bribe makes a calculation. She trades off the potential benefits to her of accepting the bribe and undertaking a corrupt act against the potential costs to her of doing so. (A similar analysis can be made of the person offering the bribe.)

If she refuses the bribe, she receives her usual pay and enjoys what we might call the moral satisfaction of resisting a bribe. If she is corrupt, she of course receives the bribe. But she also suffers the "moral cost" of being corrupt. Like the moral satisfaction of refusing the bribe, the moral cost of accepting it may be high or low, depending on the person, the situation, the organization, and the culture.

By accepting the bribe the official also runs a risk: there is some chance she will be caught and punished. She has to weigh this prospect when making her decision. The penalty could include the loss of her pay and her job, a penalty, disgrace, and so forth.

Here, then, is the official's simplified choice according to our first economic metaphor:

If I refuse the bribe, I receive my pay and the moral satisfaction of not being corrupt.

If I accept the bribe, I receive the amount of the bribe but "pay" a moral cost. There is also a chance that I will be apprehended and punished, in which case I will also pay a penalty.

So, I will accept the bribe if the bribe minus *the moral cost* minus *[(the probability I am caught and punished)* times *(the penalty for being corrupt)]* is greater than *my pay* plus *the satisfaction I get from not being corrupt.*[20]

Let us briefly consider the pieces of this calculation. Notice how each aspect of the official's calculation can in principle be altered through government policy.

■   *Pay.* Low pay encourages corrupt behavior. As we saw in Chapter 7, in many developing countries government officials must supplement their pay in some fashion in order to feed their families. An opposite effect occurs if pay bonuses can be earned by discovering corrupt behavior.

■   *Moral satisfaction and moral costs.* Although the subjective evaluation of illicit acts depends on many factors, some of them idiosyncratic, it may be the case that policies such as a code of ethics and changing an organization's "culture" can raise or lower the costs.[21]

■   *The size of the bribe.* Here we must include the economic calculation of the corrupt citizen. He will offer a bribe only if the service is thereby obtained more cheaply than through normal channels (where the "price" may include waiting and the costs of uncertainty, or where in the case of an illicit service it may not be available). Economic logic suggests that the size of the bribe will be related to the monopoly power of the official, the demand for the service being provided, the probability of the citizen's being caught and punished, and the size of the punishment if the citizen is caught.[22] To the extent an official enjoys monopoly power and discretion over whether a service (licit or illicit) is granted or how much is granted, she has more opportunity to receive a bribe, whether she asks for it or waits for it to be offered. Among other things, then, reducing monopoly power and limiting discretion will tend to reduce corruption.[23]

■   *The probability of a corrupt official's being caught.* Being caught depends on whether the illicit act is detected, which in turn depends on the system of information and enforcement. Better information may include such things as special investigations, undercover agents, citizen hot lines, computerized records, and more—as we will see later in the chapter.

■   *The punishment, if caught.* Stiff penalties will tend to reduce corruption, other things being equal. They may include firing, fines, and imprisonment, but also rebukes, negative publicity, loss of professional standing, transfers, and so forth.

Since public policy and management can affect all these variables, it follows that they influence the prevalence of corruption.

Much recent economic theory concerns itself with the principal-agent problem and its extensions, including the problems of implementing a "unified governance structure," which includes incentives, information systems, decision rules, hierarchical structures, and the control of "influence activities."[24] The complexity of the problem of a real principal like Plana soon outstrips available models, but one can usefully continue with economic metaphors. For heuristic purposes, I have found it useful to put into five categories the principal's tools for controlling corruption:

1.   selecting the agents (and training them)

2.   altering the incentives facing agents and clients (for both efforts and results)

3.   collecting and processing information on the agents' and clients' efforts and results

4.   restructuring the agent-client relationship (for example, reducing monopoly powers, clarifying rules and procedures to circumscribe agents' discretion, changing decision making, and indeed, redefining the mission of the organization)

5.   raising the moral costs of corruption (for example,

with ethical codes and changes in the organizational
culture)

Production functions connect each of these anticorruption
tools with changes in the levels and location of various types of
corruption. The principal needs to know how big a reduction in
corruption he is likely to get for how extensive (and expensive) a
policy change (a factual question about the production functions),
and how much this reduction is worth compared with the direct and
indirect costs of the reforms themselves (an evaluative question,
which also of course has factual elements).

The evaluative question is complicated and exceeds our current ability to model and estimate. The benefits of reducing corruption should be evaluated in terms of efficient allocation (static),
better incentives (dynamic), political legitimacy, distributional
equity, and other dimensions. The costs of anticorruption measures
will be gauged in terms of money, but also in terms of politics,
organizational red tape, and organizational culture. Moreover, the
principal cares not only about corruption but also about the primary
business of his agents and agency (for example, collecting taxes,
convicting criminals, or distributing pharmaceuticals). The principal
is also involved with other agents in other "games." These may
interact with his efforts to reduce corruption, and he has to be
attentive to these externalities.

Metaphorically, the policy analytic problem plays out this
way. First, the principal analyzes his organization. He examines the
agents' behavior (and the corrupt public clients') and estimates
where and how much corruption occurs. Experience as well as
theory indicate that an organization is most vulnerable to corruption
at points where agents enjoy greater monopoly power over clients,
have greater discretion over the provision of a licit or illicit service,
and take actions that are more difficult to monitor. Reducing monopoly power is a key element in the literature on rent seeking. A
stylized equation holds: corruption = monopoly + discretion −
accountability.

Second, the principal evaluates the various costs (and possible
benefits) that different kinds of corrupt activities entail, and to
whom.

Third, he determines the various policies through which he
can affect the calculations of potentially corrupt officials and citizens. He imagines enacting these policies and asks, "As I turn the
dial and spend more resources on them, how do various kinds of
corruption respond and how much does turning the dial cost?" To

allocate his resources efficiently, he must choose the appropriate types of corruption to attack and the appropriate types and levels and sequences of anticorruption policies to employ. In the first instance, he should look for a type of corruption that is important but relatively cheap to address. For political purposes, it is often important to begin a campaign against corruption with actions that can make an impact in six months—even if not against the most serious form of corruption.

An anticorruption campaign should not be pushed so far that its costs outweigh the benefits in reduced corruption. Reducing corruption is only one of the ends he seeks, and it is a costly one. This point deserves underscoring in a chapter about corruption. Because its prevention, discovery, and prosecution are costly, the optimal amount of corruption is not zero. The optimal campaign against corruption must balance reducing corruption against such considerations as cost, morale, red tape, and reducing official discretion.[25]

Using these metaphors has proved useful with policy makers in developing countries. Table 8-2 is a heuristic framework designed to help policy makers think more creatively about ways to control corruption. Notice how it uses economic intuitions without a mathematical model.

Justice Plana made moves in each of the areas described in the framework, as Table 8-3 summarizes. (The other successful cases I have studied of reducing corruption can also be usefully assimilated in this framework.) As Plana described it to me, his strategy had three parts.

First, establish a new performance evaluation system with the help of BIR employees and link incentives to it.

Second, collect various sources of information about corrupt activities.

Third, fry some big fish—that is, punish the high-level violators. This later step signaled to the BIR and the public that the rules of the game had changed.

Within three years, Plana had knocked out the internal market for jobs and extortion, greatly reduced *arreglos* and internal corruption, and reduced *lagay*. Tax revenues were up, and even those opposed to Ferdinand Marcos lauded Plana's sensational success.[26]

INFORMATION

In fighting corruption, Justice Plana emphasized information and incentives; this recalls Thomas Schelling's reminder that "an organization, business or other, is a system of information, rules for decision, and incentives." As political economist Susan Rose-Ackerman writes:

> All public bureaucracies must resolve two fundamental problems. First, they must specify individual tasks in a way that is consistent with each official's information-processing capabilities, and, second, they must motivate officials to carry out their duties conscientiously. It is pointless for low-level officials to know what they ought to do if they are not motivated to do it and equally futile to design a sophisticated motivational system that is ineffective because bureaucrats lack crucial information.[27]

Information about corruption is of course difficult to obtain. Bribery is rarely proved; accusations of bribery may be abundant and motivated by considerations other than the truth. Legal activity in this area may be a misleading indicator. One society may exhibit virtually no legal response to widespread corruption, whereas another society may define corruption and prosecute it in ways that may suggest that it is everywhere when in fact it is relatively scarce. Garnering data, the first step of any anticorruption effort, therefore faces great difficulties. Unlike many other policy issues, the information sought will probably not include survey data, economic indicators, and the like. More ingenious, indirect means must be devised.

In Plana's case and in the successful anticorruption efforts I have studied, policy makers used a variety of information-gathering devices:

- finding "heroes" within the organization—people known to be clean—and having them examine a sample of cases, decisions, or offices for evidence of corruption (and more generally of inefficiency)
- convening inquiry commissions, as proved so successful in 1989 in Zimbabwe
- using undercover agents
- devising new, often indirect measures of corrupt behavior (for example, the spending habits or wealth of top officials, the prevalence of illegal activities that would be abetted by official corruption)
- involving the public through devices ranging from hot lines to citizens' committees to random samples of clients

TABLE 8-2

Controlling Corruption: A Framework for Policy Analysis

A. Select agents.

    1. Screen out the dishonest (using past records, tests, predictors of honesty).

    2. Exploit outside "guarantees" of honesty (use networks for finding dependable agents and making sure they stay that way).

B. Set agents' rewards and penalties.

    1. Change rewards.

        a. Raise salaries to reduce the need for corrupt income.

        b. Reward specific actions and agents that reduce corruption.

        c. Use contingent contracts to reward agents on the basis of eventual success (e.g., forfeitable nonvested pensions, performance bonds).

        d. Link nonmonetary rewards to performance (training, transfers, perks, travel, publicity, praise).

    2. Penalize corrupt behavior.

        a. Raise the severity of formal penalties.

        b. Increase the principal's authority to punish.

        c. Calibrate penalties in terms of deterrent effects and breaking the culture of corruption.

        d. Use nonformal penalties (training; transfers; publicity; blackballing; loss of professional standing, perks, and travel privileges).

C. Obtain information about efforts and results.

    1. Improve auditing and management information systems.

        a. Gather evidence about possible corruption (using red flags, statistical analysis, random samples of work, inspections).

        b. Carry out "vulnerability assessments."

    2. Strengthen information agents.

        a. Beef up specialized staff (auditors, computer specialists, investigators, supervisors, internal security).

        b. Create a climate in which agents (e.g., whistle-blowers) will report improper activities.

        c. Create new units (ombudsmen, special investigatory committees, anticorruption agencies, inquiry commissions).

   3. Collect information from third parties (media, banks).
   4. Collect information from clients and the public (including professional associations).
   5. Change the burden of proof, so that the potentially corrupt (e.g., public servants with great wealth) have to demonstrate their innocence.
D. Restructure the principal-agent-client relationship to leaven monopoly power, circumscribe discretion, and enhance accountability.
   1. Induce competition in the provision of the good or service (through privatization, public-private competition, competition among public agents).
   2. Limit agents' discretion.
      a. Define objectives, rules, and procedures more clearly and publicize them.
      b. Have agents work in teams and subject them to hierarchical review.
      c. Divide large decisions into separable tasks.
      d. Limit agents' influence (change decision rules, change decision makers, alter incentives).
   3. Rotate agents functionally and geographically.
   4. Change the organization's mission, product, or technology to render them less susceptible to corruption.
   5. Organize client groups to render them less susceptible to some forms of corruption, to promote information flows, and to create an anticorruption lobby.
E. Raise the "moral costs" of corruption.
   1. Use training, educational programs, and personal example.
   2. Promulgate a code of ethics (for civil service, profession, agency).
   3. Change the corporate culture.

In addition, *participatory diagnosis* proves surprisingly useful: that is, working with officials from corrupt institutions in the analysis of corrupt activities. In my experience, as long as one is not looking for particular individuals who are corrupt, it is surprising how much information about corruption can be obtained from officials within a supposedly corrupt organization. They are able and willing to identify places vulnerable to corruption, even to design workable changes.

TABLE 8-3

**Applying the Framework for Controlling Corruption:
What Justice Plana Did**

A. Selected agents.
   1. Investigated past records to weed out the dishonest. Used professional criteria for recruitment and appointment. Created new rules against nepotism.
   2. Exploited external "guarantees" of honesty by using military and civilian intelligence personnel as information agents.
B. Set agents' rewards and penalties.
   1. Rewards: Installed a new performance evaluation system, which provided incentives for more efficient, less corrupt tax collection. Cleaned up the personnel transfer system. Used prizes, travel, perks, praise as incentives.
   2. Penalties: Dismissed and prosecuted high-level violators. Raised the pain of dismissal by publicizing the names and stories of offenders.
C. Obtained information about efforts and results.
   1. Implemented a red flag system for identifying possibly corrupt agents. Installed another system to spotlight possible tax evaders.
   2. Strengthened the role of information agents (Internal Security Division, Fiscal Control Division). Appointed a special staff of senior "heroes" and young, outside CPAs to investigate suspicious cases and some randomly selected cases.
   3. Used third parties to obtain credible information (Commission on Audit monitored tax remittances; intelligence agents inspected financial records of BIR officials; conducted undercover operations).
   4. Did not use clients or public, but did involve the media heavily.
   5. Did not change the burden of proof.
D. Restructured the principal-agent-client relationship to leaven monopoly power, circumscribe discretion, and enhance accountability.
   1. Used performance monitoring and targets for tax collection to stimulate competition among agents.
   2. Limited agents' discretion: centralized handling of large cases; instituted more controls over remittances, stamps, and so on; increased use of banks to collect funds; made some changes in tax laws; improved supervision.
   3. Rotated field agents geographically.
   4. Did not redefine the organization's mission, product, or technology.
   5. Did not organize taxpayers or civic groups.
E. Raised the "moral costs" of corruption.
   1. Held "reorientation seminars" and set pristine personal example.
   2. Promulgated values of public service.
   3. Changed corporate culture: supported the toastmaster's club, glee club, athletics, morning masses at the BIR, participatory management in creating new performance evaluation system.

INFORMA I ION IN VENEZUELA, THEN AND NOW

In 1882, the minister of finance told Congress: "Venezuela doesn't know what it owes and to whom. . . . The books of the country are behind by twenty years. . . . No system of control exists. . . . We don't know what we have nor what we export. . . . We simply don't know."

"A hundred years later," notes the Venezuelan writer Gustavo Coronel, "the Controller General of the Republic would say almost exactly the same thing."

In 1982 the controller general summed up the situation of the Venezuelan public sector. "He defined it," reports Coronel, "as a system 'totally out of control.' He felt frustrated because his numerous denunciations of administrative fraud had fallen on deaf ears and because those denounced continued enjoying the acceptance of the Venezuelan society 'at all levels.'. . . The reigning chaos in the country offered fertile grounds for acts of corruption of all kinds. It was not in vain that Arturo Uslar Pietri, at this same time, said that Venezuela had produced an anti-miracle, the conversion of immense petroleum riches into social misery."

Coronel estimates that over the past fifty years, about a third of the country's petroleum resources went to foreign companies ("for what was essentially licit work"), a third "was invested in the country," and the other third "went into the hands of the scoundrels [los pillos], some with highborn names and others born in the barrios, all sharing the same objective of personal enrichment at the expense of an immense mass of good, resigned people."

SOURCE: Gustavo Coronel, Venezuela: La Agonía del Subdesarrollo (Caracas: Litografía Melvin, 1990), 139–40, 146, my translation.

Table 8-4 shows one result of participatory diagnosis by officials in the city government of La Paz in late 1985. It was the first step in what proved to be an effective campaign against corruption.

The greatest enemy of corruption is the people. This is why almost every new government—elected or not—justifies itself by promising to combat the corruption of the previous regime. Even though individual citizens participate in corruption, the people as a whole despise it and understand the corrosion of incentives that it entails. Successful campaigns against corruption involve the public. For example, take Hong Kong's Independent Commission against Corruption (ICAC).

When started in 1974, the ICAC had three main components. The Operations Department investigated, arrested, and helped prosecute the corrupt. The Corruption Prevention Department stressed prevention and worked with government agencies to determine where organizations were most vulnerable to corruption. The ICAC had the power to "secure" changes in working procedures in

TABLE 8-4

Participatory Diagnosis in Action: Analyzing Corruption in the La Paz City Government, 1985

Type of Corruption	Value (millions of U.S. dollars)	Who Benefits	Who Is Hurt	Causes	Cures
Tax evasion (all kinds)	20–30	Evaders	Recipients of city services; nonevaders; future paceños	Hard to pay; taxes too high; low penalties; no reviews of cases	Make easier to pay; lower rates; raise penalties and enforce them; review cases
Tax *arreglos* (all kinds)	5–10	Corrupt taxpayers and officials	Recipients of city services; nonevaders; future paceños	Lack of computerization; low effective penalties; no reviews; pay through municipality; low pay	Computerize; raise penalties; review cases; pay through banks; raise pay; raise incentives to collect
Extortion	0.5–1	Corrupt officials	Direct victims	Difficult rules, rates, and procedures; hard-to-report extortion; low penalties; no reviews; low pay	Simplify rules, rates, and procedures; hot line for public reports; raise penalties; review cases; pay through banks; raise pay
Speed money	0.5–1	Some taxpayers; corrupt city officials;	Most taxpayers via slowdowns; reputation of city government	Difficult procedures; lack of computerization; pay through municipality; low penalties; no surveillance; low pay	Simplify procedures; computerize; pay through banks; raise penalties; surveillance and "whistleblowing"; raise pay
Theft (city property, parts, "boot" fees by police)	0.5–1	Thieves; some who don't pay vehicle taxes	Recipients of city services; trust in police	Lack of inventories; poor decentralization; low penalties; no reviews or surveillance	Computerize inventories; decentralize responsibility; conduct spot checks and surveillance
Procurement	0.5–3	Corrupt officials and winning suppliers	Recipients of city services	Lack of information on prices; no reviews; low penalties; low pay	Verify prices; review cases; raise effective penalties; raise pay of decision-making officials
Reporting late to work; phantom workers	0.1–0.2	Malingerers	Morale and reputation of city government	No surveillance; low penalties	Conduct surveillance; raise penalties and enforce them

government agencies in order to reduce the opportunities for corruption. Many of its activities can be analyzed with the framework of Table 8-2.[28] The third component was the Community Relations Department. It gathered information and support from the people.

The ICAC installed hot lines and complaint boxes where the public could report corruption and inefficiency. A radio call-in show became popular, as citizens vetted their complaints. The ICAC visited schools and workplaces. It set up offices in the barrios. These offices joined together employees of the ICAC; members of the barrio council or local government; and citizens, meaning housewives, and business people but, importantly, *representatives of civic associations*. Notice the components: central government, local government, and citizens and their associations.

Six citizen oversight bodies acted like boards of directors over various of the ICAC's activities. The civic associations brought both competence and credibility. Take auditors' and accountants' associations, for example: their members knew a lot about detecting corruption. They also had a reputation for honesty and, because they are not of the government, for independence as well.

In societies where irresponsibility and inefficiency have been widespread, credibility is of central importance. The citizenry may have arrived at the sad point of simply not believing or trusting the government. Here the involvement of the people is crucial, for several reasons.

First, the people can be an invaluable *source of information* about where corruption and inefficiency occur. They can be tapped for reports of isolated cases as well as chronic problems—they know where government is working and where it is not. This does not mean, of course, that every anonymous accusation of corruption is to be believed. In fact, most are false. But a trustworthy body with technical competence to investigate corruption can sift through the reports it receives from the people, looking for patterns and for cases that are important and systematic. This is what the Independent Commission against Corruption did in Hong Kong—with the people's involvement.

We have just mentioned the second and third reasons why the involvement of the people is important: *trustworthiness* and *competence*. Government may have too little of either, at least in the short run, to make much of a difference without the people taking part.

A final reason is *sustainability*. On the one hand, corruption is frequently a major issue in election campaigning. Polls in many developing countries support what many experienced politicians say: there are few issues about which the everyday individual feels more disgust than corruption. Indeed, cynics may exaggerate corruption's prevalence and importance: all of government may be lumped together as bribe-takers, self-servers, twisters of their public obligations to suit their private pockets. In any case, it is now routine for the perpetrators of coups d'état to excuse their actions as necessary to overcome the corruption of the previous regime.

At the same time, it proves difficult to form a political constituency for an anticorruption effort.[29] Unlike lobbies for, say, soya production or education, no well-organized citizens' group has a clear stake in fighting corruption. Moreover, civil servants find it threatening to countenance an anticorruption campaign in their midst. Even honest ones may fear being tarred with a reckless accusation; and dishonest ones, some perhaps induced to bribery by their inadequate pay, will lay obstacles in the path of efforts to uncover and punish their illicit activities. It is possible to launch an anticorruption campaign during a wave of public resentment, but keeping the campaign going—institutionalizing public concern—proves difficult.

INCENTIVES

Regarding incentives, many of the ideas of Chapter 7 apply. But I wish to underscore several points.

Successful campaigns against corruption tend to begin with the positive. *After* an agency's employees have participated in defining objectives, performance measures, and so forth, and after their incentives for good performance have been improved, then the attack on corruption can begin, inherently a negative undertaking. "You cannot just rush into an office," Justice Plana told me, "as if you were a knight in shining armor and assume everyone is a crook. Then, you don't get cooperation." After agents feel helped and involved, anticorruption efforts have a greater chance of succeeding: creating information systems to detect it, enhancing incentives to discover and prosecute it, and stiffening the penalties for those who partake in it.

When performance measures become more available, incentives should be linked to them. This is hardly a new idea. Adam Smith observed: "Public services are never better performed than when their reward comes only in consequence of their being performed, and is proportioned to the diligence employed in performing them."[30]

As Justice Plana explained to me, reforming incentives was his first priority:

> We needed a system to reward efficiency. Before,
> inefficient people could get promotions through gifts.
> So, I installed a new system for evaluating
> performance. I got the people involved in designing
> the system, those who did the actual tax assessment
> and collection and some supervising examiners.
> [Incentives were] based upon the amount of
> assessments an examiner had made, how many of his
> assessments were upheld, the amounts actually
> collected—all depending on the extent and type of the
> examiner's jurisdiction.
>
> In no time, the examiners were asking for more
> assignments and were more conscious of their work.

Reforming incentives faces many obstacles, even in the private sector.[31] In the public sector, difficulties of measurement, civil service rules, budget problems, and politics add further complexities. Yet, as indicated in Chapter 7, recent years have produced examples of incentive reforms that enhance productivity and discourage corruption.

As noted in Chapter 7, in many cases team-based or even organizationwide incentives may be more feasible than individual incentives. Penalties are, of course, crucial. Surprisingly, in many countries the only punishment for those guilty of corruption is the loss of the job. But leaders and administrators can do more and can be strategic about punishment. Just as positive incentives include money but go much further, penalties can include restrictions, transfers, the loss of discretion or autonomy, peer pressure, and the loss of professional status. Publicity can be used to highlight those in the wrong. Sometimes this sort of punishment is the most feared.

For example, in the Philippines Judge Plana knew it would take two years to convict corrupt officials. He went ahead with that legal process, but he also let the press have lots of information about the transgressors and their offenses. The resulting torrent of investigative reporting led to shame (and three heart attacks), which both deterred corruption and helped to change the popular belief that the big boys are exempt.

The choice of penalties (and of those to be penalized) should be made with an eye on cracking what might be called the culture of corruption. When corruption is systematic, cynicism and alienation spread widely. Experience with successful anticorruption campaigns suggests that a severe penalty to a "big fish" is one way to begin to subvert that culture. The big fish must be an important and publicly prominent figure, as well as one whose punishment cannot be interpreted as a political vendetta. For this last reason, it is best that the first big fish should come from the political party in power.

CONCLUDING REMARKS

These remarks about information and incentives comprise only a schematic treatment of a complex problem. We have barely touched an emerging economics literature that describes the state as a rent-seeking, opportunistic monopoly that serves its own interests.[32] Nor have we considered the moral and political dimensions of phenomena called corrupt.[33]

Instead, we have explored, as in other chapters, the insights that can be gained by applying the economics of information. The principal-agent model is important only when the agent has information that the principal does not (more precisely, has better or cheaper information). We saw in Chapter 7 that information is at the heart of the incentives problem in the public sector, and now we have added a new twist. The principal has to gather information not only about the goods the agent produces but also the bads. Penalties and the probability of being caught grow in importance.

I have also tried once again to illustrate the usefulness of a certain sort of policy analysis. One begins by unpacking the concept, disaggregating the types of corruption. What is usually a paralyzingly sensitive subject is approached by highlighting not the moral failures of individuals but the structural failures of information and incentives. A simplifying model yields not an optimizing model under restrictive assumptions, as is often the case in economic analysis, but a framework that might stimulate the creativity of policy makers and managers in the context of their unique circumstances. Examples illustrate that reality greatly exceeds our ability to model it, but that nonetheless successful change is possible—and is at least partly intelligible through our lens.

9

DECENTRALIZATION
AND
INTEGRATION

HIGHLY CENTRALIZED government has coincided with a certain view of the role of the state. As an extreme example, consider Africa. Countries with socioeconomic environments as different as those of Ghana and Kenya and the Ivory Coast and Mali—to mention only a few examples—have followed a similar pattern of centralized power. Democracy was replaced by a single-party or no-party system. National planning and administration controlled all public goods and services. Local government was given no independent juridical authority and virtually no resources. The executive branch dominated the legislature and judiciary. Even "decentralization" somehow came to mean central control, as in Zambian President Kenneth Kaunda's definition of "Decentralization in Centralism" as "a measure whereby through the party and government machinery, we will decentralize most of the party and government activities while retaining effective control of the party and government machinery at the centre in the interest of unity."[1]

Africa's overcentralization of power was perhaps understandable. When the African countries became independent, they inherited a centralized colonial model and as new nations they needed to establish as well as proclaim sovereignty.[2] More to the point of our concern with the state's role in economic development, centralization was consistent with prevailing economic models favoring state-led growth. It would take, the argument went, a strong central authority to mobilize and manage the nation's economic resources.

Now that the pendulum has swung toward a reduced role of

the state in the economy, so too do we see a greater interest, in Africa and elsewhere, in decentralization. That word's many uses cover politics as well as administration, ranging from the devolution of power to independent local authorities to the deconcentration of administrative responsibilities within the central government. Decentralization has not proved easy. In the 1970s many developing countries experimented with decentralization but failed.

One of the most celebrated efforts was Tanzania's *ujamaa* brand of decentralized development. It attracted unprecedented foreign financing—especially from the World Bank and the Nordic countries. The government established development authorities at regional, district, and village levels to coordinate central government activities, planning, and local initiatives—along with parallel organizations of the country's single party at each level. Deliberative assemblies were also created at each level. The results were disastrous. Between 1969 and 1983 real rural living standards in Tanzania declined at an average annual rate of 2.5 percent.[3] The new organizations became money traps as the governing councils ran afoul of the same corruption and inefficiency that plagued the central government, and macroeconomic policies were disastrous. In 1984 former Tanzanian president Julius Nyerere reflected on the failures:

> There are certain things I would not do if I were to
> start again. One of them is the abolition of local
> government and the other is the disbanding of the
> cooperatives. We were impatient and ignorant. . . .
> The real price we paid was in the acquisition of a top-
> heavy bureaucracy. We replaced local governments
> and cooperatives by parastatal organizations. We
> thought these organizations run by the state would
> contribute to progress because they would be under
> parliamentary control. We ended up with a huge
> machine which we cannot operate efficiently.[4]

In poor countries, decentralization has often become another form of central control. Real decentralization faces many obstacles. In rural areas, infrastructures are underdeveloped. Communications and logistics are difficult. Most important, at least according to much of the literature on decentralization, is the lack of local talent and initiative. "Many decentralization programs fail to improve either economic or administrative efficiencies," concludes a recent review by the World Bank. "This failure is frequently attributed to the absence of adequate managerial and technical capacity at the local government level." This attribution has its own consequences: "That, in turn, most often leads to advocacy of programs for improving public sector management capacity at local levels which are unnecessarily comprehensive, too long-term, costly, and unlikely to satisfactorily achieve their objectives. Thus, such a response is self-defeating."[5]

And so debates over decentralization swirl in vicious circles. The results of overcentralized government in Africa have been almost uniformly negative in Africa, as a recent volume edited by James Wunsch and Dele Oluwu documents in gruesome detail. But decentralization has not worked well there either, as cases as diverse as Kenya, Senegal, Zambia, Tanzania, and Liberia reveal.[6] Africa is an extreme example perhaps, but many other parts of the developing world face similar problems. If neither centralization nor decentralization as currently practiced tends to work well, might it be worthwhile to go beyond the debate over centralization itself and examine the conditions in which decentralization would be effective?

DISCRETION AND THE PRINCIPAL-AGENT-CLIENT MODEL

How much discretion should one allow the district office, the local agent, the regional government? On what should the decision depend?

Recall the principal-agent-client model encountered in Chapter 8. Consider the principal to be the central government, the agent the local office, the clients the local citizens. Granting discretion to the agent usually allows greater opportunity for shirking and corruption. But discretion may also enable the agent to respond efficiently to changing conditions, nonstandard requests, and local variations. Discretion—in different versions of the problem of decentralization: authority, sovereignty—is at the heart of the problem of decentralization. (Another version, considered below, is how the principal should allocate authority to the clients.)

Similar issues arise in every large organization, public or private. The principal must decide the optimal degree of delegation. The trade-offs may be particularly severe in the public sector. A preoccupation with corruption, argues public policy professor Steven Kelman, has tended to stifle discretion in public management in the United States.

> It can easily create a situation where government organizations become rule-based, not because such

rule-boundedness is the best way to produce effective
performance given the particular conditions in which a
given government organization works, but because
such rule-boundedness is seen as required to avoid the
scandal that would arise if our standards of probity
were violated. . . .

A bias against discretion can be seen in American
political science literature on government
organizations. . . . Even as sensitive an observer as
James Q. Wilson refers to "controlling discretion" as
"*the* problem of administration." Writers about
business organizations, by contrast, stress the need for
an environment where initiative and achievement are
encouraged.[7]

Kelman might have gone further in his citations. A venerable tradition *defines* political institutions in terms of the restriction of discretion, "as an impersonal system of rules and offices that effectively
binds the conduct of individuals involved in them."[8]

But why does the difference Kelman cites exist between public
and private management? The principal-agent-client model emphasizes the flows of information and incentives among the three parties. When the principal has ample information from both agents
and clients about what the agents are doing—their efforts and
results—and also has powerful incentives and disincentives under
his control, then he can delegate a great amount of authority. The
agents will not abuse this authority, because the principal will have
the means to learn about abuses and punish them. There will be little
need for cumbersome rules or red tape, since the principal can easily
measure the outcomes attained and reward them accordingly.

Notice, too, that under some conditions the principal may
delegate his principal's role—which we defined as pursuing the
public interest—to the *clients*. When the agents provide clients with
services that are easily judged as to quality and quantity and do not
involve important external effects, then clients can be given vouchers by the principal and empowered to shop for the best services,
public or private. If information is plentiful and competition can be
forthcoming (for example, there are not important economies of
scale in providing the service), this sort of decentralization has
promise. Public services may be privatized.

In this same highly stylized fashion, consider the other extremes along these dimensions. Suppose information about efforts
and results is scarce. Suppose that the principal has little ability to

affect the agents' incentives, because of civil service rules, syndicates, and the lack of resources. Under these conditions, decentralization is risky. Without information and appropriate incentives, agents will tend to be lethargic in providing public services, to be seen as "lacking capacity." (They may, however, energetically turn instead to corruption, here exhibiting considerable capacity.)

Now let us consider the principal's relation to the clients. Under what conditions can the principal's responsibility for managing public service provision be decentralized to the clients themselves? Problems will emerge if the quantity and quality of public services are hard for clients to gauge, if the goods are public in the economic sense that one client's consumption does not impede another's, or if one client's consumption creates externalities for other clients.

The proposition would be that many public services in developing countries fall toward these latter extremes—hard to measure and therefore information-poor, with weak incentives, involving public goods. In contrast, private services tend to be more readily measurable, have incentives more easily linked to results, providing private goods. One implication is that the differences observed between public and private sectors in decentralization and discretion are better understood in terms of differences in information and incentives than as the results of differences in training or as aberrations of administrative law.

For those interested in effective decentralization, these points have two implications. First, the optimal degree of decentralization should depend on features of the environment. As Samuel Paul observes,

> Some designers and researchers argue for
> decentralised structures for every programme without
> analyzing its strategy or environment. They do not
> appreciate that the degree of decentralisation should
> vary depending on these factors. They do not weight
> the gains of decentralisation against the costs of the
> increased complexity of management control and
> difficulty in finding the needed well-trained personnel
> at lower levels.[9]

Centralization has its economies. When standardization is important and economies of scale are significant, then centralization has advantages. But experience shows that discretion at the local level is most useful when local variations in conditions and people's preferences are large, and require local adaptation of services; when speedy local decisions are needed; when uncertainties are large; and when local demand for the service must be mobilized and local participation garnered.[10]

The successful public programs studied by Samuel Paul behaved consistently with this logic. And as Paul points out, they took it one step further. Often, centralization and decentralization are spoken of abstractly and with regard to "control" or "authority" over the whole organization. Instead, one may profitably apply the logic of decentralization to the various *functions* within an organization. "Decentralisation does not mean that all functions are decentralised. . . . Bulk purchases, certain research and development activities, and allocation of funds are often better organized centrally, whereas operational planning, detailed service designs, and service delivery may be decentralised."[11]

Thus, a successful rural education program in Mexico centralized textbook production, testing, and standard setting but decentralized aspects of teacher selection and pay, the construction of the school building and the teacher's residence, and those portions of the curriculum linked to local economic patterns (agriculture versus fishing, for example).

A second implication concerns the role of the state. Decentralization will be easier when information can be made more plentiful and public sector incentives can be connected to results. These in turn are in part the consequence of public policies. Decentralization policies are not independent of policies to enhance information and to link public sector pay to results.

Moreover, this analysis suggests a different hypothesis about that venerable bugbear of decentralization, the shortage of local people capable of exercising discretion efficiently. Incentives and information about results are more important than training in overcoming "shortages" of local talent.

Similar points hold for decentralizing authority to the clients themselves. Privatization and other means of empowering citizens will be more likely to work when actions are taken to enrich the information available to clients and when clients are given incentive-providing mechanisms ranging from vouchers to participation in management of public services.

Successful decentralization depends in part on information: its cost, validity, reliability, symmetry, and credibility. When analyzing decentralization, we should ask, "How measurable is the public service activity, how publicly available (how costly) is information about results, how can rewards be linked to results?" And: "How

DECENTRALIZATION, INFORMATION, AND INCENTIVES IN RURAL CREDIT IN INDONESIA

Critics of subsidized rural credit point to negative results—co-optation by the rich and an inability to be commercially viable. But as economists Donald Snodgrass and Richard Patten point out, saying that positive real interest rates should be charged provides "little more specific guidance on how to carry out a credit reform" or on "what form the primary lending institution should take."

After a series of failures in creating a sustainable rural credit program, the Indonesian People's Bank (BRI) underwent major changes in 1984. "Rather than exhorting BRI to be an 'agent of development' against its own business interests, the reform tried to create a Smithian situation in which profit opportunities would induce BRI to work for the good of society." Interest rates were set at 30 percent, which would enable BRI to make a profit. But this macroeconomic reform was not enough:

> *While the opportunity for BRI to make a profit is undoubtedly stronger institutional motivation than simply being acclaimed as an 'agent of development,' it would have been naive to assume that this profit opportunity alone would motivate all of BRI's employees to carry out their duties enthusiastically and effectively and thereby make the program a success. For the goal to be reached, it would be necessary to devise a set of incentives and sanctions that would induce BRI employees at all levels to work hard to achieve the overall objective.*

Under the new KUPEDES program, village banking units were given authority over loans. Accounting reforms at the village level provided realistic information. Cash management rules were liberalized. Training took place. But most important, "Village unit staff members were given the opportunity to earn a cash incentive payment if they increased efficiency and were energetic in looking for additional credit and savings customers. The payment was geared to the profitability of the unit and its success in attracting savings."

The results were remarkable. Volume more than tripled in three years. After losing money in the first year, KUPEDES became profitable and, by 1988, 82 percent of the village units were operating at a profit.

The system did not result in as many small loans to first-time borrowers as hoped: "While refusing to deal in very small loans, BRI has shown a strong preference for larger repeat loans to borrowers who have repaid in the past." This conservatism, Snodgrass and Patten speculate, may be a result of less-than-ideal BRI personnel promotion policies, which do penalize staff for problems (arrears or misuse of funds) but where "it is less clear that their status will rise along with the profits generated by the village units." Though the program is not perfect, rural credit is now available for small borrowers in Indonesia. With the equivalent of $310 million outstanding at the end of 1988, the KUPEDES program "dwarfs all other small loan programs in developing countries except perhaps those in India."

SOURCE: Donald R. Snodgrass and Richard H. Patten, "Reform of Rural Credit in Indonesia: Inducing Bureaucracies to Behave Competitively," Development Discussion Paper no. 315 (Cambridge, Mass.: Harvard Institute for International Development, November 1989): 4, 5, 29, 43–44, 49, 52

can public policies make those activities more measurable, make information less expensive and more publicly available, and create incentives linked to outcomes?"

BOLIVIA'S SOCIAL EMERGENCY FUND

In the domain of centralization, Bolivia's Social Emergency Fund (FSE) has taught some grand lessons that need to be generalized. One is this: if an organization develops strong, centrally administered quality controls and follow-up, it can efficiently decentralize both the formulation of projects (to local communities) and their construction (to the private sector).

Another lesson concerns talent. The FSE had excellent, highly motivated personnel. It attracted them with the mystique of service, a flexible bureaucracy, good pay, and promotions that depended on achievements. Even with good pay and excellent computers and communications equipment, the FSE's overhead costs were below 4 percent of the value of the public works it financed. (In comparison, the United Nations charges other donors more than 7 percent for administering their aid projects.) The FSE had higher apparent costs than the usual government agency, but was that much more efficient.

The Social Emergency Fund was founded in the aftermath of Bolivia's free-market economic reforms. Bolivia's leaders recognized that the social costs of stabilization and liberalization would be enormous. The FSE was to serve as a conduit for emergency funds to employ displaced miners and others affected by the radical economic reforms. Its mission was to create jobs through socially useful public works, especially for the poorest.

A first effort to start the FSE foundered, according to a historian of the fund, "for a series of reasons having to do with the organizational part of institutions"—in other words, bureaucratic wrangling.[12] In the context of Bolivia's highly centralized polity, all that the fund accomplished was to design forms for the submission of projects from the field. In a year, not a penny was spent.

Enter businessman Fernando Romero as the fund's new head, in January 1987. As an emergency organization with a three-year life span, the fund was given political and administrative independence, and Romero had a free hand to hire, pay, and fire its employees. Offering wages roughly equivalent to those in the private sector and expounding the mission of the fund with eloquence, Romero soon attracted a team of young, highly trained idealist-activists. As

the fund expanded, it kept this mystique: a well paid, highly motivated team dedicated to helping the poor.

The FSE's political and administrative autonomy enabled it to
pursue what was for Bolivia a radical new strategy of funding civic
works. Communities were asked to submit proposals for small public works, the repair and construction of everything from rural roads
to water supplies to sewerage to schools to health posts. Proposals
could be submitted by city and town governments, regional governments, nongovernmental organizations, and certain state enterprises. The actual works would be carried out by private contractors
named by the proposal-submitters. Many of the contractors were in
the informal sector. Thus, the design and supervision of local
projects was delegated to localities, and the actual execution of the
works was in private hands.

The FSE was an emergency program, and in the interest of
speed, competitive bidding was not required for these small
projects. But competition entered in other ways. Proposals were
carefully evaluated by FSE staff. Competition among the submissions ensured that only technically sound projects were funded,
at least after the first round of grants. During the evaluation, an FSE
staff member would visit the community and submit a report to
headquarters. Remarkably for a Bolivian institution, staff members
spent much of their time in the field. Evaluators would typically visit
ten sites a week. They verified the fit of proposed projects to local
needs—did reality correspond to what was requested? These technical reviews in the field, and in a more condensed fashion in La Paz,
helped the FSE avoid problems that have plagued some decentralized development efforts. For example, Indonesia's Subsidi Desa
program funded projects that individual villages were responsible
for proposing and formulating,

> and yet they frequently lack the technical expertise to
> effectively undertake this task. This deficiency has
> become evident in the sometimes unwise selection of
> projects and in the poor construction of others. Thus,
> in one survey of 122 villages in Java and Bali, a large
> number of the peasants interviewed indicated their
> reservations about the economic value [of] the projects
> and durability of their construction.[13]

The FSE compared each proposal's estimated costs with norms
the fund's headquarters quickly developed for each type of construction in each region. Proposals with estimates higher than the
norms had to be justified before proceeding.

ON STANDARDS OF PERFORMANCE

In his classic book The Achieving Society *(1959), psychologist David McClelland distinguished different ways to insist upon quality performance.*

McClelland noted Aramco's successes in subcontracting in third world countries and attributed it to information and appropriate incentives. "Subcontracting or industrial estates as mechanisms do not automatically work unless someone is insisting on high standards of performance from the entrepreneurs. . . . But as we pointed out . . . such standards are by no means universal. There are many instances of government enterprises in underdeveloped countries which have been allowed to operate inefficiently for years because no effective method for insisting on high standards of achievement have been developed."

But the quality standards should be based on results, not on plans. "Just as dangerous as no standards is what is sometimes called the 'cost accountant's' or 'banker's mentality,' which insists that an enterprise be thoroughly sound and involve little or no risk before an investment is made in it. . . . Accordingly, stress should be placed on picking the right man—as it was in Aramco, since Bultiste knew the Arabs he was dealing with well—leaving him free to operate if he has a plan that makes a moderate amount of sense, and then evaluating his actual performance rigorously after he has had a chance to show what he can do."

SOURCE: *David C. McClelland,* The Achieving Society *(New York: Van Nostrand Reinhold 1961): 433, 434.*

The FSE had "almost an obsession with examining costs," recalls Fernando Campero, former executive subdirector of the fund and coauthor of a forthcoming book on its development. "Given the great flexibility that the government conceded to us by not requiring us to enter into a bidding process, we had the great preoccupation that this freedom might bring as a consequence not only corruption but also a great inefficiency in the assignment of resources. The first objective in our evaluations was trying to have some control and to reduce the costs of the projects."[14]

As the volume of projects increased and the fund's confidence grew, evaluations included estimates of social benefits as well as the careful assessment of costs.

In the process the fund learned something that I find both remarkable and heartening. The first round of project submissions from certain cities and rural areas were of poor technical quality. Staff from the fund worked with the unsuccessful submitters to explain criteria and technical standards. Private sector contractors who would carry out the works had an interest in working with the communities on proposals, adding their technical skills. The second round of submissions was greatly improved, and by the end of the first year, excellent proposals were being submitted by organizations thought to "lack capacity."

"When we demanded high quality projects, we got them," one FSE staffer told me in 1988. "We did not insist on huge amounts of paper, and the contractors could help. Everyone knew we had good, computerized cost estimates and that we would be evaluating the projects before, during, and after their execution." The incentives were there for effective, decentralized performance.

Information was crucial to the fund's success—information about projects and about how well its own staff was doing. "A prerequisite for achieving internal and external credibility," note Fernando Campero and Gerardo Avila in their forthcoming book on the FSE, "was transparency, that is, the FSE ought to maintain a quality and level of information sufficient to absolve any doubt concerning the method of investment or the final destination of the resources."[15]

Because various foreign donors—from the World Bank to the Dutch government—funded the FSE, they also watched carefully how the money was spent and how the FSE worked. They were given access to all information, which no doubt further heightened the sense of an organization based on results.

> Transparency was important internally, given the great
> responsibility distributed among few people. The flow
> of information on the inside was essential for the
> control and monitoring of the principle variables. The
> insistence on very clear reports, imposed by the
> Executive Director from the outset, generated
> confidence in the institution, visible internally as well
> as outside the Fund. The degree of transparency
> achieved would not have been possible without a
> system of information ready for any and all [*a toda
> prueba*]. Great importance was given to information.
> No one wanted the traditional cloudiness [*nebulosa*],
> which might signify an incapacity to produce it but in
> many cases implied an unwillingness to give it.[16]

Computers were used to track the progress of each project, the flows of funds by region and category, and each staff member's work.

> The system of information enabled a constant
> monitoring of the global and specific parameters. Daily
> updating of information was done automatically in the
> process of payments, which permitted rapid detection

of any irregularities or errors committed during the process. The lists and reports showed the real state of implementation at the moment when they were printed, which facilitated decision making or needed changes.

The establishment of specific goals for each person in terms of the number of visits to make, the number and amounts of payments, the percentage of delays, and the punctual resolution of problems, facilitated the work of the whole organization and motivated each employee.

Monitoring was carried out through computerized lists and reports. The coefficient of delay was a comparison between real and planned expenditures. . . . The amounts paid out to each zone and region were also an object of constant monitoring. Individual goals were fixed at the beginning of each month, taking account of the results of the previous month, the amount of projects in execution and the average delay. At the end of every month, statistics were prepared and sent to every zone for the implementation of measures for their improvement.[17]

But information was not just computerized. Regional directors made regular field trips. Every two months, "follow-up meetings" involving all personnel were held in every zone.

In two and a half years, the FSE moved almost $200 million into more than 2,500 projects for the poor, creating about 20,000 jobs a month. Its overhead, for all the travel and information systems and the incentives for its 148 employees, came to less than 4 percent of its outlays.[18] The FSE is now being copied in twenty countries.

Many conditions contributed to the FSE's successes. It was an emergency organization, one that everyone knew would exist for only a few years. President Paz Estenssoro granted it political and administrative independence. It had a clear mission and ample funds, almost 90 percent coming from foreign aid and loans. It had an able, charismatic leader.

The FSE also decentralized effectively. But not every function: the submission of proposals and their design, construction, and supervision were delegated to the localities, which competed with each other for scarce funds. At the same time, many functions were centralized: for example, the development of general cost estimates for each type of construction, project evaluation, information systems, and negotiations with foreign donors.

Central to its success with decentralization was what the FSE did with information and incentives. It developed ways to generate and validate local information and to check costs against industry standards. Various field officers evaluated proposals, progress, and final results. Information systems were complemented by field trips and meetings. All of these activities introduced a rigor to local proposal writing and supervision: one might say, abundant information and competition made it possible for project design and implementation to be efficiently decentralized. And the local organizations— public, private, and nongovernmental—responded. As Virginia Osso and Molly Pollack concluded in their assessment of the fund:

> The second kind of unanticipated impact of the FSE
> concerns the degree of participation that was achieved
> on the part of the communities involved in the
> projects. Despite the initial lack of trust, finally the
> trust of the communities was attained. The principal
> causes of this achievement are explained by the
> philosophy implicit in the Fund's works: works
> destined to improve the living conditions of the
> poorest and, at the same time, executed by them or by
> people in similar conditions.[19]

The FSE's staff was paid well. Promotions were rapid and linked to performance, which was measured in a variety of ways— none was perfect, but taken together they proved highly motivational. The department for the promotion of projects was separated from project evaluation, which avoided possible adverse incentives. Staff members were given a high degree of autonomy, and their results were monitored and rewarded.

To what extent can the FSE model be replicated? The FSE's short-run and emergency nature, and its focus on works that were relatively easy to measure, fostered a businesslike emphasis on results, incentives linked to results, and decentralization. Its mission contrasts with many public activities of a longer duration, which deal with deep-seated problems such as education and health and whose results are not visible in months or perhaps even years. When public goods are difficult to measure and therefore difficult to link with quantitative rewards such as money, it is difficult for a principal to monitor and motivate a decentralized agent.[20]

In this case, we see tight links between decentralization, information, and incentives. Is there a lesson here? Isn't better information the key to better incentives, and aren't both crucial for effective decentralization? In thinking about decentralization, we might begin by analyzing tasks, functions, people, institutions, and other pieces of the problem along a spectrum of *information processing*. How easy is measurement? How easily disseminated and understood is the appropriate information? Where information is weak, workable proxies for unavailable measures may help, as we saw in Chapter 7. We might experiment with short-term proxies thought to be linked to longer-term benefits, such as truancy and test scores in the case of education, or indicators of services provided and rates of illness in the case of health.

Empowering clients may also help—vouchers to permit competition among schools and clinics, various forms of citizen management of social services, and so forth. Public policy may be able to enhance the "information-processing capabilities" of clients and agents—through, for example, better measures, more and more transparent information, more education, more intelligence, and better communications systems. (The checklist in the appendix to Chapter 5 is relevant here as well.)

To the extent that public policy can enhance what might be called the informational environment, decentralizing public administration will be easier and more productive.

INTEGRATION

Another organizational issue that has vexed the public sector in developing countries is the degree to which activities should be administratively integrated. In the 1970s and 1980s, "integrated rural development" was a watchword. Projects such as Ethiopia's CADU, the Philippine Bicol River project, Peru's Vigos, and Nicaragua's Invierno administratively combined extension, credit, infrastructure, health, education, family planning, marketing, and input supply.

Unfortunately, though the large literature on the subject contains "many maxims about the importance of integrating," in the words of sociologist John Cohen, "little systematic or practical thought has been given to translating this theory and the scattered case studies into a framework that can guide designers, implementors, and evaluators in the applied task of doing integrated rural development."[21] Economist Vernon Ruttan was pessimistic in his review of the literature. "Integrated rural development can be described, perhaps not too inaccurately, as an ideology in search of a methodology or a technology."[22]

Even today, there does seem to be a normative tone to many

calls for an integrated or holistic approach (good) as opposed to separation, specialization, or even making a service independent (bad)—just as for decentralization (good) versus centralization (bad). But decision makers may wonder how to begin analyzing the pros and cons of administrative integration in a concrete case. We will focus on administrative integration in rural development, but the logic applies to many other domains of public management.

Administrative integration can occur at many organizational levels. Consider four examples: integration at the level of the agency, project, clinic, and workers.

■ *Agency-level integration.* In 1970 the Indonesian government integrated family planning services. Presidential Decree No. 8 created a single agency reporting directly to the president. The new National Family Planning Board (BKKBN) would "coordinate, integrate, and synchronize the activities of the national family planning program throughout the country." The BKKBN consolidated family planning activities from the ministries of Health, Information, Education, Interior, and Religion, and from the army.[23]

■ *Project-level integration.* Ethiopia initiated the Chilalo Agricultural Development Unit (CADU) in 1968. This large project administratively combined public services in crop production, animal husbandry, forestry, extension and education, commerce and industry, water development, public health, and construction services. CADU provided these services outside the usual chains of command and line agencies in the Ethiopian government.[24]

■ *Clinic-level integration.* Haiti's Triangle Project created integrated community health centers that combined family planning, health, and other services under a single roof. Each clinic brought together a variety of diverse personnel, including medical residents, nurses, and auxiliaries but also agricultural extension workers and midwives. A medical resident exercised administrative control.[25]

■ *Worker-level integration.* The Philippine Masagana 99 rice program turned its agricultural extension agents into multipurpose workers. Despite their demanding duties in promoting the correct use of new seeds, fertilizers, and pesticides, the extension agents were given the added responsibility of promoting credit. They received a bonus for each farmer who took out a loan and another, lesser bonus if the loan was repaid on time. The agents were assigned the extra duties because they were thought to be uniquely placed to promote loans, screen out unsatisfactory applicants, and encourage repayment.[26]

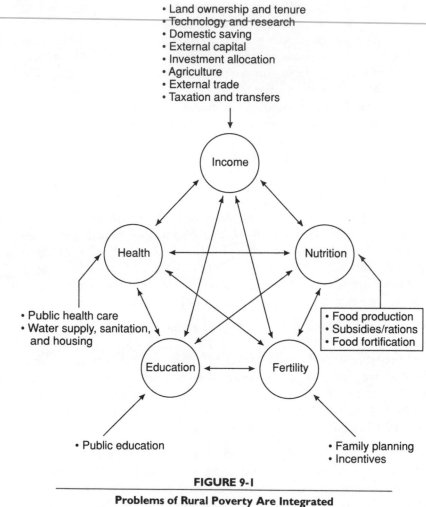

FIGURE 9-1

Problems of Rural Poverty Are Integrated

SOURCE: World Bank, *World Development Report, 1980* (Washington, D.C.: World Bank, 1980): 69.

These kinds of integration differ in many ways, and administrative mechanisms for integration vary by degree, function, and hierarchical position.[27] Without attempting to minimize these differences, we can still point to common features. In each case, the logic of administrative integration is similar.

First, the *problem* being addressed is multi-dimensional, a seamless web, a vicious circle.[28] Figure 9-1 illustrates this view. Second, therefore, the *response* must also be integrated, attacking all the problems at once; and this idea may slide into the implication

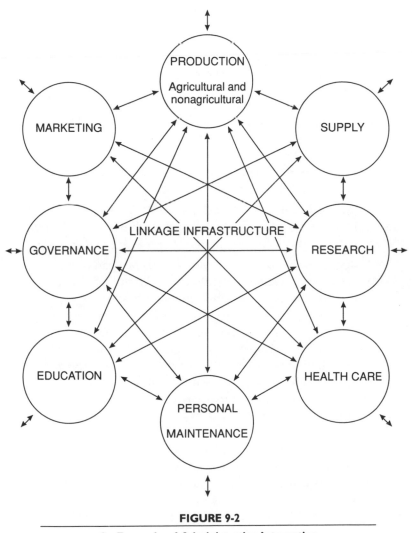

FIGURE 9-2

An Example of Administrative Integration

SOURCE: Alan H. Adelman, "Colombian Friendship Groups: Constraints on a Rural Development Acquisition System," *Journal of Developing Areas* 15, no. 3 (April 1981).

that the integration must be administrative as well. For example, Figure 9-2 depicts Colombia's FEDERACAFE program. Though specific to coffee producers, by attacking every problem under one organization it represents, in the words of one enthusiast, "a multidimensional, holistic understanding of rural social system interrelationships."[29] The ministries, the project, the clinic, the field worker—each must be *integrated*.

Integration, like coordination, is an attempt to combine forces more efficiently. Attractive though this logic may appear, experience shows that administrative integration also carries costs. Robert Wade argues:

> Put more generally, the larger the number of components to be administratively integrated, the higher the cost—in time, in friction (people do not like to be integrated), in the sacrifice of performance for control. It may be suggested that the costs increase more than proportionately with the numbers of components, especially if the components include the economic and the non-economic.[30]

Because administrative integration entails costs as well as benefits, simply calling for an integrated approach is unlikely to help us analyze specific cases. Robert Chambers presents this critique:

> "Integration" and "co-ordination" can be seen to have heavy costs as well as benefits. . . . The word "co-ordination" provides a handy means for avoiding responsibility for clear proposals. It is perhaps for this reason that it is much favoured by visiting missions who are able to conceal their ignorance of how an administrative system works or what might be done about it by identifying "a need for better co-ordination." Indeed, a further research project of interest would be to test the hypothesis that the value of reports varies inversely with the frequency with which the word "co-ordination" is used. Moreover, by using "integrated" and "co-ordinated" more or less synonymously and in alternate sentences, long sections of prose can be given an appearance of saying something while in fact saying very little indeed.[31]

"Maximizing co-ordination or integration," Chambers concludes, "would paralyze administration."[32]

Administrative integration has advantages and disadvantages. How might we help local policy makers sort them out, in order to stimulate their own analyses?

PRODUCTION FUNCTIONS

Consider two kinds of production function. The first refers to the outcome of interrelationships among different goods and services. The outcome may be as grandiose as "rural development," where the production function would combine services as broad as health, education, and agricultural extension. Schematically, rural development (*D*) is a function of public services such as health (*H*), education (*E*), rural roads (*R*), agricultural extension (*A*), and so forth:

$$D = f(H,E,R,A, \ldots) \tag{1}$$

The second kind of production function relates to the public good or service being provided. These public services can themselves be viewed as the outcome of production processes within public organizations. For example, if we are considering a public health clinic, the inputs in the production function would include capital, labor of various kinds, information, transportation services, and so forth. Schematically, the production of health services (*H*) is a function of inputs like capital of various kinds (*K_i*), labor of various kinds (*L_i*), information (*I*), and other factors.

$$H = h(K_i, L_i, I, \ldots) \tag{2}$$

I find it useful to recast arguments about integrated public services in terms of these two production functions. Table 9-1 presents a series of questions that have proved useful to policy makers in thinking through the pros and cons of various kinds of administrative integration in the public sector. Let us consider the framework piece by piece.

COMPLEMENTARITY AMONG PUBLIC SERVICES

Complementarity in the first sort of production function is a popular reason for "integrated rural development." The production function for rural development exhibits complementarity among public services such as water, agricultural extension, roads, health, education, and credit. More narrowly, in agriculture the marginal product of fertilizer often depends on the levels of other factors of production, such as water, seed varieties, pesticides, and other inputs.[33] Determining these complementarities in practice (as opposed to the agricultural experiment station) is not easy.[34]

If complementarity does exist, can consumers themselves integrate the goods and services without the government having to carry out administrative integration? That inputs are complementary to their welfare does not entail the integration of the suppliers of those inputs. As one expert pointed out, "The major requirement is that such services be *simultaneously* available and it is frequently possible for that to be achieved without administrative integration."[35] Ordinarily, economic reasoning assumes that clients—

TABLE 9-1

1. Complementarity among public services
   a. Which goods and services exhibit complementarity? To what extent, at what levels of output? Focus attention on outputs whose synergies are most marked.
   b. Why can't consumers themselves integrate the goods and services optimally?
      - Externalities among consumers
      - Transaction costs
      - Consumer ignorance

      How would the integration of the supply of the goods and services overcome these problems? Might other measures be preferable (such as providing information, adjusting prices, education)?
2. Economies of combined inputs for producing public services
   a. Reallocating resources across agencies
      - Does administrative integration allow resources to be reallocated among agencies?
      - If so, with what resulting efficiencies? Consider the "comparative advantages" of the different agencies in various functions (such as planning, marketing, delivery, evaluation, political connections).
      - Could the desired reallocation take place without integration?
      - Consider the risks of misallocation ("the Shaw-and-the-dancer problem," see p. 161).
   b. Economies of scale from integrating inputs
      - How large, for what functions (such as planning, research, capital equipment and other overhead, top management, delivery costs)?
      - What economies exist in the provision of collective goods (such as information, political organization, public relations)?
   c. Externalities
      - To what extent do agencies affect each other via externalities? Consider especially the external effects of lumpy investments in capital, space, and time, such as infrastructure.
      - How well can independent agencies adjust to externalities without integrating (such as information exchange, changing prices, and so forth)?
3. The creation of a monopoly
   a. What benefits might accrue from the monopoly powers ensuing from integration? Consider increased bargaining leverage in relation to local citizens and clients, the provincial and national governments, and donors of foreign aid.
   b. What negative consequences might ensue? Consider the ease of co-optation by elites, corruption, politicization, and excessive expansion, as well as resistance by line agencies.
4. Overcoming transaction costs via integration
   a. Do independent agencies engage in transactions with each other, analogous to the purchase of inputs and the sale of outputs? If not, this argument for integration does not apply.
   b. How would administrative integration lower these transaction costs and to what extent?
5. Allowing financial diversification via integration (portfolio effects)
   a. To what extent would such financial benefits follow from administrative integration?
   b. Could the same benefits be obtained more efficiently through financial markets, investments, and so forth?
6. Direct financial costs of integration (such as the costs of starting an integrated organization, new personnel costs, changes in staffing patterns, training, information and publicity, and so forth)

Integrating Public Services (continued)

---

7. Indirect and managerial costs of integration
   a. How large are learning costs (for changes in budgeting, personnel, political linkages, standard operating procedures, evaluation and information systems, and so forth)? Consider the costs for clients as well as employees.
   b. How serious will bureaucratic resistance be? Consider the legitimacy and power of the integrating authority, the similarity of missions among the organizations and individuals being integrated, and possible conflicts of politics and culture.
   c. Are the managerial tools available for inducing agencies to integrate effectively? Consider incentives, authority, information, control over work loads, and career paths.
   d. How large are the returns to specialization? To what extent is specialization sacrificed in the attempt to integrate? Consider the technical aspects of the production function, but also the role of routine, measurable outcomes, morale, and so forth.

---

in this case, rural farmers and households—know best about complementarities, which may vary according to individual preferences and conditions.

Thus, farmers' choices and the market itself can be the integrating mechanism. But rural markets may malfunction in ways that administrative integration can ameliorate.

1. Externalities among Consumers. What one farmer does may affect another's productivity—for example, through practices that affect erosion, the use of water, and the control of pests. When the incentives individual farmers face do not reflect these externalities, administrative integration may improve the results. For example, a program might "integrate" the purchase of cows with mandatory vaccination and dipping services. Another might require farmers to buy pesticide along with seeds and fertilizer. (An alternative, of course, is to institute optimal prices and taxes.)

2. Transaction Costs. Clients may save time and travel costs by obtaining services from a single supplier—or at least from collocated suppliers. This is a major argument for combining services in a single agent, clinic, or project. Simply putting spread-out rural services in a single place led to "in many ways the most remarkable results" of the celebrated Comilla rural development project in Bangladesh.[36]

3. Consumer Ignorance. Thirty years ago, experts in rural development often cited tradition-bound and ignorant rural people as an obstacle to development. This is no longer in fashion. Today one tends to hear that rural people know best what they need and what works for them. Actually, both positions may have validity. Farmers may indeed "rationally" respond to the prevailing incentive structure, but this structure may itself contain encrusted constraints, empirically derived habits of distrust, and unreliable or biased sources of information and knowledge.

An example of a kind of integration overcoming such "ignorance" occurred during Pakistan's green revolution in wheat. The ideal mixture of fertilizers for the new wheat variety was four parts nitrogen to one part phosphate. Phosphatic fertilizer was available separately on the market, but it was more expensive and had not customarily been used with the old wheat varieties. In certain soils, in the short run, using nitrogenous fertilizer alone had about the same effect as the recommended 4:1 mixture. But over a period of years, the exclusive use of nitrogenous fertilizers led to lower yields by altering soil characteristics. After five years of the green revolution, farmers in certain areas of Pakistan suffered exactly this outcome. They complained that the new seeds were not of good quality. In response, fertilizer suppliers premixed the fertilizers in the 4:1 proportion—taking the integration of these factors out of farmers' hands.

Other examples of supply integration that overcome "ignorant" consumer preferences may be found in credit schemes. Instead of theoretically optimal cash transfers to creditworthy farmers, who would then integrate inputs according to their perceptions of needs and complementarities, the Masagana 99 program in the Philippines and the SRDP program in Kenya tied credit to packages of agricultural inputs. Fertilizer and pesticide chits were given instead of pesos or shillings. Loans were provided only for special varieties of livestock or particular sorts of machinery. In Korea, farmers receiving loans on the IR 667 program were required to attend classes on the best cultivation methods for the new rice variety—a less heavy-handed form of integration, but an example of the same principle.

Integrated supply is not the only way to overcome consumer ignorance. Education and informational activities may be preferable, such as local experimentation and demonstration projects. Examples include the Rural Academy of the Comilla project in Bangladesh, local experimentation and demonstration, using locally elected model farmers as in Ethiopia's CADU project, and Korea's remarkable educational blitz mounted on rice farmers. And if consumers are not in fact as ignorant as public officials think, educa-

COMBINING STRENGTHS MAY END UP
COMBINING WEAKNESSES

Organizational mergers or integration are sometimes justified by the logic of one institution's strengths complementing another's. It may work out the other way around, as a famous anecdote reminds us in another context.

One evening at a dinner party, George Bernard Shaw was seated alongside a celebrated and beautiful dancer. She was flirting with him recklessly. "My dear Bernard," she said, "Wouldn't it be simply wonderful if you and I should have a child? Just imagine—a child with your brain and my body?"

To which Shaw responded, "But what if it should be the other way around?"*

*Traditionally, the dancer is alleged to have been Isadora Duncan. Her sister Irma denies it. "As for that anecdote which connects her name with George Bernard Shaw, he himself admitted that the 'dancer' in question was not Isadora. The latter had no occasion to meet G. B. S. nor did she correspond with him. Her letters and writings give ample proof of her own native intelligence and wit." Irma Duncan, Duncan Dancer: An Autobiography (Middletown, Conn.: Wesleyan University Press, 1965), 159.

tional interventions still enable them to decide; it is gentler and more enabling than integrated solutions that take choices out of their hands.

ECONOMIES OF COMBINED INPUTS FOR
PRODUCING PUBLIC SERVICES

Integrating the agencies that produce public services may result in several kinds of economies in the second kind of production function mentioned above.

1. Resource Reallocation. Private firms that merge often justify the action by saying that each firm can profit from the strengths of the other. In the merger between two pharmaceutical companies, Merck with Sharp and Dohme, it was said that Merck had a strong research organization, whereas Sharp and Dohme had an effective sales force. By integrating, resources that are in effect underutilized in one firm are shifted to a more productive combined use.

Economists have been skeptical of this logic. Empirical research seems to show that instead of the weaker unit profiting from the stronger one, the process often works the other way around.[37] I call this "the Shaw-and-the-dancer problem" (see box above).

2. Economies of Scale.   A common rationale for pursuing integrated rural development is the supposed paucity of trained managers. Combining functional agencies under a single chief may exploit economies of scale in management. Economies of scale may also be realized by integrating common organizational functions such as research and development, finance, legal services, political functions, marketing, and information gathering. Integration may reduce redundancy. If agencies separately replicate part or all of a common task, then after integration what was done many times need only be done once. If the Department of Water and Power has established a village council to obtain the views of local residents, it may seem nearly costless for the Bureau of Extension Services to utilize the same mechanism. Collective goods will be produced in suboptimal amounts by independent, nonintegrated organizations. We examine below some of the diseconomies that integration may create.

3. Externalities in Production.   One agency's lumpy decisions in space and time may affect the operations of another. The analysis of such spillover effects is a classic topic in development planning. Direct and indirect spillovers, first-order and second-order effects, technological and pecuniary externalities, forward and backward linkages: these are part of the parlance of project analysts. But how to include them in designing an integrated project is controversial theoretically and difficult empirically.[38]

When externalities exist, it may be possible to share information and change incentives so that independent agencies will make the right choices. Joint planning may be called for—indeed, this is a fundamental argument for planning—but the administrative integration of various agencies is not necessarily implied. A key question is whether mutual adjustment by individual agencies is rapid and relatively costless. If so, then there is little need for integration.

> Interdependence by itself does not cause difficulty if the pattern of interdependence is stable and fixed. For in this case, each subprogram can be designed to take account of all the subprograms with which it interacts. Difficulties arise only if program execution rests on contingencies that cannot be predicted perfectly in advance. In this case, coordinating activity is required to secure agreement about the estimates that will be used as the bases of action, or to provide information to each subprogram unit about the activities of the others.[39]

SOME ADVANTAGES OF RURAL MONOPOLY

Administrative integration can create a monopoly of rural services, which in turn may permit beneficial bargaining. The Mahatma Gandhi Cooperative Lift Irrigation Society in Andhra Pradesh, India, combined water with agricultural inputs such as fertilizer and seeds. It also provided credit. Early on, the society had problems with certain farmers, such as those whose land happened to be the first to be irrigated, who refused to allow their land to be mortgaged. Other farmers were reluctant to repay loans to the society. But because the society had "in its control all the inputs a member needs—seed, fertilizer, credit, and most important, money," it could lever a recalcitrant farmer.

"Without the cooperation of the society he can do little," reports Robert Wade. "This is what the people of the hamlet found out when they decided not to allow their already developed lands to be mortgaged."

Its "monopoly power" through integration turned out to be one of the reasons the society became what Wade called "a success story" in rural development.

SOURCE: *Robert Wade, "Leadership and Integrated Rural Development: Reflections on an Indian Success Story,"* Journal of Administration Overseas *17, no. 4 (Fall 1978): 248.*

Mutual adjustment will be easier if information is widely available, and if rewards depend on results.

THE CREATION OF A MONOPOLY

It may be advantageous for separate agencies to present a united front. As opposed to a set of independent actors that can be pitted against one another or fragmented in negotiations, the integrated unit can in theory bargain for better outcomes in negotiations with local citizens, the regional or national government, or foreign donors.

Of course, creating integrated monopolies also entails costs and risks. A single organization may be easier for local elites to co-opt, as has been argued for the Comilla project and in Tanzania.[40] Or it may become an ethnic battleground, as in the Sudan, where for this reason Richard Huntington recommended that "rather than one overall Abyei Development Organization, several single-purpose development groups be formed. . . . The closeness of these groups to practical matters and their multiplicity would minimize the negative effects of all-or-nothing fights for control.[41] Or monopoly power and discretion may be misused, as in the case of Indonesia's state-owned oil company Pertamina. During the oil boom, it "integrated" into schools, road-building, even luxury hotels; but it ended up overextended and broke.

OVERCOMING TRANSACTION COSTS VIA INTEGRATION

In Chapter 3 and the appendix to Chapter 5, we saw that forward and backward integration can help resolve problems of asymmetric information and incentives to mislead—at least in theory. In the newly integrated organization it is hoped that information will be shared and incentives aligned, as if among brothers.

So we must ask, Do the entities to be integrated interact with each other and encounter such problems? If so, before integrating we should consider the rest of the checklist in Chapters 3 and 5, which presents problems with and alternatives to integration.

ALLOWING FINANCIAL DIVERSIFICATION VIA INTEGRATION (PORTFOLIO EFFECTS)

In the private sector, sometimes firms merge to take advantage of portfolio effects—combining assets or activities whose risks and returns are not perfectly correlated. Presumably, this argument is less relevant to the public sector. Risk sharing is a common rationale for cooperatives, credit unions, and other sorts of integrated structures; but integration across government agencies would seem to have few portfolio effects.

SOME COSTS OF ADMINISTRATIVE INTEGRATION

Because of the theoretical benefits we have just reviewed, integration can make conceptualizers swoon. "It is apparent from this list" of external effects, writes economist Tibor Scitovsky in a classic article, "that vertical integration alone would not be enough and that complete integration of all industries would be necessary to eliminate all divergence between private profit and public benefit."[42] Practical people may also be attracted. In a given situation, one may more easily perceive what seem to be the costs of a lack of integration—the misunderstandings, the failures to coordinate, the duplications—than the costs of potential integration or the benefits of staying separate.

In the event, almost every integrated rural development effort has resulted in higher costs than anticipated. Some of the costs can be measured directly in currency, but others involve reduced effectiveness because of management problems.

DIRECT FINANCIAL COSTS OF INTEGRATION

Creating a new organization, committee, staff, or council costs time and money. So does training a multipurpose worker, sharing data and reports and impressions, and designing and implementing joint incentive and evaluation systems.

INDIRECT AND MANAGERIAL COSTS OF INTEGRATION

In addition to monetary expenses, there are costs in managerial currency. Without entering into the large literature on bureaucratic behavior, we can readily recount some of the difficulties to be overcome. Organizations differ in budgets, organizational styles and traditions, connections to local and national clients and powers, personnel systems (pay scales, prescribed duties, career lines), and standard operating procedures. Creating and then learning the new administrative order entails costs not only for employees but for clients as well.

Bureaucrats may perceive integration as an invasion of their turf. In addition to dead-weight or start-up costs, interorganizational conflict often ensues. Bureaucratic battling has been blamed for the failure of India's Community Development Movement in the 1950s and for many problems with integrated rural development. These costs will be greater the weaker that the legitimacy and power of the integrating authority become, the less that integration helps each participating organization by its own standards, and the more different these separate standards turn out to be. The resistance and conflict are not just among organizations but also among personalities. Careers are built on the fight over who gets to control budgets and workloads. Administrative integration jumps squarely into that ring.

We should again ask whether appropriate incentives are available to induce integration. Without financial incentives in the short run and career incentives down the line, managers may be unable to motivate agencies and personnel to integrate in meaningful ways. Once again, information and incentives are crucial to success.

Note, too, that integration tends to forgo specialization. Consider this advice from a business-school textbook:

> *The effective solution to any integration problem is the one that costs the least and that does not seriously undermine the effectiveness of the specialized subunits. . . .* More than one well-intentioned company president has managed to "get his people to start pulling together," but in the process, made them less effective at their respective specialized tasks.[43]

Specialization has its own returns: familiarity, expertise, and savvy. Often routines are more readily established, outcomes more easily measured, and uncertainties reduced. Integration is not just more, it is different. Managing an integrated organization often requires qualitatively different skills and systems. Rarely will two organizations merge and find that one's old management system suits the new integrated unit. In rural development, where many complicated ends are sought, integration may be taken to imply overwhelming requirements for a "holistic" approach, for learning and flexibility (both of which are complex), for a committed and highly capable staff.

David Korten's review of integrated family planning can be analyzed with the framework of Table 9-1. Despite the theoretical attractions, integrating family planning with health clinics turns out to be managerially expensive. Korten concludes:

> Integration in itself is not likely to improve the acceptance of family planning and indeed may result in serious deterioration in program performance. . . . It should be clear that integration is not a panacea for poor program performance. . . . Indeed I would suggest as a tentative hypothesis that on the whole, integrated programs require stronger management to maintain the same level of performance as a comparable vertical program.[44]

CONCLUDING REMARKS

The purpose of our analysis has not been to condemn administrative integration, but to help us overcome a kind of simplistic fascination with it. "A multifaceted problem requires an integrated response," we tend to say. If this is not a tautology but implies an *administratively* integrated response, then this bit of common sense may lead us astray. Administrative integration comes in many varieties; none is right or wrong per se. The merits of various means of integration depend on a host of situationally specific considerations. The framework in Table 9-1 is designed to help policy makers think more creatively about the alternatives.

The analysis connects to our earlier work. As in the case of decentralization, we see that we should think in terms of *functions*, not in the first instance of entire organizations. Choices about what functions to decentralize or integrate, and how much, should depend, in different ways, on the nature of the services being produced and the task environment. Success hinges on good information and incentives.

Some features of the "informational environment" are beyond our control. For example, some services are simply harder to measure than others. So, too, may incentives be difficult to affect in the short run.

But often governments can take steps to enhance information and make incentives more flexible. If so, decentralization will be easier and more efficient. We may also be able to avoid some of the costs of administrative integration by providing an information-rich environment and appropriate incentives so that independent agencies and the citizens they serve are able efficiently to do their own "integrating." Administrative reform, so often thought of in terms of training and organization charts and administrative law, may be usefully refocused in terms of information and incentives.

10

POVERTY AND ETHNIC GROUPS IN DEVELOPING COUNTRIES

IN CHAPTER 2 WE examined an often overlooked characteristic of Bolivia: the country's poor are disproportionately members of indigenous ethnic groups.[1] The country's national plans scarcely mention this fact. Documents from international agencies such as the World Bank and the U.S. Agency for International Development also neglect it.[2]

In this regard, Bolivia's situation is dramatic but not unique. Most developing countries are plagued by poverty coupled with ethnic inequalities. Around the globe, ethnic and political borders seldom correspond. In almost a third of the countries of the world, the largest ethnic group represents less than half the total population. In fifty-three countries there are more than five significant ethnic groups.[3] Racial and other groups often differ in economic access and success, in educational opportunities and attainments. Often the result is perceived injustice and social tension, and sometimes violent conflict.

As this book goes to press, the most dramatic examples are the "national problems" being experienced in Yugoslavia, Romania, and the Soviet Union. The movement toward democracy and free markets seems to have kindled ethnic tensions—and not just in Central and Eastern Europe. Many African countries fear that democracy will breed destabilizing parties organized along ethnic and tribal lines. In many parts of Asia and in some parts of Latin America, calls for decentralizing government are interpreted as ways for ethnic and other groups to gain more control over government.

I wish to focus on a particular aspect of ethnic diversity—the existence of economic and educational differences among ethnic groups. I believe that many countries will discover, after undertaking free-market reforms, that ethnic inequalities take center stage in public policy. Indeed, these inequalities may even increase in the short run; certainly, with freer markets and democratic participation, the inequalities will become more noticed and controversial. Governments will be forced to face up to the reality that poverty *within* third world countries is ethnically concentrated.

This has always been one of the "secrets" of underdevelopment, hidden and, indeed, suppressed. With economic and political liberalization, I believe it will increasingly come out into the open. Greater pressures will build to adopt public policies to reduce economic and educational inequalities among groups (ethnic, tribal, community, castes, religious). The ethics of different policies will be debated; and, with luck, the debate will also include a strategic analysis of what sorts of policies reduce ethnic inequalities under what conditions. It is toward this debate that this chapter and the next two are directed.

ETHNIC INEQUALITIES IN LATIN AMERICA

The Latin American countries as a whole have exhibited transient conceptions of ethnicity. Miscegenation has been the rule, with relatively small numbers of white colonists arriving, often without families, and interbreeding with the indigenous people and with imported black slaves. Numerous studies have documented through serological and other means the great extent of miscegenation. For example, even in one supposedly "pure" Quechua community in the Peruvian Andes, an analysis of blood group antigens showed that about 15 percent of the population was "the product of Indian-Negro mestizaje."[4] Both biologically and socially, ethnic divisions in Latin America tend not to be sharp. It is often said that today an "Indian" may transcend his racial background and "become" a mestizo by adopting certain norms of language, dress, and behavior; and it is said in countries such as Brazil that "money whitens," meaning that social class rather than racial heritage determines one's status. Perhaps because of the large degree of intermixing, Latin America is noteworthy in that ethnic fissures have seldom led to secessionist movements or to racial violence.[5]

Nonetheless, race and color are crucial for understanding Latin America. Social discrimination exists even in countries that have prided themselves as being free of prejudice, such as Brazil and Costa Rica.[6] More important, in most Latin American countries blacks and Indians are at the bottom of the economic and political order, mestizos are in the middle, and "whiter" groups are at the top.

> Stratification correlates with racial ancestry in almost all of the nations. That is, the privileged classes are largely of white background and/or are lighter skin-colored than the less affluent strata. . . . Urbanization and industrialization have done little to improve the situation. The class structure in most racially heterogeneous cities is closely correlated with color. . . . The Caribbean nations, all of which are former European colonies, reveal an even greater emphasis on color and race than elsewhere. Whites and/or mulattoes occupy the dominant positions, even in predominantly black societies such as Haiti and Jamaica.[7]

In the words of one specialist, "Minority control of the land and the non-white people who work it remains the core institution in many different nations" in Latin America.[8]

GROUPS IN AFRICA

Black Africa presents a different situation. Despite what appears to some Westerners to be racial homogeneity, many African nations suffer from ethnic and tribal inequalities. Except in Somalia, Lesotho, and Swaziland, diversity is the rule. Kenya is said to have forty-six ethnic groups, the Congo more than seventy, and Nigeria and Zaire at least two hundred each.[9] Anthropologists have shown that differences among Africans are surprisingly large in terms of physical characteristics such as lip size, shape of head and nose, and hair texture; in cultural and linguistic terms, of course, the ethnic variations are even greater. In many African societies people with lighter-colored skin have higher status.[10]

African independence movements often featured elements of racial and cultural pride, an us-versus-them quality with the Europeans on the other side. (In some countries, more recently, "them" has meant the Asians.)

It was hoped that after independence the new African states

would be able to exploit this solidarity against the colonialists to mend internal ethnic and tribal cleavages. Unfortunately, this has not occurred in most countries. Instead, subnational cleavages and inequalities have remained or become more pronounced. Movements that began by being territorial and inclusive ended up being ethnic and exclusive.[11] In the words of the Soviet expert R. N. Ismagilova, "Not only did ethnic conflicts in African countries fail to disappear, but in recent years they have even markedly increased."[12] The most important factor predicting military coups in Africa is a country's ethnic diversity.[13] When political parties exist, they are usually organized along ethnic lines. Indeed, the establishment of one-party states is often justified as a means of overcoming purely ethnic politics.

"Ethnic particularism," concluded political scientist Seymour Martin Lipset, "still accounts for tensions in every black African state, save Somalia."[14]

ASIA'S ETHNIC COMBINATIONS

Asia is perhaps the most ethnically complex region. "All the major races are represented in Asia," note three Soviet scholars, "the Mongoloid, the Europeoid, the Negroid, and the Australoid."

The Mongoloids are subdivided into three groups: the Northern, Eastern, and Southern Mongoloids. The first of these groups includes the Mongols and certain peoples of Northeast China; the second—the northern Chinese and the Koreans; the third embraces various mixed and intermediate forms linking the Mongoloids and the Australoids: the southern Chinese, Indonesians, Filipinos, peoples of Indochina, and the Japanese belong to this group (the Japanese type, which includes also Ainu elements, is characterized by a somewhat different combination of traits).

The Europeoid race is represented in Asia by various types of its southern branch (the Armenoid, Indo-Afghan, and other types); these types are prevalent among the peoples of Southwest Asia and northern India.

Comparatively small groups of Australoids are scattered over many regions of Asia. The Veddoid type is to be observed among the Veddas of Ceylon, the Bhils and various Dravidian and Munda-speaking groups in India and among some small peoples of Southeast Asia (the Senois, Toalas, etc.); the Melanesian and Papuan types—among East Indonesian peoples; the Negrito type—among the Filipino Aetas, the Semangs of Malaya and the Andamese; the Ainu type—among the Japanese Ainus. A South-Indian type originated in the zone of early contacts between the southern branch of the Europeoids and the Veddoids. This is mainly represented among India's Dravidian peoples.

In the southern coastal regions of the Arabian Peninsula there are representatives of the Negroid race.[15]

In Asia these racial combinations interact with linguistic, religious, and geographical differences to create a remarkably rich and sometimes explosive ethnic mix. Miscegenation has been common for millennia in Asia and sometimes has led to the development of separate races such as the Japanese.[16] The Soviet expert N. N. Cheboksarov stated that the Indian subcontinent is populated by the product of miscegenation "from the most ancient times" between indigenous Australoids and southern Europeoids and various groups of Mongoloids from Southeast Asia. He also observed: "Nowadays in East Asia and Oceania it is difficult to distinguish between intermediate racial types remaining here from the period of ancient racial homogeneity and metisated forms which arose later as the result of interaction between Australoid and Mongoloid populations."[17]

In many countries of Asia, economically and politically backward groups are identified as belonging to, or shading toward, the indigenous or Australoid groups. The Scheduled Tribes of India are one example.[18] The Indian caste system is not explicitly based on race, but the upper castes tend to have lighter skin and the lower castes tend to be darker.[19] A reversal of this correlation is considered unusual and even sinister. A proverb in Northern India states: "A dark Brahman, a fair Chuhra, a woman with a beard—these three are contrary to nature." The word for the four fundamental castes is *Varna*, which literally means "color."

Ethnic inequalities are pronounced in Asia. Ethnic Chinese have tended to achieve disproportionate power, despite official persecution and occasional violence against them.[20] Sri Lanka is torn by ethnic strife. In Southeast Asia, ethnic inequalities are severe in Burma, Thailand, Malaysia, Singapore, Laos, Cambodia, Vietnam, the Philippines, and Indonesia.

Thus, in most countries of the developing world, ethnic inequalities underlie grave social problems. Bolivia is not alone. In most developing countries, economic and educational gaps among ethnic groups constitute a serious, long-term issue.

GROUP INEQUALITIES AND
PUBLIC POLICY

Recognizing this, what should be the roles of the state in remedying ethnic inequalities? If governments such as Bolivia's do not face up to the ethnic correlates of poverty, their antipoverty policies are likely to fail. This is an assumption, not an established truth; perhaps it stems from my experience as a North American. This assumption does not specify what policies a state should adopt in order to overcome ethnic inequalities. It does imply that we should think hard about these issues and not hide them or wish them away.

What should be the role of the state with regard to educationally and economically backward groups? What might Bolivians learn from the varied experiences of other developing countries? Given the extent of ethnic inequalities in the third world and the variety of strategies governments have adopted when faced with such problems, one might expect an abundant literature on these questions. But surprisingly little has been written from a policy perspective. There are abundant ethnographic descriptions and analyses of ethnic politics. But if one asks what policies work best for reducing ethnic inequalities, one finds little of use in the literature.[21] What follows in Chapters 11 and 12 is a provisional attempt to provide a framework for policy analysis.

11

THREE STRATEGIES
FOR OVERCOMING
ETHNIC INEQUALITIES

WHILE I WAS VISITING Brazil in late 1984 to study ethnic inequalities, the great novelist Jorge Amado received a literary award. He used the occasion to speak on Brazil's "racial question." The government always denied that the country had racial problems, but Amado underlined the inequalities. What could be done about them? The gist of his argument was assimilation through miscegenation. "It is necessary to repeat," Amado concluded, "that only one solution exists to the racial problem: the mixture of races. All the rest, whatever it may be, leads irremediably to racism."[1]

Most governments would recoil from such a radical view. They pursue "assimilation" by other means—linguistic, political, cultural, or economic. Many leaders have given priority to the formation of a nation through a lingua franca, a common polity, a unified culture, and an integrated national economy, even though they also talk of "preserving" local cultures and languages. Underlying these goals is an assumption, or perhaps a wish. With the assimilation of separate languages, politics, cultures, and economies, ethnic inequalities and conflicts will eventually disappear.

This logic has been followed by diverse regimes, ranging from colonial powers to independent nations of varying ideologies. En route to the assimilationist goal, Lenin noted, it may be necessary to pass through a transition period that stresses the self-determination of "nations"—a term often meaning "peoples" or "ethnic groups" in Marxist writings—but "this is not equivalent to the acknowledgment of federalism as a principle. The objective of socialism is not only to put an end to the fractioning of humanity into small states and to the isolation of nations, it does not consist only in bringing the nations closer, but also in fusing them into one."[2]

A practical issue in assimilation strategies is—without countenancing Jorge Amado's solution—how best to accomplish this "fusing into one."

PERU'S STRATEGIES
OF ASSIMILATION

Peru is not a typical case—no case is—but it does illustrate the use of several means of assimilation. "All of Peru's problems," wrote Victor Alba in 1977, "center upon one fundamental problem—the need to convert a country into a nation."[3] In an attempt to assimilate its Indian population, over the years the Peruvian state has used land reform, educational and language policies, and political reforms. How well have these efforts succeeded in overcoming ethnic inequalities?

According to the census of 1972, 68.3 percent of Peruvians spoke Spanish as their mother tongue at that time, whereas 26.6 percent spoke a language in the Quechua family, 2.9 percent Aymara, 1.1 percent another indigenous language, and 0.4 percent a foreign language. The "mestizos" are an amalgamation of people of different origins ("white," Indian, and black). They tend to live in the coastal zone and are Catholics. Mestizos are said to be bonded by the consciousness of not being Indians. People in transition from Indian to mestizo status—as Indians learn Spanish, migrate to the towns, and become petty craftspeople or domestic servants—are called *cholos*.

The indigenous groups can be separated into those of the mountains and those of the jungle. The latter groups number around 200,000. Among the highland Indians the most numerous are the Quechua, of whom by the criterion of mother tongue there were slightly more than three million in 1972. The other highland group is the Aymara, of whom about a third of a million reside in Peru, primarily near the shores of Lake Titicaca.

The Aymara and the Quechua are alike in many ways. They tend to be subsistence farmers in the Andes, living in communities where much of the land is held in common and where social relationships are based on reciprocity. Members of the community perform services for one another (*ayni*) without requiring payment, expecting that they will get help when they need it. Both Aymara and Quechua have intermingled pre-Colombian rites with Christianity.

At the same time the Aymara and Quechua are distinct ethnic groups. Their languages are mutually unintelligible. Although both claim to be descended from the Inca, each has its own history. Intermarriage is rare.[4] So is political and economic cooperation.

Under the Spanish colonial regime, Indian labor and land was exploited. Indians could not be enslaved or sold, but they had to pay tribute and, except as members of local communities (*ayllus*), were not permitted to own land. The state isolated the Indians to prevent them from rebelling. *Castas* divided colonial society into racial groups, with each *casta* having a different legal status.

The Indians were the objects of fervent missionary activity. At the local level they were allowed to govern themselves in the *ayllus*, provided they paid their taxes. After independence, efforts were made to end the more blatant ethnic separatism and exploitation. The Indian tribute was banned in 1854. But, colonial rules no longer protected the *ayllus*. Large landowners in the highlands were able to encroach on the Indians' land, and the state did little to counteract this. Some experts believe that the Indians were actually better off under the paternalistic exploitation of the colony than they were after independence. "At the end of the nineteenth century," wrote Bernard E. Segal, "the gap in power, option, and social possibility between Peru's Indians on the one hand, and her white and mestizo population on the other, was greater than at any time before."

> Only at independence did the Enlightenment
> challenge the ideas that status determined right, that
> options and privilege, restriction and prohibition were
> dependent on rank, and that rank depended upon and
> reinforced ethnicity. Yet independence and the shift in
> doctrine had disastrous consequences. It did away
> with those portions of Spanish law that provided
> Indians with a special status and helped insulate them,
> however tenuously, from the depredations that
> higher-ranking groups were always ready to visit upon
> them.[5]

After Peru's defeat in the 1879 war with Chile, many intellectuals came to believe that one of the causes of Peruvian weakness was the relegation of the Indian population to the fringes of society. The result was a movement known as *indigenismo*. Slowly the discrepancies among the rights allowed to *criollos* (the descendants of the

Spanish colonizers), mestizos, and Indians began to be removed. In 1909 a law prohibited the state from requiring free labor from the Indians. In 1916 another law was passed—and implemented in 1923—that decreed a minimum wage for Indians. The Constitution of 1920 recognized the *ayllus* as legal entities. And beginning around the turn of the century, organized efforts were made to teach Indians the Spanish language. After 1900 most governments—especially that of President Manuel Prado (1939–1945)—expanded educational facilities in the highlands and promoted the learning of Spanish.

RECENT POLICIES

In more recent times, successive Peruvian governments have pursued efforts to assimilate the Indians. These undertakings may be grouped into several categories.

Politics.   Historically, Peru has been governed in a highly centralized manner. The country is divided into departments, which are further subdivided administratively. Under military rule from 1968 to 1980, prefects appointed from Lima administered the departments. In 1979 an elected assembly promulgated a new constitution. It granted illiterates the right to vote, which benefited mainly Indians. Moreover, it contained a commitment to decentralization. The departments would henceforth (1) have jurisdiction over public health, housing, highways, public works, agriculture, mining, industry, trade, social insurance, work, and to some extent education; (2) manage their own budgets, financed in part by the central government and in part by local taxes; and (3) have a regional assembly, a regional council, and a regional office of the prime minister. Only two-fifths of the Regional Assembly would be elected members, and for them the voters would be the provincial mayors. The other three-fifths would be "delegates of the institutions representative of the economic, social, and cultural activities of the region."[6]

It is too soon to judge the effects of these changes. Peru's civil unrest and the economic collapse beginning in the late 1980s have derailed many plans. We can note that none of these political changes makes explicit allowance for ethnicity. For example, no seats are reserved for Indians.

Agrarian reform.   A number of policy measures have been undertaken to improve the lot of subsistence farmers, most of whom are Indians.

Beginning in 1958 and lasting through 1965, Indians throughout the highlands illegally occupied land belonging to *hacendados*—land the Indians claimed was historically theirs. At the height of this movement, some 300,000 peasants participated. The movement was quelled by agrarian reform legislation in 1964 and, in a brief guerrilla movement in 1965, by the army. President Fernando Belaúnde's efforts at agrarian reform in the 1960s were limited by political opposition, the exemption of "efficient plantations and haciendas," and a small implementing agency. Only about 375,000 hectares of a total of some 23,000,000 hectares of agricultural land were transferred.[7] Perhaps in an effort to keep the Indians from migrating to the cities, between 1963 and 1968 the government recognized more than 600 indigenous communities, which thereby gained exemption from most taxes and the right to "first priority" to government assistance.[8]

President Belaúnde's initiatives also included *Cooperación Popular*, which combined the resources of several ministries in an attempt to give technical assistance to subsistence farmers and to encourage self-help. University students were to add their efforts to Cooperación Popular during their vacations. In its first year, this program built some 2,600 kilometers of roads, 2,000 community buildings, and 500 schools. But funding was a problem, and in 1966 the Peruvian Congress cut off appropriations.[9]

According to most observers, Peru's efforts at agrarian reform in the 1960s yielded meager results. Almost 400,000 peasant families remained landless, and in the highlands the haciendas continued to predominate. The program may, however, have had a political impact: the immediate danger of Indian land invasions was headed off.

After the military coup of 1968, the reformist government gave great emphasis to helping the indigenous peoples. President Juan Velasco presented the agrarian reform law with these words:

> Today, the Day of the Indian, the Day of the Peasant,
> the Revolutionary Government is making the best of
> all tributes to him by giving the whole nation a law
> which will end forever an unjust social order. Today,
> Peru has a government determined to achieve the
> development of the country by the final destruction of
> ancient economic and social structures that have no
> validity on earth.[10]

Under this law about 11 million hectares were to change hands by 1976. All landholdings larger than 150 hectares on the coast and 200 hectares in the highlands were to be expropriated. Sugar plantations were included. Outside experts called it the most ambitious land reform in Latin America outside Cuba.[11]

The government's original idea was to divide the expropriated land into private plots for peasants—mostly Indians—to farm. To the government's surprise, many peasants fared less well economically than when they had worked as employees on the large haciendas. Their resistance, coupled with the increasingly ambitious aims of the revolutionary government, led to a more radical policy emphasizing cooperatives. These came in two forms: the fully collectivized agricultural production cooperatives and the social interest agricultural societies. The latter were a compromise between parcelization and collective agriculture. They combined former estate laborers and surrounding "communities." The cooperatives ended up receiving the lion's share of state support, at the expense of peasant communities and peasant-run enterprises. Despite their financial advantages, most cooperatives failed; Peruvian scholars have blamed managerial inefficiency and bureaucratization.[12]

With the onset of hard times in the latter part of the 1970s and the discrediting of radicals during the Morales Bermúdez government, agrarian reform was quieted. The efficiency costs of previous efforts were sinking in. From 1971 to 1978 agricultural growth had averaged only 1.8 percent per year. Migration from the highlands continued at the rate of about 1 percent per year. Although in 1975 a law had been promulgated extending expropriation to estates of 50 hectares or more, it was never implemented.

In the 1980s the new civilian government of Belaúnde did not try to undo land reform, although it disapproved of some of the methods that had been used to carry it out. The government preferred to emphasize private enterprise and efficiency, instead of the problems of the largely Indian peasantry. The Agricultural Promotion Law of November 1980 opened the way to a dissolution of the cooperatives.[13]

Language Policies   Ambiguity has marked recent policies toward the Quechua and Aymara languages. On the one hand a widely shared goal is the eventual transition into Spanish, on the other is a desire to respect indigenous languages.

For example, the General Law of Education of 1972 seemed to state that native languages should be used as means to facilitate literacy in Spanish. But later the law declared: "In consequence, bilingual education will seek to avoid the imposition of any single culture, but rather promote the uniform appreciation of the cultural pluralism of the country."[14] The Constitution of 1979 required that education above the primary level be in Spanish. But the same Article 35 desired that the study of "aborigene languages" be promoted and guaranteed the right of Indian communities to receive primary education in their own languages.

In 1972 Quechua became an official language of Peru and a Roman alphabet was prepared. But no Indian languages have been used in government documents. Technical problems inhibit their use. First, Quechua has no tradition as a written language. "The written Quechua that now exists," notes political scientist Jorge Domínguez in a personal communication, "is not the heritage of the Incas but of zealous heirs of Pizarro. For this reason, a Quechua speaker is doubly illiterate in his own language and in Spanish." Second, Quechua is a language family, with some versions as different as Spanish and Portuguese. Newspapers and even radio have therefore not replaced oral communication within small regions.

EFFECTS ON ETHNIC INEQUALITIES

How well have these various policies worked in assimilating the Indians of Peru? The question does not admit a definitive answer, and not just because longitudinal data are lacking. Still, it is worth reviewing several dimensions of the current status of the indigenous peoples of Peru.

Politics. Throughout most of Peru's history, the political system has been centralized, which has meant that the Indians were ruled from Lima, by people of a different ethnic group. Even today in the highland communities where Indians form a clear majority, they rarely rise to positions of authority outside the *ayllus*. The mestizo minority continues to provide the mayors and municipal councillors. Some observers believe that the Indians have accepted this political exclusion despite its disadvantages because it has allowed them to preserve their ethnic identities through self-government in the *ayllus*.

"The most salient political characteristic of the Indian peoples of Guatemala and Peru, for example," Charles W. Anderson concludes, "is their capacity to resist cultural assimilation into the Hispanic part of the society."

> Sequentially, they have maintained their cultural
> integrity against the efforts of the Spaniards, the
> Church, the governments of the independent nations,

and the modern-day technical assistance experts. It is not the will of the Indian that has been frustrated in his confrontation with Western civilization. It is rather the "modernizing elites" who have been powerless to create the nationally integrated, economically developed, Westernized societies to which they have aspired.[15]

The rise of the Shining Path guerrilla movement in the 1980s has been interpreted not only as an ideological but also as an ethnic movement.

Economics. Ethnicity and economic welfare continue to correspond closely in Peru. The oligarchy, middle classes, tradespeople, and the organized working class tend to be mestizos, whereas the subsistence farmers and servants are almost all Indians. Anthropological studies indicate that in the highlands the social relations between Indians and mestizos are still characterized by ethnic distrust and discrimination.[16]

Although direct measurements of income by ethnic group are not available, to Peruvians it is apparent that the Indians remain at the bottom of the income distribution. Existing data about economic inequalities are harsh indeed. Peru's income distribution is among the most unequal in the world. Economist Richard Webb's study is dated, but it is the only careful analysis I know of Peru's income distribution. He showed that in 1961 the bottom 40 percent of the distribution had only 9 percent of the country's personal income, whereas the richest 10 percent had 49 percent of the income. In 1961 the income per capita was $716 for Lima, $463 in the coastal region excluding Lima, and $246 in the highlands. Between 1950 and 1966, earnings in the modern sector grew 4.1 percent a year, whereas among small farmers the yearly growth rate was only 0.8 percent.[17]

Did agrarian reform in Peru help the Indians? Most observers now conclude that the reforms made little difference. "The agrarian-reform legislation that was aimed at peasant communities raised expectations, but changed relatively little," according to one study.[18] It is nonetheless true that in some ways the situation of the Indians has changed markedly over the past thirty years. Many of these changes took place independently of agrarian reform. Already by the end of the 1960s about 80 percent of the peasants had their lands "rent free"; participation in markets had grown dramatically with the opening of roads since the early 1950s; and about 90 percent of peasant children of primary school age were in school.[19]

Sadly, the changes did not seem to make the Indians significantly better off in economic terms. Sociologist Julio Cotler estimates that land reform increased the incomes of the poorest 25 percent of peasant families by less than half a percent.[20] The percentage of the land held by small landholders called *minifundistas* rose from 10.6 percent to 12.9 percent, while the *ayllus'* holdings went from 35.2 to 36.8 percent. Cristóbal Key concluded: "The redistributive capacity of the agrarian reform was . . . quite limited," a verdict also reached in a study by Peter Cleaves and Martin Scurrah.[21] Economist José María Caballero put it this way: "Semisubsistence production and highland agriculture in general remain stagnant. . . . Taken overall, the Andean peasant economy is maintaining itself at a level of simple reproduction, at least during the past two decades: output, yields, accumulated capital, incomes, and population have grown little or not at all.[22]

Education. Illiteracy has fallen over time, and most of the improvement has been among Indians. Illiteracy in Spanish in Peru as a whole dropped from 51 percent of those fifteen or older in 1950 to 39 percent in 1961 to 29 percent in 1970. Moreover, in 1940 only about 32 percent of those whose mother tongue was an Indian language could speak Spanish. By 1961 this figure had increased to about 50 percent and by 1972 to about 57 percent.[23]

Nonetheless, large educational disparities persist. According to the 1972 census, even in urban areas Quechua and Aymara speakers were about twice as likely as those with Spanish as their mother tongue to have had no education. They were only a third as likely to have attended university.[24]

Although data are scarce, it appears that decades of state policies to assimilate the Indians have failed to remove huge inequalities in political power, poverty and economic well-being, and education. Like all Peruvians, Indians are better off than they were fifty years ago. But ethnicity remains highly correlated with poverty, disease, and poor education.

NONINTERVENTIONIST BRAZIL

Other developing countries have adopted a range of policies to deal with ethnic inequalities in education, income, and employment. At one extreme of the policy spectrum is Brazil. Over the years successive Brazilian governments have simply denied that ethnic problems exist and consequently have undertaken no ethnically based policies at all.

The 1980 census reported that about 54 percent of the Brazilian population was white, 39 percent brown (*parda* or mixed race), 6 percent black, and less than 1 percent yellow. Some experts think the percentage of *pardas* is much higher. A survey by the United Nations estimated that "70 to 75 percent (of the population) was constituted of Negroes (blacks or *miscegenados*)."[25] Since in many studies respondents classify themselves, various biases and inconsistencies are introduced. In any case, Brazil has large numbers of nonwhites—so many that government officials promoting relations with Africa tout Brazil as "the second largest African nation," trailing only Nigeria in its number of people of Negro descent.

Official reluctance to examine the race question has a long pedigree. In 1899 by order of Rui Barbosa, a liberal, all documents pertinent to slavery were destroyed, in order to erase "the black stain of Brazilian history."[26] By political decision racial data were not included in the 1960 and 1970 censuses.

Indeed, far from admitting that any racial problem exists, Brazil's politicians have lauded its unique success as a multiracial state. I have traveled throughout Brazil and been struck by the free mixing of the races, by a sort of ideology that race is irrelevant. More important, several distinguished social scientists have also been impressed. In a classic study sociologist Donald Pierson noted that "Brazil is one of the more conspicuous melting pots of races and cultures around the world where miscegenation and acculturation are obviously going on." After the emancipation of the slaves in 1888, Pierson argued, the relations between whites, blacks, and mulattoes were determined by social and economic factors, not race. As blacks and mulattoes improved their socioeconomic standing, they would have no problems in being fully assimilated. Racial discrimination was not a central issue.[27]

Sociologist Gilberto Freyre agreed. The only discrimination in Brazil was socioeconomic. Race relations in Brazil were different from those in other countries. The Portuguese colonists were less bigoted than their Anglo-Saxon counterparts, in part because Portugal itself had long been a place of ethnic mixing with Arabs, Jews, and Africans. Consequently, Freyre said, the Portuguese more freely "mingled their blood" with that of African slave women. "Every Brazilian, even the light-skinned, fair-haired ones, carries about with him on his soul, when not on soul and body alike—for there are many in Brazil with a mongrel mark of the genipap—the shadow, or at least the birthmark, of the aborigene or the Negro." Freyre goes on to proclaim "the influence of the African, either direct or vague and remote. In our affections, our excessive mimicry, our

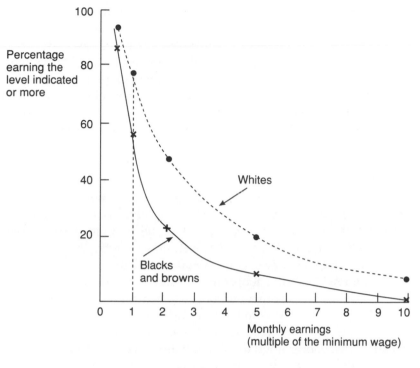

FIGURE 11-1

Monthly Earnings of Males over Ten Years of Age, by Color

SOURCE: Author's calculations based on *IX Recenseamento Geral do Brasil-1980*, vol. I, tomo 4, no. I (Censo Demográfico Dados Gerais-Migração-Instrução-Fecundidada-Mortalidade) (Rio de Janeiro: IBGE, 1983), Table 1.6. The figure includes only those males ten or older who in fact had earnings. Of the whites, 24.2 percent did not have any monthly earnings; the corresponding figure for blacks and browns was 27.9 percent.

Catholicism, which so delights the senses, our music, our gait, our speech, our cradle songs—everything that is a sincere expression of our lives, we almost all of us bear the mark of that influence."[28]

The Brazilian etiquette of race relations seems unique.[29] Despite this accomplishment, critics have questioned Brazil's success in overcoming ethnic inequalities. For example: "At present the black man's position in Brazil can only be described as being virtually outside the mainstream of society. He is almost completely unrepresented in any area involving decision making."[30]

Only recently have data become available to analyze the extent of racial inequalities in Brazil. Figure 11-1 depicts monthly earnings by different racial groups. Given Brazil's ethos of equality, the gaps are remarkable. Of those who reported earnings in the 1980 census, about 44 percent of the blacks and browns earned less than the minimum wage, compared with only 24 percent of the whites. At the other end of the earnings spectrum, whites were overrepresented. About three times the proportion of whites as nonwhites earned between five and ten times the minimum wage. About five times the proportion of whites earned more than ten times the minimum. On average white wage earners earned a little more than twice as much as blacks and browns.

A survey in 1976 of 120,000 households throughout Brazil provides richer data for analysis. Holding the level of education constant, whites earned about one and two-thirds as much on average as nonwhites (see Table 11-1). Regression analysis was used to adjust earnings differences for education, occupation, and four measures of parents' socioeconomic background. With all these factors statistically equated, whites would still be predicted to have incomes from 1.4 to 1.6 times higher than nonwhites.[31]

Nonwhites also lag in educational terms. According to the 1980 census, nonwhites were about twice as likely to have had no education as whites. At the other end of the spectrum, whites were more than three times as likely to have attended university.

Within Brazil these statistics are not widely known. Perhaps because data concerning ethnic inequalities have seldom been collected, over the years Brazilian governments have not given policies an ethnic focus; or perhaps the causal arrow runs the other way. Even after the emancipation of the slaves in 1888, no public programs were developed explicitly for the former slave population. Consequently, according to some scholars, the economic situation of

TABLE 11-1

Income by Education and Race in Brazil, 1976

Level of Education	Average Income (cruzeiros)		Income Ratio (nonwhite:white)	Total Number (percentage white)
	Whites	Nonwhites		
Illiterate	1,734	1,174	0.68	4,661 (46)
Literate[a]	2,985	1,674	0.56	3,720 (60)
Elementary	3,769	2,122	0.56	3,753 (68)
Junior high	7,790	2,891	0.37	576 (71)
Senior high	9,742	5,557	0.57	228 (80)
College	10,900	6,801	0.62	255 (89)

a. Literate but has not finished elementary school.

SOURCE: Author's calculations based on data in Carlos A. Hassenbalg, "Race and Socioeconomic Inequalities in Brazil," Série Estudos no. 13 (Rio de Janeiro: IUPERJ, March 1983).

blacks actually deteriorated after emancipation.[32] As in most countries, a law bans discrimination based on race or color; it was passed in 1951. Beyond this, Brazil's approach has always been racial laissez faire. "Brazilian society left the Negro to his own fate, laying upon his own shoulders the responsibility for re-educating himself and for making the adjustments to the new patterns and concepts created by the advent of free labor, the republican regime, and capitalism."[33]

One critic notes a conspiracy of silence about ethnic inequality, including but going beyond government officials:

> There has been a consistent if perhaps not entirely intentional alliance of politicians, administrators, the aristocracy, academics, workers, artists, and others— politically and ideologically at variance though they might be—vis-à-vis the plight of the black Brazilian: for their own reasons they all refuse to recognize that the special problems the black person encounters as a result of his colour and his heritage require special attention.[34]

Another expert attributes this reluctance to "the 'inferiority complex' which is prevalent throughout Brazilian culture, and which developed during the long period of Indian and Negro slavery and of dependence on the outside world."[35] No doubt this attitude is a factor in many countries that are reluctant to acknowledge ethnic inequalities.

As the outset of this chapter, I cited Jorge Amado's belief that the only cure for racial inequalities would be racial mixing. Brazil has certainly experienced ample miscegenation, and overt racism and discrimination seem not to be widespread. Nonetheless, as we have seen, ethnic inequalities in income, employment, and education are glaring.

INTERVENTIONIST MALAYSIA

In contrast to Brazil's see-no-evil attitude, other governments have been interventionists when confronted with ethnic inequalities.[36] For example:

- In India the constitution and various state laws reserve places for "backward castes and tribes" in higher education, the civil service, and the legislature.[37]

- Nearly all the cultivable land in Fiji has long been reserved to ethnic Fijians.

- Indonesian public policy requires that at least a fifth of the shares in new companies must be held by *pribumis*, or non-Chinese Indonesians. The admission of Chinese to universities is subject to a quota. In the allocation of subsidized credit, preference is given to non-Chinese.

- Tanzania adjusts examination scores so that students from different tribes are more evenly represented in school and university enrollment.[38]

- Sri Lanka alters the scores on examinations taken in different languages, even in subjects like mathematics, so that the same percentages of Sinhalese as Tamils are admitted to university.[39]

Malaysia provides perhaps the world's most spectacular example of a government intervening to reduce ethnic inequalities—or what the authorities call "racial differences." Unlike Brazil, the topic is discussed with surprising frankness, even in official circles. Consider, for example, this analysis:

> For the basis of the Malay claim to discrimination [that is, to preferential treatment] is not man-made law but inherent human behaviour. It has been pointed out that races are not only distinguished by colour, physiognomy, language and culture, but also by their character. Inherent racial character explains the rapid recovery of Germany and Japan after their defeat in World War II. [Other examples follow.] . . .
>
> It explains why the Malays are rural and economically backward, and why the non-Malays are urban and economically advanced. It is the result of the clash of racial traits. They are easy-going and tolerant. The Chinese especially are hard-working and astute in business. When the two come into contact, the result was inevitable. . . .
>
> I contend that the Malays are the original or indigenous people of Malaya and the only people who can claim Malaya as their own and only country. In accordance with practice all over the world, this confers on the Malays certain inalienable rights over the forms and obligations of citizenship which can be imposed on citizens of non-indigenous origin.[40]

The author of this passage, Mahathir bin Mohamad, later became the prime minister of Malaysia—a position he still holds.

Bumiputera, or sons of the soil, make up about 58 percent of the population of peninsular Malaysia's fifteen million inhabitants; most of them are ethnic Malays and Muslims.[41] About 32 percent of peninsular Malaysians are of Chinese descent—virtually none Muslim—and about 10 percent had ancestors who came from India, mostly Tamils, mostly non-Muslims. Unlike Brazil, very little inter-marriage has occurred across racial or religious divides.

Peninsular Malaysia—the largest part of the country, and the one from which most of the data below are drawn—was placed under "indirect" British rule beginning in 1874. Tin mining and rubber plantations began to boom. "The local Malay population, for various political, cultural, and economic reasons, either was not prepared to enter or was prevented from entering into the rapidly expanding export-oriented primary sectors."[42] Penniless Chinese and Indian laborers were imported—the Chinese for the mines, the Tamils for the rubber. Malays remained predominantly rural and agricultural, ruled by the British through the Malays' own heredi-tary, quasi-feudal leaders.

Over the years the British instituted a series of legal measures to protect the Malays from the "more rigorous drive of the other ethnic groups," in particular the Chinese. The Malay Reservations Enactments, passed in different Malaysian states during the 1910s, set aside certain areas of land for Malay ownership. Preferential treatment was given to Malays in education and government ser-vice. As independence approached, citizenship wrangles accumu-lated, affecting many Chinese and Indians. Many Malays wanted their language to be declared the only permissible language of in-struction and government, and these issues continue to smolder today.

At independence in 1957, Article 153 of the constitution pro-vided that Malays would receive preferential treatment in public employment, scholarships, and permits and licenses for business. It was decreed that at least half the land in each state be held perpet-ually under Malay ownership. One reason for these policies was to preserve past Malay privileges. "Even more important, however" said the leader of the Malayan Chinese Association before indepen-dence, "is the indisputable fact that as a race the Malays are econom-ically backward and well behind the other races in this field. . . . An economically depressed Malay community will never be able to achieve the desired degree of cooperation with the substantially more prosperous non-Malay communities."[43]

But during the 1960s the historical economic gaps between the Chinese and the Malays remained. As the economy grew at a 5.7 percent pace from 1957 to 1970, Chinese incomes continued to average about double those of the Malays, and only part of this difference could be explained in regional or rural-urban terms.[44] By 1969 Malays controlled only about 1 percent of limited companies (in contrast to about 33 percent by "other Malays" and 62 percent by foreign interests).

Nonetheless, Malaysia remained democratic and its economy continued to grow. An American political scientist published a book in 1969 that proclaimed Malaysia's victory over ethnic strife.

> Malaysia's most significant achievement is in racial
> cooperation. Combining communal parties into an
> Alliance has worked effectively. A similar compromise
> on the explosive issue of national language has
> avoided the violence that occurs in many countries.
> Malaysia seems to have discovered a way of
> permitting three ancient cultures to continue their
> great traditions but to work together in harmony. It is
> this that makes Malaysia so significant in the world.[45]

Soon this verdict seemed premature. In 1969 a series of violent racial incidents rocked the country. With the specter of nearby Indonesia's racial slaughter of 1966 in mind, the Malay-dominated government decided to redouble its efforts to close the Malay-Chinese gaps. By 1971 the government instituted the "New Economic Policy." One of its two principal objectives was "restructuring Malaysian society to correct economic imbalance, so as to reduce and eventually eliminate the identification of race with economic function." Malaysia thereby inaugurated what may be the world's most vigorous program of preferential treatment.[46]

The new ethnic preferences went well beyond Malaysia's former practices. They were informed by hypotheses about ethnic differences that would shock many Western politicians—as they did some Malaysians. I have already cited some of the prime minister's views. At about the same time, a group of Malay intellectuals under the leadership of the secretary general of the principal Malay political party brought out a book called *Revolusi Mental*. It criticized "Malay economic ethics in contrast to those of the Chinese."

> Chinese success is attributed to Chinese self-reliance,
> diligence, and acquisitive drive; the Malay psychology
> is presented as lacking in these qualities. In addition,
> the book asserts, Malays have certain misconceptions

of religious beliefs and are easily contented. This leads
to a lack of persistent effort in work and to
dependency on others, chiefly on government
agencies. . . . Thus progress could only be achieved
through a revolution in mental attitudes, leading in
turn toward economic advancement through self-
reliance. In other words, the Malays would have to
change from a culture-oriented to an economic-
oriented society.[47]

Public policy did not tackle psychology, however. Instead, it
instituted a series of quotas favoring Malays as part of a broad
package of pro-Malay policies.

Consider education. Under the New Economic Policy, the universities adopted for the first time informal racial quotas. Ethnic
preference in financial aid policies was expanded. The University of
Malaya made Malay—officially renamed *bahasa Malaysia* or Malaysian language—its official language. New universities and technical
colleges were founded to cater primarily to *bumiputera;* tertiary enrollment rose from 8,505 in 1970 to 37,838 in 1985.[48]

In employment, the government pushed "targets" of 40 to 50
percent for Malay employment in private firms. The public sector
expanded its hiring of *bumiputera*. For example, the Malaysian Administrative and Diplomatic Service was legislated to require a three-
to-one or four-to-one ratio of Malays to non-Malays in many top
positions.

Perhaps most remarkable were initiatives in the ownership of
productive enterprises. The target of the New Economic Policy was
that 30 percent of total business ownership should be in Malay
hands by 1990. This evolved into the requirement that all new businesses had to have at least 30 percent Malay participation. A second
initiative was public sector ownership on behalf of individual *bumiputera*. The National Corporation holds assets in trust for eventual distribution to *bumiputera*. Its wholly owned subsidiaries are in
insurance, construction, engineering, securities, properties, and
trading; it also has joint ventures in mining, hotels, containerization,
and other fields. The National Equity Company purchases interests
in individual companies and sells shares to ethnic Malays on nearly
risk-free, highly profitable terms.

Special efforts were made to help *bumiputera* entrepreneurs.
New racial quotas were applied to public procurement. Bank Bumiputera was set up to give loans to ethnic Malays. Other organizations such as the Urban Development Authority, the Malaysian
Industrial Finance Berhad, various state economic development

corporations, the Rural and Industrial Authority, and the Council of Trust for the Indigenous People (MARA) all had special programs favoring *bumiputera*.

Public debate over these measures was modulated in several ways. The media were kept in check—for example, with requirements for Malay ownership of many non-Malay newspapers. In 1971 a constitutional amendment forbade the public discussion of special rights for *bumiputera*.

RESULTS

The gap was closed in higher education. The Malay share of enrollment at public universities increased rapidly from 43 percent in 1970 to 67 percent in 1972. *Bumiputera* remained underrepresented in the sciences, a fact attributed to the superior examination scores of Chinese students and the relatively greater job opportunities for Chinese in technical employment, which is not as subject to ethnic quotas.

Two unintended results of the shift in enrollment were a fall in standards at the universities and an exodus of Chinese students abroad. The academic preparation of students has declined. Graduates are having trouble finding jobs. According to one estimate in 1987, thirty-five thousand graduates were unemployed. More than nine-tenths were *bumiputera*.[49]

As the quotas for *bumiputera* went into effect, many Chinese and Indian students were forced to emigrate. By the mid-1970s as many students from Malaysia were enrolled abroad as in the country's own universities. In 1987 there were about 40,000 students at the tertiary level in Malaysia, compared with some 65,000 Malaysians, mostly non-*bumipetera*, studying at the tertiary level in other countries. "This large government-sponsored and privately financed Malaysian student population overseas cost the country an estimated Malaysian $1.5 billion in foreign exchange in 1986."[50]

Employment patterns changed somewhat. The percentage of Malays among citizens employed in "administration and management" rose from 24 percent in 1970 to 32 percent in 1979, before dropping to about 28 percent in 1980, where it remained through 1988.[51] As the number of "registered professionals"—such as architects, engineers, accountants, and lawyers—doubled in the 1980s, the percentage of Malays rose from 15 percent to 25 percent of the total. (The Chinese percentage fell from 63 percent to 58 percent.)[52]

A recent review by two economists with the Malaysian Institute of Economic Research is sobering:

Despite the increasing supply of *Bumiputera* professionals and skilled labour, they are still disproportionately represented in lower skilled categories. They made marginal advancements into the professional and technical occupations. By 1975, they accounted for 48 per cent of those employed in this category (a large percentage of whom were teachers and nurses) compared with 47 per cent in 1970 in Peninsular Malaysia. An overwhelming percentage of Bumiputeras are still in agricultural occupations, and their share by the end of the decade, will remain at about three-quarter [sic]. *Bumiputera* representation in key occupations has not shown very rapid progress as by 1990 they are estimated to reach only about 46 per cent compared to about 44 per cent in 1980. When the proportion of registered professionals (e.g. doctors, architects, engineers and lawyers) are taken into account their underrepresentation is even more glaring; by the end of 1988 only a quarter of the registered professionals were *Bumiputera,* compared to 58.4 per cent and 14.3 per cent noted by the Chinese and Indians respectively.[53]

Malay ownership of productive resources grew. Ownership by Malay individuals and trusts rose from 2.3 percent in 1969 to 20 percent in 1988 (see Figure 11-2). This significant increase fell well below the target in the New Economic Policy (NEP) of 30 percent by 1990.[54] In absolute terms Malay ownership lagged far behind that of Chinese and Indians. For example, from 1971 to 1980 ownership by these "other Malaysians" grew by about M$8.3 billion, compared with a growth of about M$3 billion for total ownership by *bumiputera.*

As Figure 11-3 reveals, during the first ten years of the NEP the gap between Malay and Chinese incomes had not closed.[55] After that, there was some progress, especially during the recession of 1985–86. Some experts attribute the closing of the gap during the recession to the Malays' greater reliance on agriculture, which is less affected that commerce and industry by economic swings. (In 1988 Malays made up 78 percent of those working in agriculture, compared to 75 percent in 1970.)

Preferential programs tended to favor the already well-off segments of the Malay population. Within the Malay group, the distribution of income worsened slightly.[56] Educational quotas favored well-to-do *bumiputera.* For example, whereas Malay students from

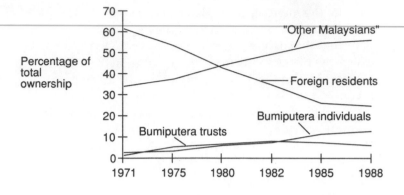

FIGURE 11-2

**Share of Ownership Held by Various Groups,
Malaysia, 1971–1988**

NOTE: Ownership calculations are based on the par value of shares issued and paid up in limited companies and value of net assets of local branches of foreign incorporated companies.

SOURCE: Various Malaysia Plans and Mid-Term Reviews; Kamil Salih and Zainal Aznam Yusof, "Overview of the New Economic Policy and Framework for the Post-1990 Economic Policy" (paper presented at National Conference on Post-1990 Economic Policy, Malaysian Institute of Economic Research, Kuala Lumpur, 1989); Robert Klitgaard and Ruth Katz, "Overcoming Ethnic Inequalities: Lessons from Malaysia," *Journal of Policy Analysis and Management* 2, no. 3 (1983). Slight discrepancies in the 1985 data have been resolved in favor of the *Mid-Term Review of the Fifth Malaysia Plan* (1989).

families in the lower income brackets—63 percent of the population—received 14 percent of the university scholarships, Malay students whose families were in the top 17 percent of the income distribution received slightly more than half of all scholarships awarded to Malays.[57] If one calls the top 5 percent of the *bumiputera* income distribution "upper class" and the bottom 63 percent "poor," then for every one chance that a poor household has for being awarded a government scholarship, a rich household has 21.[58]

CONCLUDING REMARKS

Few poor countries provide as much racially specific data as Malaysia, and few countries have tried as hard to close the economic and educational gaps. During the 1970s Malaysia's economy grew an average of 8 percent a year. In the 1980s, things slowed down, and critics began to question the New Economic Policy.

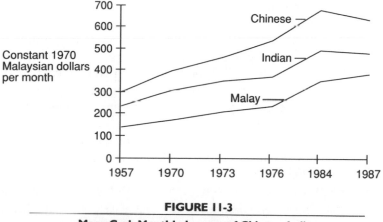

FIGURE 11-3

Mean Cash Monthly Income of Chinese, Indian, and Bumiputera Households, 1957–1987

SOURCE: Various Malaysia Plans and Mid-Term Reviews. Author's conversions of 1988 figures to real 1970 Malaysian dollars, based on data in *Fifth Malaysian Plan* and *Mid-Term Review of Fifth Malaysian Plan.* See also note 55.

Two Malaysian economists recently addressed this question. "Comparing the national economy to the other NICs [newly industrialized countries], including Thailand," Kamal Salih and Zainal Aznam Yusof observed, "Malaysia indeed experienced a lower economic growth rate" over the past twenty years. Many factors were responsible, and it is hard to blame the difference on the New Economic Policy. One estimate by the World Bank was troubling. The contribution of the so-called residual factor to national output fell from 28 percent in 1970–1975 to 14 percent in 1975–1980 to −21 percent in 1980–1983. The residual factor is "a measure of efficiency, innovation, technology and skills," the authors say. Another study using a different methodology calculated the residual factor for the whole period at 17–20 percent—which is one-third the corresponding percentage in other Asian newly industrialized countries. "This shows how much the problems of wastage, inefficient management, and shortcomings in skill and manpower, and technological development, need to be addressed under the post-1990 economic policy."[59]

Nonetheless, Salih and Yusof say, "on the second issue whether Malaysia's economic growth over the two decades would have been better without the implementation of the NEP, the counter argument is that this is the price we are willing to pay in order to achieve better distribution of wealth and incomes, and political stability."[60]

Yet, to many Malaysians, progress in overcoming ethnic inequalities has been disappointing. In 1989 the executive director of the Malaysian Institute of Economic Research concluded that despite two decades of economic growth (averaging 6.1 percent per year) and the preferential policies, economic inequalities between Chinese and Malays had grown.[61]

The NEP may have slowed but did not halt Malaysia's economic growth, which many other developing countries would envy. (When the NEP seemed to constrain growth and foreign investment in the mid-1980s, it was loosened.)[62] The NEP's ethnically based policies may have helped to stabilize Malaysia politically. Ethnic violence has not reemerged. Democracy persists. When one compares Malaysia to other countries where ethnic conflict flared in the late 1960s, these are blessings.

Preferential programs interact with the role of the state in Malaysia. In the 1960s and 1970s, the strategy of heavy state involvement in the economy gave the government's preferential programs a wide swath. With the recession of 1985–86, the government shifted economic strategies. A greater role was given to the private sector and to foreign investment. Public spending was cut from a planned M$74 billion in 1987 to only M$47.7 billion. Government hiring was frozen; so, therefore, were those strong preferences for *bumiputera*. As part of a general policy of deregulation, the government relaxed rules about the restructuring of private enterprises to meet ethnic goals. Ethnic requirements for foreign investment were also eased. Exchange rates were liberalized, and interest rates were dropped. Government credit programs for *bumiputera* were cut by 57 percent. Government plans for equity acquisition and new investment on behalf of *bumiputera* ownership were slashed by 42 percent.[63] It is likely that the government's efforts to help *bumiputera* will turn toward such things as entrepreneurial training and will rely less on public subsidies and state-owned enterprises.[64]

Although the government is justly proud of having fulfilled the NEP's twenty-year objectives for reducing absolute poverty, it is concerned by shortfalls in the racial restructuring of the economy. The problems of ethnic inequalities, states the 1989 *Mid-Term Review of the Fifth Malaysia Plan*, require

> new approaches and rethinking of strategies towards
> effective participation of *Bumiputera* in all economic
> activities. With continued regional disparities, growth

in less-developed states will be promoted through better urban-rural linkages. The challenges ahead would entail policy shift [sic] that will nurture self-reliance, resourcefulness, and positive commitment among all Malaysians, particularly the lagging.[65]

12

THE EVOLUTION, MAINTENANCE, AND REDUCTION OF ETHNIC INEQUALITIES

IN PERU, BRAZIL, AND MALAYSIA, economically and educationally backward ethnic groups have made progress in absolute terms over the years. But in all three cases, surprisingly large ethnic inequalities have persisted.

This is not good news. When I began studying Brazil and Malaysia a decade ago, I hoped to be able to document success. Ethnic conflict was minimal in both countries, and their economies were on the move. But after studying both, I find that neither has been notably successful in overcoming ethnic differences. Certainly, other developing countries cannot simply copy Brazil's official indifference (and unofficial mestization) or Malaysia's interventionism and hope that ethnic inequalities will be quickly reduced.

In the absence of a clearly successful model to emulate, we need to delve deeper into the ethnic dimensions of poverty and possible remedial measures. Unfortunately, this topic has been overlooked or suppressed in the practical literature on economic and political development. For example, ethnic issues are not mentioned in any of the twenty-two course syllabi on economic development in U.S. universities compiled by Edward Tower.[1] Nobel prize–winning economist Jan Tinbergen reflected on the subject in "a philosophical interlude" in his review of three decades of work on economic development. Among the determining factors of development were "racial differences."

"Objective scientific treatment of this subject is obstructed, however, by the emotions aroused by two extreme views: one assumes a priori that the subject is taboo; the other, that whites—and even more particularly, German-defined Aryan people—are superior in all respects."[2] Tinbergen added in a footnote, "I am calling this section a philosophical interlude, because I do not think that research on these questions has a high priority."

Many factors inhibit such research. The concepts of race and ethnicity are analytically slippery, and data in developing countries are scarce. Most people interested in economic and political development are untrained and perhaps afraid of the anthropological and biological fields that might throw light on ethnic differences. All of us fear unintended consequences of treading into such sensitive subjects. In this century race has been enmeshed with preposterous, sometimes criminal ideologies and actions. We worry that studying ethnicity and development might lead to misunderstanding or misuse, perhaps to ethnic intolerance. Or to defeatism.

The fear of fostering defeatism may underlie Tinbergen's idea that race matters in economic development but research on the topic does not deserve priority. But like it or not, ethnicity is intimately associated with poverty and disadvantage in many developing countries. Presumably, ethnic inequalities are affected by public policies toward education, employment, infrastructure, markets, and affirmative action. I believe an important challenge is to understand how and how much, and under what circumstances.

TWO EXTREME VIEWS OF ETHNIC INEQUALITIES

Thinking about ethnic inequalities has been varied and has metamorphosed over the years, but I think it is fruitful to begin by contrasting two extreme views.

Crudely summarized, one extreme view asserts that members of certain groups tend to be stupider, lazier, and more vicious than members of other groups. As a consequence of their bad behavior, these groups disproportionately end up uneducated, poor, and sick. Their economic and educational backwardness is the result of their characteristics and behavior, as reflected through markets and merit systems.

Another extreme view disagrees saying, true, some groups are less educated, poorer, and less healthy than others. But this backwardness is not the result of differences in intelligence, diligence, or virtue. Rather, these groups are uneducated, poor, and sick because it suits a dominant group to keep them that way. The dominant group exploits their backwardness, profits from it. To do this, the dominant group distorts markets and merit systems in discriminatory ways. Economic and educational backwardness is the result of discrimination and exploitation.

These two extremes are caricatures, but we may recognize in them what might be called different intellectual reflexes. Upon observing that poverty has ethnic correlates, the first view tends to see the reflection of behavioral differences. The second view tends to see the machinations of an exploiting group, which manipulates ostensibly fair markets and meritocracies to its advantage.

The first view is seldom expressed in writing these days, but anyone who has spent time in Bolivia or in many other developing countries is sure to have heard something like it. At one time, it was the dominant view. Yale historian Emilia Viotti da Costa notes:

> Everywhere, we find the same remarks about the natives, from Puritans in New England, planters in Virginia, missionaries in Brazil, and slave traders and royal bureaucrats in Africa. The natives lived like beasts, they said. They did not value property; they were lazy and promiscuous; they had bad manners, ate strange food, and were superstitious and filthy, treacherous and inconstant and unreliable, violent and addicted to lying.[3]

In short, the "natives" are backward because of the way they behave. They have little human capital. The market and the meritocracy reflect this, and the natives end up at the bottom of the society.

Notice that this argument need not be racist. Behavior has many causes. Indeed, as Viotti da Costa points out, the Europeans who first encountered the natives were not racists.

> No matter what the mechanism, it is clear that the arguments about the natives' inferiority were not initially cast in racial terms, at least not in the way we conceive of racism today. The superiority of the colonizers and the inferiority of the Indians or Africans were defined not in biological but in religious and cultural terms.[4]

Only later did this first view take on the racist character we now associate with colonialism.[5] The older view was that without religious and cultural change, the natives would remain educationally and economically at the bottom. The later view was that even religion and culture had their limits with people who were congenitally stupid, lazy, and devious. Perhaps a modern version would not talk about ultimate causes at all. It might put the problem more operationally: no matter what public policies are adopted, behavioral change of importance to the economic and educational success of different groups takes a long time—without hypothesizing whether the deep reasons for behavioral backwardness are cultural, racial, or some others.

If this first extreme view tends to be skeptical of programs aimed at changing ethnic group differences in behavior, it also tends to be pessimistic about the prospects of reducing ethnic inequalities in educational and economic outcomes. Freer markets and better merit systems will reduce arbitrary differences, but they will in the end reflect faithfully group characteristics that have economic and educational importance. For example, if members of one group tend to be less intelligent than members of another group, even a perfect educational meritocracy will result in group inequalities.

The second extreme view disagrees. Crudely characterized, it asserts that the behavior of educationally and economically backward groups is not to blame; rather the discriminatory behavior of the dominant group or groups is responsible. A powerful group seizes upon irrelevant cultural and biological attributes to discriminate against the backward group, thereby keeping the backward group subservient and impoverished. The powerful group may be a class or another ethnic group, may be national or international, or may be men in relation to women—or a combination of these. In all these cases, group inequalities should be attributed to exploitation by the dominant.

Only superficially and misleadingly are the characteristics or behavior of different groups to blame. If there are objective differences among groups, the second view tends to be optimistic that educational and other policies can change them, and rather easily. This is because whatever differences do exist are small in size and epiphenomenal in nature: they do not result from deep differences but from discriminatory economic and educational structures.

Although I have presented only a caricature, I think many readers will recognize that something close to this second extreme is nowadays the predominant view among those who write about the developing countries. For example, according to the Guatemalan historian Severo Martínez Peláez:

> Oppression *made* the Indian problem and has
> conserved it as such. Historically the Indians are a
> product of the colonial regime, a result of the

oppression and the exploitation of the natives . . .
and the persistence of an indigenous majority today,
when labor markets have replaced forced labor, is
caused in the first place by the inertial action of four
centuries of servitude.[6]

Similar arguments are heard around the world. The indigenous people are in no way responsible for, in Martínez Peláez's words, their present "sum of organic and cultural deficiencies."

And these deficiencies persist, according to this second view, because exploiting groups profit from the poverty of the disadvantaged group. This argument can be taken to remarkable extremes. The limiting version states that even policies with the apparent aim of improving the lot of the disadvantaged are in truth veiled ways of improving the lot of the advantaged. Consider this Costa Rican example:

The different reactions with respect to the indigenous
problem, beginning with social Darwinism, racism and
liberalism and up to the distortion of revolutionary
postulates, as well as the different attitudes that are
adopted toward the problem, such as paternalism and
messianism, have been nothing more than the
conscious or unconscious justification of the
discrimination and exploitation to which the
indigenous population of America and of course the
aboriginal minority of Costa Rica have been subjected.[7]

In the second view, racial hostility usually plays a pivotal role in perpetuating the poverty of certain groups. The discriminators use racist theories of innate inferiority to justify their own discriminatory behavior, which on conventional grounds would be illegitimate. After a while, the racial stereotypes and dislike may become self-perpetuating. Some extreme models yield situations where, although the "backward" group is on average as productive and intelligent as the dominant group, the dominant group never learns this because of its prejudiced beliefs.[8]

Exactly how the members of the dominant group collude—and indeed how they profit from discrimination—has often been left unclear. Sociologists tend to find it so obvious that an exploiting group benefits that describing the mechanisms and estimating the magnitude of the gains are unnecessary.

Economists tend to be more skeptical. Wouldn't the forces of competition tend to bust any effort by a dominant group to collude? Wouldn't an unprejudiced employer make more money than a prejudiced one, and therefore in the long run wouldn't the unprejudiced take over the market? Regarding the lack of progress by U.S. blacks in the eighty years after emancipation, Richard Freeman posed rhetorical questions typical of the economic thinking:

> Why didn't nondiscriminating white businessmen, workers, or consumers take advantage of the profit possibilities of associating with black workers? . . . What prevented *black* businessmen or skilled workers from undercutting their discriminatory white competitors and eventually eliminating market discrimination? Capitalism was relatively successful among oriental Americans; why not among black Americans?[9]

Freeman rejected explanations based on difficulties of replacement due to turnover costs or on job-market signaling. He argued that public policy in the southern states discriminated against blacks for many years in school spending, public services, and employment. The public sector, in other words, was not part of the competitive market: it was monopolistic and racist. In this way, Freeman believes, the continued economic backwardness of U.S. blacks can be accounted for, but not through arguments of market discrimination or exploitation.

Gary Becker's influential analysis of discrimination showed that, under conditions of competition and perfect information, firms that do not discriminate racially will be more profitable than those that do. Eventually, therefore, the discriminators will be driven out of business.[10]

If the second view is correct—that economically important behavioral differences among groups are small or nil—then an attractive remedy for ethnic inequalities is competition: let market forces drive racial prejudice away. Unfortunately, holders of the second view often maintain, dominant groups will not let fair markets or fair merit systems operate.

A THIRD VIEW OF THE EVOLUTION OF ETHNIC INEQUALITIES

Let me propose now a third view. It explains the persistence of ethnic inequalities as the result of (1) preexisting behavioral differences among groups and (2) poor information in markets and merit systems. This approach plays down racial dislike and conspiracy. It has an open mind about the changeability and relevance of the behavioral differences that may exist among groups and individuals (see Table 12-1).

Let us begin with a hypothetical story, as we did in Chapter 3. Imagine a geographical area containing a number of small subsistence economies. Suppose that the borders of these primitive economies are the same as or smaller than the borders of individual tribes or ethnic groups. Transactions therefore take place within tribes and groups. In effect, these primitive economies are already ethnically segregated because they are homogeneous, and there is perforce little room for ethnic discrimination. This may have been the situation in many developing areas before the colonial period.

Now consider the long transitional period between these primitive economies and a fully modern, industrial economy. During the transition the tribes and groups come into ever greater contact with each other. The market expands, and commodities that used to be consumed at home or traded with one's fellow villager are now sold at distant points. Economic transactions occur across formerly segregated groups of people. Since many of the groups differ in language and customs, transactions between groups entail new costs and uncertainties. Moreover, different groups enter the transitional economy with different constellations of comparative advantage. By dint of their original geographical locations, groups differ in their

TABLE 12-1

Three Models of Ethnic Inequality

Aspect	First Model	Second Model	Third Model
Relevance of behavioral differences between groups to economic and educational success	Important	Unimportant	May be important
Ease of changing behavioral differences (e.g., human capital formation)	Difficult	Easy	No position
Dominant group profits from ethnic inequalities	Unlikely	Greatly	No, but individual actors discriminate rationally
Role of racial prejudice and hate in perpetuating group inequalities	Small	Large	Inessential
Effects of more competition and better merit systems on group inequalities	Remain or grow larger	Become smaller	Depends on information and how markets and merit systems work

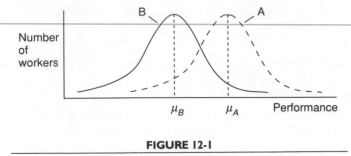

FIGURE 12-1

Overlapping Group Distributions of Performance

Although the distribution of performance of group A lies to the right of the distribution of performance for group B, the distributions overlap considerably, and many B's have higher performance than many A's. If an employer knows only that $\mu_A > \mu_B$, he will hire nothing but A's, and this will exacerbate group inequalities.

skills as herdsmen or fishermen or farmers. For any number of reasons, some ethnic groups are better prepared for industrialization than others. They may have been less subject to slavery and colonialism (or more?), closer to trade routes, more exposed to the dominant language, or more likely to have had access to formal education. Therefore, tastes and capabilities differ across groups in economically and educationally important ways. It is not that all members of one group have one trait and all members of another group a different trait. Think instead of overlapping distributions, as depicted in Figure 12-1.

For many possible reasons, then, in the transition away from primitive economies—in the process of economic development that we observe today—different groups may objectively differ in their costs of transactions, the kinds of jobs they like and are good at, and how well they fit into the new national economy. Such group differences are a fundamental fact in most developing countries. Under these circumstances what might be called "institutionalized discrimination" can flourish.

To see how, we introduce another feature of a developing economy: poor information. As we argued in Chapter 3, in the long transition from primitive to modern economy, the span and scope of the market expand more rapidly than do market information systems and institutions that safeguard contracts, distinguish and reward variations in quality, and promote credit. A similar mismatch occurs in government. The powers of the nation-state expand more quickly than its systems of management information and accountability. In developing countries, a notable characteristic of both markets and governments is their informational deficiencies.

Consider the labor market in our hypothetical developing economy. A national labor market has emerged. But it lacks much of the informational infrastructure we associate with advanced economies: credible job testing and certification, job banks, employment training, and labor exchanges. The labor market is imperfect in other ways. It is often difficult or impossible for employers in developing countries to pay employees according to productivity or to fire unsatisfactory workers. Consequently, deciding whom to hire is an economically crucial decision.

Posit a profit-maximizing employer. He is about to hire new employees for a particular job at a given wage. For now, let us assume he must consider the wage as fixed. This is an artificial assumption but one that does reflect the difficulty in developing countries of adjusting pay to performance—as we saw in Chapter 7.

Suppose the employer has no racial preferences: to him, a person is a person. He simply wishes to predict which candidates will be the most productive employees. If he were in a textbook economy with perfect information about the productivity of each candidate, he would have no problem. He would look at Figure 12-1 above, rank candidates by productivity, and hire from the right-hand tail of the distribution of productivity. Under these pleasant conditions, the employer would not care about the distributions of productivity of group A and group B: he would gain nothing by knowing the ethnic group to which an applicant belongs. That piece of data would have no economic value given that the employer had perfect information about each individual's productivity.

Unfortunately, our employer finds himself in our hypothetical, information-poor developing economy. He possesses meager data about each candidate's likely productivity. To make the analytical point sharper, let us go to the extreme of supposing the employer has *no* credible information on individual candidates. But he does know that because of past practices and past accidents, different ethnic groups differ *objectively* in their tastes, propensities, and capabilities.

In terms of Figure 12-1, this means that the employer knows about the distributions of the productivity of group A members and group B members—or at least that on average group A members have higher productivity than group B members—but he cannot discern the place of any individual candidate in those distributions. He can, however, easily tell whether a candidate is a member of group A or group B.

Unlike the textbook case of perfect information, in our developing economy we expect the profit-maximizing employer to use the information conveyed by group membership in deciding whom to hire. In the absence of better information, the profit maximizer will discriminate: he will tend to hire people from group A. The result is institutionalized discrimination, not based on ethnic hostility but on the rational calculation of profit maximizers when information is imperfect.

Even where there is economic competition, the workings of the labor market can reinforce and even exacerbate preexisting group differences, if information is imperfect and it is difficult to adjust pay to performance.

INSIGHTS ON DISCRIMINATION AND ETHNIC INEQUALITIES

Like the first two views, this third view of ethnic inequalities is a caricature. It makes extreme assumptions about information and the employer's ability to adjust wages and dismiss unsatisfactory workers. In reality, employers will be able to observe or gather some useful data about each candidate's likely productivity. Employers may be able to offer different wages to different employees, depending on their expected productivities. Or in the best case, an employer may be able to adjust a worker's wage, or in the limit fire him, depending on his actual performance on the job. If so, the institutionalized discrimination I have been depicting will be mitigated.[11]

Although extreme, the third model qualitatively captures important features of the ethnic problem in developing countries. We have been discussing labor markets but most of the logic and the lessons also apply to markets for credit, business partners, housing, and so forth. Let us consider a few phenomena that are consistent with the third model:

■ Ethnic groups differ not only in poverty but in some
    characteristics and behavior relevant to economic and
    educational performance. This is a fundamental fact in
    many developing countries.[12] Acknowledging it is by
    no means racist. Existing differences may have a wide
    variety of causes, as Donald L. Horowitz showed in
    his monumental study of ethnicity. But it does no
    good to deny objective differences: "Whatever the
    exact mix of causal factors, it is abundantly clear that
    ethnic groups have not had uniformly distributed
    opportunities and have not performed uniformly even

when the opportunities have existed. The result is that groups are unequally advantaged."[13]

■ The onset of a national administration or the creation of a national and competitive labor market does not necessarily lead to a reduction in ethnic inequalities. The colonial period in many countries marked the first establishment of a large-scale state apparatus, and it often led to an accentuation of both the perception and the fact of ethnic differences.[14] The Brazilian example is interesting: "the creation, consolidation, and growth of the competitive social system did not help" the newly emancipated slaves overcome their economic handicaps.[15] Contrary to the optimism of some economists, there is ample evidence that ethnic tensions and inequalities are frequently exacerbated rather than removed by the onset of competitive markets.[16]

The third model captures this phenomenon. It says that if, for whatever reasons, groups differ objectively in performance and if information on individual performance is scarce and expensive, then we cannot count on free markets for labor or fair merit systems to drive out discrimination. Laissez faire may not be enough. *If information is poor enough and it is difficult to vary wages according to performance, then the forces of competition may even reinforce ethnic inequalities.*

■ Racial hatred is not pronounced in many Latin American countries where, nonetheless, ethnicity and poverty are correlated.

The third model is consistent with this phenomenon. It posits that irrational discrimination, such as racial hostility or ethnic "tastes" favoring one group over another, may play no part in the problem of ethnic inequalities. As we saw, an employer may have no intrinsic preference for one ethnic group over another, yet may rationally hire members of groups with higher expected productivity. *Discrimination can exist without ethnic hostility.*

■ Return for a moment to the second model discussed above. It attributed ethnic inequalities to prejudicial behavior by a dominant group, which invents irrelevant reasons to exclude certain groups. If,

contrary to the first and third models, these reasons
have no economic correlates—for example, if the
groups discriminated against are really as productive
as the dominant groups—then the remedies are
competitive markets and fair meritocracies. *In well-
functioning markets the forces of competition and selection by
merit should over time drive away irrational discrimination
and thereby ameliorate ethnic inequalities caused by this
behavior.*

■ Nonetheless, a competitive market under conditions of
imperfect information and objective group differences
may yield institutionalized discrimination. When this
occurs, the group that is behind will lose. But it is not
true that in this situation the discriminating employers
will gain. If someone gave employers better
information to predict the performance of individuals,
they would be delighted to have it, because the
average quality of the workers hired would go up. *If
"exploitation" means earning higher profits through
discrimination, then we conclude that institutionalized
discrimination can exist without exploitation.*

■ As more and more data become available about the
performance of individual workers, the informational
value of group membership in predicting a worker's
productivity goes down. It makes less and less sense
for an employer to practice institutionalized
discrimination. *Information is crucial for understanding
and overcoming discrimination.*

TOWARD A FRAMEWORK FOR POLICY ANALYSIS

This discussion suggests a possible framework for organizing our
thinking about the possible roles of the state in reducing ethnic
inequalities.

Consider these four features of the problem:

1. Ethnic groups differ in political power, education,
    employment, ownership, and income. In particular,
    poverty has stubborn ethnic correlates.

2. Ethnic groups also objectively tend to differ in certain
    behaviors and characteristics relevant to economic and

educational performance. The problem of ethnic inequalities cannot entirely be explained away as the product of the discriminatory tastes or nefarious plots of a dominant group.

3. Especially in developing countries, information is imperfect. The variables used to predict later performance (job records, tests, professional standards, grades, credit ratings, and so forth) and the measures of later performance itself (production, merit ratings, academic achievement, even profits) may be nonexistent or inexact. They may contain systematic biases against certain groups. Moreover, it is difficult to pay people according to their actual productivity, reward farmers for the actual quality of what they produce, or pay contractors according to the quality of the work they carry out.

4. Economic and political decisions are at least partly made on the basis of predicted and actual performance. This is simply a postulate of rationality in the marketplace and in the merit systems found in schools and government. The result of such rational behavior is that disproportionately few decisions favor the groups that are backward—and the groups may therefore remain so.

If this characterization is correct, then we may use the same four headings to organize remedial measures. Table 12-2 presents a checklist for policy analysis.

The objectives of this framework should be clear from other chapters. It is not a complete treatment of the problem. Instead, the framework is designed to stimulate a rethinking of a complicated, emotionally charged issue. If it succeeds, policy makers will be better able to generate and scrutinize alternatives. The framework tries to make sure that certain promising possibilities are not over-looked. Its goal is to provoke creativity, not to pronounce judgments on the ultimate desirability of policy alternatives or offer answers for a particular case.

Let us work our way through the framework. We will allot more space to preferential treatment (option 4d in Table 12-2). Doing so does not imply that preferential treatment is normatively superior or likely to have the greatest impact on ethnic inequalities, rather that the subject seems particularly prone to controversy.

TABLE 12-2

Overcoming Ethnic Inequalities:
A Framework for Policy Analysis

1. Directly reduce existing group inequalities in social outcomes like power, employment, ownership, and income—or deflect attention from those inequalities.
   a. Transfer resources from one group to another.
   b. Conceal inequalities or reduce awareness of them.
      (1) Suppress information about ethnic inequalities.
      (2) Emphasize subethnic divisions.
      (3) Emphasize variables that exhibit small or no ethnic inequalities.
      (4) Emphasize other divisions (e.g., class, nation, religion).
2. Reduce underlying group differences in behavior and human capital.
   a. Allocate disproportionate resources to education and training for backward groups.
   b. Invest in other programs that change behavioral characteristics (e.g., nutrition, health, language, socialization)
   c. Decide whether to target policies under 2a and 2b on ethnic groups or on the undereducated, poor, and backward of whatever ethnic background.
3. Improve information and market functioning.
   a. Improve information about individuals (educational, economic, and so forth).
      (1) Use variables to predict performance (credit ratings, tests, grades, professional standards, and so forth).
      (2) Use variables to measure performance once hired, enrolled, given credit, and so forth.
   b. Improve information about groups.
      (1) Increase information about actual as opposed to stereotyped group differences in social outcomes and behavior/human capital.
      (2) Improve knowledge of predictive relationships between indicators of behavior/human capital and social outcomes.
      (3) Correct bias in variables used to predict and to measure performance.
   c. Improve markets so that individuals can be rewarded on the basis of performance.
      (1) Liberalize hiring rules.
      (2) Overcome incentive myopia.
      (3) Liberalize firing rules.
4. Change or influence where and how economic and political decisions are made.
   a. Segregate decision making (e.g., let each ethnic group make its own policies).
   b. Change the language through which decision making is done (e.g., instruction, entrance examinations, official languages).
   c. Do not allow group information to be used in decision making (e.g., antidiscrimination laws).
   d. Require that group information be used in decision making, but in a redistributive way (e.g., preferential treatment, affirmative action, ethnic quotas).

1. *Reduce ethnic inequalities in power, education, employment, ownership, and income—or deflect attention from these inequalities.*

Seldom do countries employ the option 1a: the straightforward intergroup transfer of economic and political attainments. Analogies do exist in the relationship among nations: for example, one country's assets may be nationalized by another. In some cases, Indians in the United States and aborigines in Australia have successfully reasserted collective ownership over the lands and resources seized by whites in former times. Malaysia specifically said it was not redistributing existing resources, but the fruits of future growth.

Usually the prevailing system of taxes and transfers redistributes income toward the poor. Since certain ethnic groups are disproportionately poor, even tax and transfer systems that take no note of ethnicity will make a difference to the interethnic distribution of income.

Option 1b suggests that the government may try to conceal or reduce awareness of ethnic inequalities. The idea is that ignorance or distraction may muffle the political repercussions of ethnic inequalities. Thus relevant data may be suppressed or simply not be collected. As we saw, Brazil historically has been reluctant to publish data on racial inequalities. But in this regard Brazil is hardly exceptional among developing countries. Bolivia publishes virtually no data on income, education, or health by ethnic group; nor does Peru. In some African countries it is illegal to examine and openly discuss tribal inequalities.

A government may deflect attention to subethnic cleavages. One technique is to decentralize power to the provincial level, hoping that subethnic divisions at that level will reduce consciousness of ethnic inequalities at the national level. "Where groups are territorially concentrated," observes Donald L. Horowitz, "devolution may have utility, not because it provides 'self-determination,' but because, once power is devolved, it becomes somewhat more difficult to determine who the self is."[17] Decentralization is most likely to achieve this result if the provinces are ethnically homogeneous, if subethnic cleavages are strong, when it is done prior to rather than after an explosion of ethnic conflict, and if secessionism is not an issue.[18] Devolution of course has other costs and benefits that must be contemplated. Pursuing them here would take us too far afield; some of the administrative aspects were analyzed in Chapter 9.

Policies may also emphasize what ethnic groups have in common. Governments may stress the culture and history that groups share rather than the cultures and histories that distinguish them. Indonesia's creation of *Pancasila*, the national ideology of unity in diversity, has provided a common denominator among the country's hundreds of ethnic groups. The principle of "one person, one vote" may be given emphasis—unless groups start to notice that under this scheme the majority ethnic group dominates.

Finally under the first heading, ethnic inequalities may be minimized by focusing on other cleavages. Marxists say class rather than race is the important divide. To Marx, ethnic consciousness and "chauvinism" were "a means of hindering the international cooperation of the working class, the first condition of its emancipation."[19] Perhaps not incidentally, fomenting class consciousness would have the benefit of reducing an economically backward group's consciousness of the ethnic aspects of its backwardness.

2.   *Reduce underlying group differences in behavior, human capital, and so forth.*

Governments may act in many ways to try to augment the human and other capital of backward groups, thereby changing the behavior and characteristics that seem to handicap group members in education and economic competition. Examples include public investments in education and training, health and nutrition, credit and entrepreneurial assistance, and the material infrastructure of living and doing business.

It is obviously crucial here to know the benefits and costs of such undertakings, including—but of course not limited to—their effects on ethnic inequalities. Unfortunately, social scientific research has been disappointing in this regard.

Take the case of education. It is often said that the long-term answer to ethnic inequalities is education. Two crucial empirical questions are (a) To what extent are various kinds of later economic success functions of the quantity and quality of education provided, when other relevant variables are taken into account? and (b) How much does it cost to increase the quality and quantity of education (in general and for the group in question)?

Even after decades of research on these questions in the United States, the answers remain controversial, in part because of their political sensitivity. The general finding, however, seems to be that current ethnic differences in measured learning ability and in later incomes are only slightly affected by the quality of the educational system (student-teacher ratios, educational levels of the teachers, library and laboratory facilities, dollars spent per student, and so forth).[20] The quantity of education obtained—for example, the years of schooling completed—does play a positive, if modest, role in improving later economic success, other things being equal. In the Brazilian case we examined above, the evidence indicated that equating white and nonwhite years of education would reduce the white-nonwhite income gap by about 10 percent.[21]

3. *Improve information and market functioning.*

Option 3a is crucial. A key factor is the availability of information about individuals—their achievements, abilities, and propensities—and about opportunities for schooling and work. When such information is scarce and unreliable, labor markets and educational systems malfunction. Economic agents and decision makers will rely on stereotypes, even though inexact. This is one reason why institutionalized discrimination flourishes in the developing world: groups differ in language, economic skills, and education, and information is poor.

If reliable and valid information is available to predict the performance of individuals, then selecting workers, contractors, students, and so forth will not result in "rational discrimination." If we are able to measure the productivity of individual employees—and if economic institutions allow wages to equal marginal products—the selection problem itself is minimized in importance, and again institutionalized discrimination is reduced. (Analogous points hold for discrimination in markets for credit, higher education, and so forth.)

The government may consider collaborating with the private sector in several ways.

- It may help develop, disseminate, and certify better job-related and education-related information, including tests, performance measures, employment records, and the like.

- Personnel systems in the public sector need strengthening. Information is the key.

- Job banks and assistance to labor markets could enhance the ability of job seekers and employers to find the right match—and could help to mitigate discrimination and ethnically segmented labor markets.

- The government may also take measures to make privately supplied information more credible, such as enforcing laws that prohibit "false advertising" or false credentialing. (See Chapter 3 and the appendix to Chapter 5.)

- Government policies that encourage easy hiring and dismissal of employees make the selection problem

less important; consequently, they also lessen
institutionalized discrimination. So do policies
affecting "sticky wages" (such as minimum wage laws)
and what we called in Chapter 7 "incentive myopia."
To the extent that pay can be linked to performance,
the economic motivation for employers to discriminate
in hiring is reduced. (See the policies discussed in
Chapter 7.)

All these measures have a common theme: find policies that
make it possible to communicate and reward in the marketplace
information about individual "quality" in the broad sense. Such
measures will reduce the economic motivation for using group information in economic decisions, thereby dismantling institutionalized
discrimination.

Two additional points emerge under the heading of improving
information.

Option 3b reminds us that the government can work with the
private and nonprofit sectors to *correct bias in measures of predicted or
actual performance*. "Bias" here refers to measures that systematically
understate one group's potential or actual achievement compared
with that of another.

For example, members of one ethnic group may on average
obtain higher scores on a selection examination than members of
another group. This fact in itself does not show that the examination
was biased in the predictive sense. "Bias" would be indicated if, on
average, people from different ethnic groups who had the same
score on the exam ended up with different levels of performance
later on. An example would be a university entrance examination in
Spanish, which might be a language more familiar to one group than
another. The members of the second group might, if admitted to
university, come to master Spanish equally well and do as well as
the members of the first ethnic group. If this were generally the case,
their examination scores would underpredict their later performance and would therefore be biased against them.

Bias can be discovered through research. Statistical analysis
can estimate the relationships between (a) the examination scores or
other criteria used for selection to (b) measures of later performance.
The idea is to set up separate prediction equations for each different
group. Then one tests the assumption that the two prediction equations are the same. If they are not, there is evidence of bias.

If such bias is discovered, it can be corrected in several ways. In
the case of the examination, it might be made available in several

languages, or points might be added to the scores of members of the second group—exactly enough points to render unbiased the predictions of later performance. Sometimes particular questions or parts of the selection criteria are biased and can be removed. In other cases an entirely new selection or measuring process needs to be devised.[22]

If bias is found and corrected, one can reduce group inequalities and simultaneously increase efficiency. This is a happy result. Alas, it is not the usual one. For example, in a number of cases of ethnic groups performing differently on entrance examinations or intelligence tests, studies show that test bias does not account for more than a small fraction of the differences.[23] Nonetheless, I have documented two cases in developing countries of predictive bias against females.[24] Bias demands investigation in every case where group differences in performance are found: Is the measure of performance itself biased?

Subcategory 3c reminds us of a third possible informational initiative. In addition to the provision of individual information, it may be useful to *supply information about the distributions of performance and attainments across groups.* (See the example from Sri Lanka in the box on the next page.

4. *Affect where and how economic and political decisions are made.*

"Rational discrimination" arises in part because decision makers base their choices on predicted or actual performance. Such discrimination might be avoided if decision makers were not allowed to choose on those bases.

First, the geographical scope of choices might be restricted. Recall that ethnic discrimination in the third model emerged when the economy and polity expanded beyond local geographical and ethnic bounds. A possible "solution," then, is not to allow the economy or polity so to expand. For example, political control might be devolved to small, ethnically homogeneous units. Decisions about appointments, spending, and so forth would then be "segregated" within the ethnic group. The cost would be the reductions in whatever benefits ensue from a more extensive polity or economic market, such as economies of scale and standardization.

Second, language may be specified, which often affects on ethnic groups. If Spanish is the official language but Quechua is not, one group is obviously disadvantaged in entering public life. Peru has made Quechua an official language, but Spanish is still exclusively used in government documents and government business. The choice of one or more languages for entrance exams, university instruction, and so forth may affect ethnic inequalities.

GROUP INFORMATION IN SRI LANKA

After the violence between Sinhalese and Tamils in July 1983, concerned citizens of various ethnic groups (those two plus Muslims and Burghers, the descendants of Dutch colonists) and political persuasions met and agreed that "Semi-truths tear at the fragile fabric of a united Sri Lanka." These citizens believed that many people in Sri Lanka, especially Sinhalese, held exaggerated views of the Tamils' educational and economic circumstances. For example, the Sinhalese nationalist Cyril Mathew, minister of industries and scientific affairs, wrote in 1970:

> A fact that should be especially mentioned here is that the wholesale and retail trade, which about sixty-eight years ago was in the hands of the Sinhalese in Colombo as well as in the Uva, Sabaragamuwa and Central regions, is now completely in the hands of Indian nationals [i.e., Tamils]. This has not happened spontaneously, but is the result of an organized move by Indian trade unions and other organisations to supply Indians with cash and other necessities to purchase Sinhalese-owned business enterprise and buildings. . . . In the central market in Colombo, which is at Pettah, the local Sinhalese traders do not own even 5 per cent of the trade. The power is almost entirely in the hands of Indians, Borahs, and Sindhs [sic].[25]

In August 1983 Mathew said during a constitutional debate, "The Sinhala people want to know what you are going to do? They [Tamils] are like maharajas here. A Sinhala trader cannot even get a finger in. It is this injustice which has been festering like a wound for twenty five years."[26] To counter this sort of rhetoric, the interethnic group of concerned citizens put together a report that summarized available data about Tamil-Sinhalese differences in employment, income, education, and ownership. It turned out that Tamils were under- and not overrepresented in public sector employment, even at higher levels. Tamils were overrepresented in higher education, but not "over ten percentage points of their ethnic proportion in the population. Popular perception about Tamil students in the coveted faculties of medicine, law and engineering usually place their participation at 50%."[27] The report did not specifically address Mathew's assertions about traders, but it did show the occupational distributions by ethnic group nationwide, it discussed the credit system (the main sources being state and foreign-owned banks), and it showed that in the most extensive list of private sector companies only about 20 percent of directors, chairmen, and partners-proprietors were Tamil. (Tamils made up a little over 18 percent of Sri Lanka's population.) Obviously the report's underlying presumptions were that people were misinformed about group inequalities and that if better information were available, ethnic tensions might be reduced. In the latter hope the authors of the report appear from later events to have been overly optimistic. Their presumptions, however, may have application in other countries where stereotypes and myths lead to exaggerations of ethnic inequalities.

The third subcategory is not to allow the rational discriminator to use group information. Most countries of the world have anti-discrimination laws. Unfortunately, such laws are hard to enforce against discrimination of the economic kind we have been discussing. It is hard to know how decisions were made.

4d. *Preferential treatment: A special category of policies.*

We may think of preferential treatment as the *requirement* that ethnic group status affect economic and political decisions, but in a way that favors the disadvantaged group. As noted above, examples of preferential programs abound in the developing world. The pros and cons of preferential treatment have been widely debated in the developed countries and in India, but seldom in Latin America and Bolivia. Though the subject is controversial, it seems to me that the advantages and disadvantages of preferential treatment fall into three categories: efficiency, representation, and incentives.

By efficiency I am referring to the quality of the people selected. Recall the selection problem discussed above. If the selection criteria are unbiased, then obtaining more members of group B means replacing some more qualified candidates from group A. This costs something in performance. The marginal cost is equal to the difference in predicted performance between the last B accepted and the last A rejected.[28] This marginal cost rises as the difference in group performance increases and the percentage of applicants that can be accepted declines.

The second dimension is representation. For a variety of reasons, one may desire a greater proportion of group B members among those selected, including the diversity they bring to the privileged group and the quieting of ethnic conflict.[29] Obviously, many philosophical issues enter here as well.[30]

A third dimension, incentives, is also affected by preferential treatment. Sometimes the effects can be negative, as when aspirants recognize that ascriptive status that they cannot control determines their rewards. On the other hand, economists have shown that under plausible conditions members of both the backward and advanced groups may strive harder under group quotas.[31]

It is often of interest to ask *how the efficiency costs of preferential treatment vary with the proportion admitted from the backward group.* Elsewhere I have developed a method for displaying this trade-off between efficiency (in the sense of performance sacrificed) and representation (the proportion of the backward group selected) in preferential treatment.[32] The method is summarized in Table 12-3.

Consider an example from Indonesia. In 1982, while working

TABLE 12-3

Guidelines for Studying Predictive Bias and Preferential Treatment in Selection Policies

1. Calculate the performance costs of additional representation.
   a. Obtain the distribution of predictors for each ethnic or other group (i.e., selection criteria such as tests, prior performance, and so forth).
   b. Using regression analysis and similar tools, use the predictors to forecast later performance you care about. Perform the calculation for each group separately. (This adjusts for bias in the predictors.)
   c. Define what percentage of the applicant pool you can accept or hire.
   d. For various proportions of the backward group selected, use 1a, 1b, and 1c to calculate differences in predicted performance for the marginal person selected in each group. Adjust for unreliability of measurement.
   e. Evaluate predicted performance in terms of your utility function.
   f. Graph the marginal costs against the proportion of the backward group selected or hired.
   g. Consider qualitatively any ecological costs—for example, costs arising from disproportionate members at the bottom of the group hired or the student body being from one or another group.
2. Consider the benefits of additional representation of the backward group.
   a. For different proportions of group representation, calculate how much better it is if you replace one nongroup member with a group member. The benefits may be to workers' welfare or students' education, their later-life success, a just or mobile or stable society, or the satisfaction of constituencies. The result is your marginal benefit curve. Examine its intersection with the marginal cost curve described above.
   b. Alternatively, you may look at the marginal cost curve and ask how much predicted performance you are willing to give up in order to have one additional group member among those selected or hired.
3. Calculate the optimal degree of preferential treatment for you. Notice that the answer depends on factual questions such as the percentage of applicants you select or hire, the groups' distributions of predicted performance, and the equation you compute relating the predictors to performance. It also depends on value judgments: your utility function for performance and for group representation.

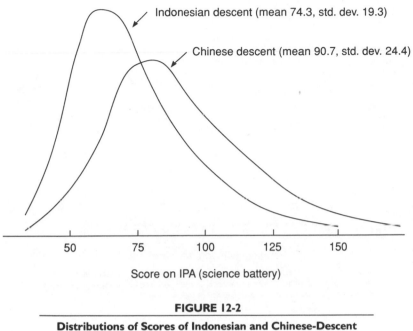

Indonesian descent (mean 74.3, std. dev. 19.3)

Chinese descent (mean 90.7, std. dev. 24.4)

50 75 100 125 150

Score on IPA (science battery)

FIGURE 12-2

**Distributions of Scores of Indonesian and Chinese-Descent
Test-Takers on IPA Science Battery, Early 1980s**

with the government on higher education policy, I discovered almost by accident the existence of a secret quota system to limit the enrollment of students of Chinese origin. A battery of examinations called the IPA is used to select students for science faculties at the ten top Indonesian universities. When students signed up for these tests in the early 1980s, they were also asked to indicate their ethnic group. Monitors looked students over to confirm this self-identification. A test-taker of Chinese descent had a red mark put beside his or her name; this mark later became an asterisk when the IPA scores were computerized. About 9 percent of those taking the battery had asterisks. Ethnic Chinese make up an estimated 3 percent of Indonesia's population.

I learned that the Chinese test-takers did better on the IPA test than ethnic Indonesians, as Figure 12-2 shows. (The Chinese mean was 90.7 and the standard deviation 24.4; for students of Indonesian descent, the mean was 74.3 and the standard deviation 19.3.) The ten universities were extremely selective, accepting only about 8 percent of all test-takers. If students had been admitted solely on the basis of IPA scores, about 30 percent would have been of Chinese descent.

The universities' admissions policies were set by the Directorate General of Higher Education, which imposed an Indonesian

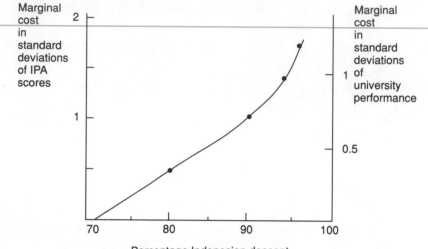

Note: Based on normal approximations assuming 91 percent of applicants are Indonesian, 8 percent of all applicants are accepted, and the equation predicting university performance is that found at the University of Indonesia in 1982.

FIGURE 12-3

Marginal Costs of Preferential Treatment for Students of Indonesian Descent

quota of 94 percent (or a maximum quota for Chinese students of 6 percent). How much did this quota cost in efficiency terms? Here are some estimates based on data from the University of Indonesia:

- The marginal cost in terms of grade-point average at the university on a scale of 1 to 4 was about one standard deviation. This means that the difference between the lowest-scoring Indonesian accepted and the highest-scoring Chinese rejected would translate into a one standard deviation difference in university performance—roughly the difference between a student at the 50th percentile and another at the 84th percentile.

- The marginal cost in terms of the probability of graduating was 0.21. The lowest-scoring Indonesian accepted had an 0.68 probability of graduating, whereas the highest-scoring Chinese reject was predicted on the basis of his test score to have had an 0.89 probability.

- The marginal cost in rupiahs per graduate was 12.3 percent higher.[33]

These calculations can be transformed into curves showing the trade-off between efficiency and representation.[34] Figure 12-3 gives an example. The left-hand scale shows how much has to be forgone, in terms of standard deviations of IPA scores in the applicant pool, to ensure that various percentages of students of Indonesian descent are admitted. The right-hand scale shows how much is given up in terms of standard deviations of university performance.

The technical aspects of these calculations are described in the references noted. I have analyzed similar curves for women and for outer islanders in Indonesia, for students from poor families in the Philippines, and for blacks in the United States.[35] Here we should focus on several general points concerning the trade-off between efficiency and representation.

Obviously, the benefits and costs are broader than university grades or costs per graduate or the percentage of Indonesians admitted. The costs and benefits will be different, perhaps even more extensive and difficult to measure, when we are analyzing preferential treatment in employment. But the qualitative point is valid: *programs of preferential treatment usually involve a trade-off*. The benefits of greater representation are purchased at the cost of lower performance among the selected group. The costs of preferential treatment, in terms of performance sacrificed, are likely to be higher

■ the larger the group differences in predicted performance. Differences of a third of a standard deviation do not turn out to matter much in most realistic situations, whereas differences of a standard deviation or more usually matter a lot.

■ the larger the proportions desired of the backward group.

■ the smaller the proportion of the total applicant pool that can be accepted.

■ the more performance matters to us (or to society). A standard deviation's difference in performance may matter greatly among top officials or on crucial technical jobs, but it may matter little on many other jobs.[36]

Since these characteristics will vary from problem to problem, even in a given country, it follows that *no one representational target is ideal for all problems*. The ideal ethnic quota in one context will cost "too much" in terms of efficiency in another decision context. In particular, there is little to be said in theory for a constant quota equal to a group's percentage of the overall population or even its percentage of the applicant pool. As Marc Galanter concluded regarding India, "In the delicate task of balancing the merit principle with other interests, a flat percentage limitation on the extent of reservations is of less use than it might appear. . . . The real impact of a scheme on the chances of others and on the merit principle cannot be known from the percentage of places reserved."[37] Without techniques such as those we have been describing to analyze the trade-off, analyses of preferential policies are likely to remain as Galanter described India's: "The courts have not penetrated beyond the superficial question of the specified amount of preference to address the real quantitative question of the net effects of preferences."[38]

EXTENSIONS

In this chapter we have covered a lot of ground. Yet at the end humility is appropriate. It is apparent how little we know about the problems of ethnic inequalities and their solutions, in Bolivia and elsewhere.

Many fundamental facts are unknown. Data are scarce and inexact about the behavior and attributes of various groups and about their economic and educational attainments. Little seems to be known about improvements over time and variations across regions of the country in question. Perhaps most important, there seem to be few clues about which policies make the most difference to ethnic inequalities—and have what costs and other benefits.[39]

We are still at the stage of problem recognition. The situation in each developing country is unique. A few have no ethnic or racial cleavages. But, as a generalization, it is fair to say that within most developing nations the economic and educational backwardness of certain groups—ethnic, communal, religious, sexual—constitute one of the two or three most troubling issues of domestic policy. And yet, one finds few scholarly efforts to appraise ways that discrimination and racial inequalities might be reduced. The fact that poverty and ethnicity are intimately intertwined in countries such as Bolivia is seldom officially recognized.

The framework for policy analysis presented in Table 12-2 and discussed in the text is an attempt to structure a rethinking of the roles of the state in the reduction of ethnic inequalities. It distinguished four broad categories of public policies.

One option in the first category denied or hid the problem of group differences in performance and results. It seems unlikely that in the long run this approach will be of much use. Nor does experience lead us to be optimistic about the feasibility or desirability of option 1a, that of confiscating the resources of the advantaged group and presenting them to the disadvantaged.

The second category focused on state interventions through which underlying group differences in human capital might be reduced. "Human capital takes many forms, of which formal schooling is the most visible but not for that reason any more important than skills, discipline, organizational talents, foresight, frugality, or simply good health."[40] If human capital is in part the product of communities—including families—then we might predict the perpetuation of human capital disadvantages, in the absence of contravening action by the state.[41] But what exactly can the state do to alleviate these disadvantages? Education and public health are clearly desirable, but we know little about the best ways, probable effects, and costs in countries such as Bolivia. Some behavioral differences may be too intimately connected with families and culture for a state to affect, or wish to affect if it could. The connections between ethnicity, behavior, and public policies are so important and so poorly understood in developing countries that they would seem a priority topic for political discussion and policy research.

A third category of public policies focused on improving information and the functioning of market institutions. We have speculated in this chapter that some of the discrimination encountered in developing countries is economically "rational." This does not mean that such discrimination is good, for it turns out to enhance whatever economically relevant inequalities already exist. The culprits are (1) imperfect information about the performance and "quality" of individuals and (2) market institutions that hinder pay from being accorded for individual performance. In an economic environment characterized by preexisting group differences in performance (for whatever reasons) and by poor individual information, profit maximizers will use the information provided by group membership in their economic decisions. The result can easily be economic stratification and a new round of group inequality. This sort of environment, and alas this sort of result, seem to characterize the transition from a primitive economy to a developed one.

This argument is both stronger and weaker than I have made it. It is stronger in extent. It applies to many economic groups besides ethnic and racial groups. Perhaps the starkest example of "groupism" in the developing world is sexism. For a variety of reasons women and men in most developing nations objectively differ in some employment-related characteristics, often because of past exploitation and discrimination. One's sex has some predictive power about one's tastes, capabilities, and career orientation.

Therefore, in the absence of good information that would help economic actors distinguish the many exceptions in both sexes, profit maximizers will use sex to decide who should get a job or a loan or a business partnership.

My argument is weaker than I have made it because in presenting what I hope is a useful perspective on the problem I have underemphasized other important causes of ethnic inequalities. The often-cited causes—plain intolerance, one group exploiting another, and so forth—have validity in many circumstances. If I had to guess, I would suppose that the informational model presented here captures only a small part of the phenomena we associate with racial discrimination and inequality in the third world.

This small part—or whatever it turns out to be—has surprising characteristics. Here are some of them:

- Discrimination can exist even under conditions of pure competition. One does not need to presume monopoly power or a conspiracy among a dominant race.

- Discrimination can exist with absolutely no racial hatred or dislike on the part of the discriminator.

- Discrimination can exist even when the discriminatory equilibrium does not make the discriminator richer or happier. Better information would make both the employer and the group discriminated against better off. There can be discrimination without exploitation.

- The forces of the competitive market can, under certain plausible conditions, increase group inequalities rather than reduce them. It can lead slight group differences in performance to become exaggerated differences, thus begetting a further cycle of inequality.

The solutions to rational discrimination revolve around ways to generate, certify, and use individual information in economic decision making and to improve the functioning of markets. They revolve around better information on the efforts and achievements of individual employees, better ways of measuring quality, and better market institutions (more flexible hiring and firing, more variable wages, more competitive markets).

The fourth category of policy initiatives focused on the loci and bases of political and economic decision making. Who should make decisions and on what grounds? Decentralization and devolution may alleviate ethnic tensions by granting to each group a measure of self-determination. Preferential treatment programs change the bases of decision making by introducing explicitly ethnic criteria.

We examined the trade-offs entailed in preferential programs. We saw that when groups differ in performance and only a few can be chosen from the combined pool, even in a perfectly informed selection process the group that is ahead in performance will be greatly overrepresented among those selected. This in turn may create social problems, misconceptions, and elitism. Public policy may wish to create more group balance, and we have developed some tools for deciding how far to go in the pursuit of preferential treatment.

The key idea was a trade-off between the benefits of more balanced representation and the costs in lower performance among those selected. The trade-off is not always there; for example, the devices used to predict or to measure performance may be biased against the disadvantaged group. In this case more balanced representation might not cost anything in performance. But this, unfortunately, is not always or even often the case. Group differences in performance are often objective and not the result of biased measures; they are the result of a variety of past and present factors. Preferential policies will therefore have efficiency costs.

As we review the framework for policy analysis, it is fair to conclude that we have uncovered no magic wand. Nor did we discover one in Chapter 11 in our discussion of Peru, Brazil, and Malaysia. Sensitive to the absence of data noted above, I would nonetheless venture several conclusions on the basis of the framework. They are summarized in Table 12-4.

Some readers might protest. "We have not considered the profound alternative of a communist revolution. Isn't the problem simply capitalism and the cure communism?" Consider this claim from a Soviet book of African studies:

> The solution of the national question, one of the most
> burning and dramatic questions in the history of
> human society, ranks high among the achievements of
> the Revolution. . . .
>
> At that same time the Party was tackling such
> tasks in the field of national relations as the complete
> elimination of national strife; . . . the establishment of
> a new form of Soviet statehood—a union of peoples;
> the establishment of fraternal friendship and close
> cooperation between them; development of the
> economy, overcoming the cultural backwardness of
> the formerly oppressed peoples and the achievement
> of actual equality in their development levels.
>
> All those tasks have been successfully
> accomplished.[42]

This argument is not heard as much in 1991 as it was a decade ago, but it is still a fair question. The evidence on ethnic inequalities in communist and socialist countries is limited. One systematic review of the available data concluded that the percentage of ethnic inequalities is as large as in "matched" capitalist countries. The inequalities examined included income, education, infant mortality, health care, and political representation. The matching was done along rough variables such as the share of the population held by the minority group, general economic level of the country, and so forth. Across the board, "the relative status of minorities is remarkably

---

TABLE 12-4

Summary of Broad State Strategies for Overcoming Ethnic Inequalities

---

1. Directly reduce existing group inequalities in social outcomes like power, employment, ownership, and income—or deflect attention from those inequalities.
   Comment: Redistribution is unlikely to be politically feasible and in any case is unlikely to improve the long-run prospects of the economically backward groups, because of differences in behavior characteristics and human capital.

2. Reduce underlying group differences in behavior, human capital, and so forth.
   Comment: Education and health problems are helpful, but we know surprisingly little in developing countries about what sorts of programs help how much at what cost. In general it seems better to boost the human capital of groups that lag rather than to try to redistribute the results of human capital differences (e.g., wealth) from one group to another. Even so, the usual sorts of public interventions do not seem able rapidly to raise economically and educationally backward groups.

3. Improve information and market functioning.
   Comment: Although "rational discrimination" may cause only a small part of the problem of ethnic inequalities, it can be countered through a variety of relatively cheap, relatively efficient measures. Such policies have few hidden costs.

4. Change or influence where and how economic and political decisions are made.
   Comment: These measures have costs (and benefits) apart from the raising up of backward groups. How well they work to enhance the long-run attainments of backward groups remains debatable, but we have outlined a methodology for beginning the analysis.

---

similar in both socialist and capitalist countries."[43] Although it is true that there are no South Africas in the communist world, ethnic inequalities apparently remain large within communist countries. (The possible exception of Cuba would be interesting to study.)

If there is no magic way to overcome socioeconomic inequalities among ethnic groups, it can be said that economic growth tends to raise the absolute level of even the most backward groups. Disadvantaged ethnic groups have advanced in absolute terms in almost every country, as we saw in the case studies in Chapter 11. But ethnic disparities are remarkably persistent. We have seen how the beginning of market competition can actually enhance these disparities, and it is important to combat market discrimination by improving the informational bases of competition and liberalizing hiring, pay, and firing practices. No doubt educational programs and public health efforts have played a positive role. Preferential treatment programs can redistribute opportunities toward educationally and economically backward groups, although usually at some cost in efficiency (and therefore in the amount of opportunities available to distribute). But I conclude that these measures are not enough or work only over the very long term.

Thus, as we approach the next millennium, we seem to have arrived at a juncture in our admittedly imperfect understanding of ethnic inequalities where we need to ask new and more fundamental questions.

If there are deep differences among groups in preferences, propensities, or productivities, can we design educational and economic technologies to take advantage of the differences, leading eventually to more equal outcomes?

Will technical breakthroughs in education—such as the use of computers and perhaps even chemical assistance to learning—make possible more rapid progress than we have yet seen in overcoming group inequalities in that domain?

Will we discover new ways of organizing the work of teams and companies that take advantage of existing cultural differences for productive ends?

I don't know the answers. But for those who wish to alleviate the plight of economically and educationally backward groups in Bolivia and elsewhere, these may be the questions for the future.

13

RETHINKING ECONOMIC DEVELOPMENT

"OUR NEOLIBERAL POLICIES, as they are now labeled, certainly have a philosophical justification," Bolivia's former president Victor Paz Estenssoro recently explained. "But it was primarily a situation engendered by realities—the inflation, the complete economic disorder, the fiscal deficit, the bad loans of the central bank—and not a decision taken for philosophical reasons."[1]

His remarks apply to many other countries that have switched from a strategy of state control of the economy to one of free markets. It is not primarily a case of ideological conversion.[2] Rather, the old strategy is perceived to have failed—the strategy that the state should dominate the economy. In 1985 Victor Paz Estenssoro at the age of seventy-eight dismantled much of the economic machinery of his own revolution of 1952. Then he had nationalized Bolivia's mines; in 1985 he closed down most state-run mines and dismissed three-quarters of the state-employed miners. In the 1950s his government had controlled prices and erected high tariffs to protect domestic producers. In 1985 his administration let most prices be determined by market forces, and tariffs were reformed. The apparent contradiction between the two strategies did not trouble Paz Estenssoro. One was right for 1952, he told me, when private markets were stagnant and the rural economy was quasi-feudal. (Neither he nor the subsequent administration revoked the land reform of the 1950s.) The second strategy was right for 1985, by which date the Bolivian state itself had become what he called "a negative force."

In its remarkable free-market reforms, Bolivia has not been alone. The trend is worldwide, and some have called it a revolution. Eastern and Central Europe and the Soviet Union are highly visible examples, but in many ways, Africa, Asia, and Latin America have been the pioneers. By 1991, more than fifty developing countries had undertaken some form of structural adjustment.

Now comes the time for adjusting to reality. The move toward freer markets, though welcome, does not magically solve the problems of poverty and underdevelopment. Since markets in developing countries are often flawed, peasants and the urban poor do not immediately benefit from economic reform. And without specific steps to help them, certain ethnic groups may remain economically and educationally backward, and discriminated against.

Under the new strategy, the state intervenes less in the economy, but it does not disappear. The government inevitably remains a principal actor in macroeconomic policy making, infrastructure, and social programs—not to mention defense and foreign policy. Successful liberalization itself requires the highly skilled public management of the privatization process, new efforts to protect the environment, policies that promote and protect competition, and the sophisticated regulation of newly freed capital markets and banking systems.[3] For free-market reforms to work, government institutions must also work. Unfortunately, in most developing countries governmental effectiveness is undercut by poor information, adverse incentives, corruption, and overcentralization.

The administration of justice is another example. Free-market dynamism requires the enforcement of contracts and property rights.[4] Here again the reforms must go beyond the macro level—that is, beyond better laws. In fact, the laws on the books in many developing countries are already state-of-the-art. But judicial systems tend to be cumbersome and corrupt. Police forces are often inept and sometimes predatory. When the rule of law is undermined, the whole system, and not just the economy, grows sick.[5]

Weak markets and ineffective governments: these are the realities to which development strategies must adjust. This means that the debate over the role of the state must go beyond the battle over how much government, how much market. If the economic reforms are to endure, they must go deeper than declaring markets to be free. Beyond market versus state we find market *and* state, indeed market thanks to state; and we must turn to the challenge of making both market and state work better.

THE CHECKERED RECORD

It is no secret that both the market and the state have functioned badly in most developing countries. I like this passage from the Turkish economist Mükerrem Hiç because his spontaneous, involuted eloquence seems to convey a widely felt frustration:

> But, the relative strength of various pressure and interest groups, doctrinaire viewpoints, historically set attitudes of various political parties may pull government interventions in the social and economic fields away from the optimum to a compromise solution and thus cause inefficiencies. Yet, the basic economic rigidities, shortages and market imperfections as well as the initially unequal distribution of income and wealth may be so acute that the inevitability of mismanagement on the part of the government may not be taken as a deciding factor to argue against government interventions to the economy. Just as equally important as the need for government interventions, however, is the fact that excessive government interventions and interventions in the wrong direction may at times create acute inefficiencies and in making the economy an "administered economy," in drifting it away from world markets and market conditions and making it "closed" instead of "open" to world markets, and in carrying reformism to excesses. Under these circumstances, therefore, the essence or the basic need for government intervention can be easily lost.[6]

Under such conditions simple diagnoses and prescriptions can easily mislead—such as noting market failures and calling for more government, or noting government's shortcomings and calling for more market. When both markets and states are weak, the question "How much government or how much market?" may be less important than "How good a government and how good a market?" As we saw in Chapter 1, neither economic theory nor empirical research offers conclusive advice about the role of the state under various conditions, despite the rhetoric of popularizers and politicians on both sides.[7] We do know that the conditions matter. For example, the literature on the effects of protectionism—governmental interference with international trade to protect local producers—

illustrates the general point that "it depends." Practical people increasingly prefer less protection—a preference I share—but the best theorists warn us of simplistic conclusions based on elementary trade theory.[8] *How* and *how well* the government intervenes often matters more than *how much*. In contrasting Taiwan's successful import substitution strategy with the failed one of the Philippines, economist Gustav Ranis concludes:

> It is this renunciation of power, or better, the more restrained exercise of power via "on the table" rather than "under the table" actions which was part of the deliberate trend toward liberalization on Taiwan. Such a depoliticization of the system implies that the government gradually learns to be more responsible and open about what it is doing, moves away from implicit taxes and covert transfers, and towards explicit and more equitable and efficient types of interventions in the economy.[9]

"The key question," concludes economist Jagdish Bhagwati, "is not whether there is governmental action in the Far Eastern economies, but rather how these successful economies have *managed* their intervention and their strategic decision making better than the unsuccessful economies."[10]

Uma Lele and her colleagues at the World Bank recently concluded a monumental series of studies on agriculture in Africa.[11] They found little support for simple answers such as "government intervention is bad (or good)." The variables that seemed to matter were again *how* and *how well*.

"The private-sector nature of cotton production in Nigeria does not appear to have made the cotton sector efficient," Lele writes in a summary of this work. "Whether privately, cooperatively, or publicly operated, cotton production in Anglophone Africa has suffered from inadequate capitalization, lack of credit, a poor record of payments for output, and in particular, lack of accountability to producers" (p. 73). Meanwhile, the public sector did well with cotton in Cameroon, thanks to "an excellent network of research on cotton in French West Africa, undertaken by the Compagnie Française pour le Développement des Fibres Textiles," which has equity interests in the Cameroonian public enterprise SODECOTON (p. 72).

Nor did Lele and her colleagues find that low taxes and stable prices were determining factors. "Coffee and tea in Kenya, cotton in Cameroon, and cocoa in Nigeria show good export crop performance under both high and low taxation levels and stable and unstable prices" (p. 74).

Lele argues that foreign aid was not particularly successful. The donors who did best were those with the most information.

> The study reveals that donors have made a surprisingly small contribution to agricultural development in Africa. Countries receiving the most aid have performed the least well, as external finance has substituted for a sound diagnosis of development problems. Even in countries that have done well, donor interventions explain only a small part of their achievements. The few success stories are accounted for by the efforts of the former 'colonial' donors (showing the importance of detailed knowledge based on grassroots experience as a source of well-planned and executed development programs) (pp. 7, 9).

Another large study of Africa is worth citing at length, because it contains a reminder that is often forgotten in today's debate over the role of the state.

> The empirical record in the early 1960s quickly proved that capitalism and foreign aid could not produce miracles that would allow countries to "skip stages of growth" (a theme repeated by African politicians in the 1960s and 1970s). The failure of capitalism in the early 1960s "to bring development to the people" led to the swift replacement of capitalism with socialism in Ghana, Mali, Guinea, and Tanzania.
>
> Agrarian socialism is now under fire because after 20 years of experimentation there are no countries where agrarian socialism is performing well. But as the pendulum swings between socialism, state capitalism, and free market forces, it is useful to point out that successful agricultural and rural development policies, programs, and projects can be achieved under either capitalism or socialism. To put all or most of the weight on ideology—capitalism or socialism—is to ignore an important lesson that has been learned over the past 30 years—namely, the ideology of economic policy is but one variable influencing the outcome of agricultural development projects, programs, and strategies.[12]

The reasons why both markets and governments tend to malfunction in developing countries are complex. We see some of them
in Chapter 2 through the example of Bolivia. Important sectors of the
Bolivian economy—mining, hydrocarbons, highland agriculture,
transportation, extralegal activities, credit, and agricultural markets—display classic market failures, such as increasing returns,
common property resources, externalities, adverse selection, and
more. Economic theory and practical experience tell us that these
sectors will generate problems if left entirely to the play of market
forces.

But the existence of market failures does not by itself prove
that the government should take over these sectors. The underlying
conditions are not favorable for efficient government either. Especially in poor countries, the public sector exhibits nonmarket failures, such as adverse incentives, corruption, and overcentralization.
The problem is not with the theory of the free market or the theory of
the efficient, benevolent state. The problem is that because the
underlying conditions are so difficult in developing countries, many
markets don't work well and much of the government doesn't work
well either. How might development policies adjust to these
realities—and perhaps go about changing them?

Another adjustment may also be necessary. Poverty is a principal concern in development strategies, or should be. Freer markets
and improved public services will in the long run benefit the poor.
But we discover in Bolivia a phenomenon found in many other
developing countries. Certain groups in the society are disproportionately and stubbornly impoverished, undereducated, unhealthy,
and discriminated against. In Bolivia's case, the economically and
educationally backward groups are indigenous peoples—the Aymara and Quechua "Indians" and various peoples of the lowlands.
Many markets do not effectively reach such groups, nor do many
political institutions, the press, or the legal system. Even as economic and political institutions are liberalized, societies stratify by
race, ethnicity, community, religion, tribe.

The ethnic concentration of poverty raises new questions
about economic development and the proper roles of the state.
Beyond the state's efforts to invest in human capital, promote distributive justice, and combat poverty through social programs,
should special steps be taken to deal with the ethnic character of
poverty and discrimination? What have we learned from experience
around the globe about public policies aimed at reducing ethnic
inequalities?

INFORMATION AND MAKING MARKETS WORK

Let us begin with the reasons markets tend to malfunction in poor countries. Not just there, of course: a central tradition in Western economics analyzes the role of the state in terms of overcoming failures in the private sector. In a comprehensive review of the literature that makes no reference to developing countries, economist Robert Inman identifies five categories of market failures: public goods, economies of scale, externalities, imperfect information problems, and unemployment. Each has been used to justify government intervention—although as Inman notes and we have been at pains to emphasize, intervention carries its own costs and failures and in any given case one must balance and blend imperfect market and imperfect government. But I wish to stress a deeper conclusion from Inman's review, his identification of a common source of market imperfections:

> Markets fail. They fail for the fundamental reason that the institution of market trading cannot enforce cooperative behavior on self-seeking, utility-maximizing agents, and cooperative behavior between agents is often required for beneficial trading. In each instance of market failure—public goods, externalities, increasing returns, asymmetric information, unemployment—agents were asked to reveal information about their benefits or costs from trades with no guarantee that information would not be used against them. Without that guarantee, information is concealed, trades collapse, and market institutions fail. Only through cooperatively sharing valued information can the preferred, Pareto-optimal allocation be achieved.[13]

In economic theory, information is at the heart of the classic problems of the market; and so it is, too, in the real world of the developing countries. It is, I believe, a defining characteristic of underdevelopment that markets struggle with poor information about the quality of goods, services, risks, and people.

In Chapter 3 we consider one example, agricultural markets. Farmers in developing countries often have little knowledge of market conditions; in one African study, three-quarters of maize farmers "had no idea of the current maize price and were unwilling even to hazard a guess."[14] Weights and measures—more generally, standards and clear rules of the game—are often imperfect or even absent. Traders often have "defective market information."[15] Quality is difficult to measure and certify, and this engenders adverse incentives for producers and consumers. As a consequence, many agricultural markets are unstable, and marketing margins are large.[16] Informational imperfections become points of leverage for oligopolists and exploiters of various stripes. For all these reasons, free-market reforms take too long to reach the poor. Structural adjustment at the macro level may leave micro structures unaffected.

Poor people (and others) adapt to these problems in many ways—for example, using interlinked transactions, reputation, various kinds of rules, family or other ties to help enforce contracts, and gifts. Scholars have analyzed the evolution of firms,[17] of norms and customs,[18] of trade associations and universities and the informational media, as responses to defects in markets, particularly problems with information. In developing countries, markets affecting the poor are often overlain with competition-restricting practices that persist in part because they provide information, reduce risk, allow credible commitments, and facilitate quality control.

As markets expand and specialize, many of the institutions and mechanisms of the bazaar and the primitive society become economically inefficient and unfair. Some scholars, observing what they deem to be "exploitation" and the restriction of trade by informationally advantaged traders, have called for controlling trade. The market is so imperfect in developing countries, they say, that it needs to be strictly regulated, if not replaced. This impulse has sometimes combined with an anticommerce worldview to produce a calamitous cycle of government interference with rural markets (see box on facing page).

Other scholars, shocked by this cycle and enchanted by the hum of the competitive equilibrium, believe in an opposite solution. One must dismantle the trade-restricting institutions not only of the state but also of primitive societies and bazaars. "If only competition were set free," they say. But the informational perspective cautions against mistaking the symptoms for the underlying causes. The reasons for the state controls and "primitive" economic institutions may run deep: among other things, informational problems may be to blame. And if information remains poor, setting markets free may result in inefficiency and injustice, especially for the poor.

As I employ it, "information" has broad coverage. It includes the data relevant to economic decisions and the ability (both societal and individual) to generate, distribute, guarantee, analyze, and

---

THE SPIRAL OF INCREASING INTERVENTION

"Basic development strategies called for industrialization, usually to be accomplished by overvaluation of exchange rates and restrictions on imports of manufacturing items. But this hurt farmers, reduced agricultural exports and increased food imports. Offsetting measures became necessary, such as subsidized fertilizer, credit, and irrigation. But these were costly and their financing required higher taxes and increased external borrowing, further overvaluing the exchange rate. Price controls instituted to help urban consumers reduced or eliminated profits of farmers and drove private traders out of the market; the solution was to give legal monopolies to marketing agencies. Prices that differed across time or regions of the country were taken to indicate inefficient, speculative, or exploitative private trading activities; the solutions were regulation of trade (margin controls, banning of trade by certain ethnic groups, regulations governing the movement or storage of commodities) and, again, parastatal monopolies. Over the years, these policies have created the attitude that all characteristics of the economy are the responsibility of government. The cycle is perpetuated; intervention begets pressure for more intervention."

SOURCE: Onid Knudsen and John Nash, with contributions by James Bovard, Bruce Gardner and L. Alan Winters, "Redefining the Role of Government in Agriculture for the 1990s," World Bank Discussion Paper no. 105 (Washington, D.C.: The World Bank, November 1990), 49–50.

---

process it.[19] The *effective use* of information in economic decisions is what matters.

In Chapter 3, we analyze one broad category of informational problems in developing countries, the measurement of the "quality" of a good or service, a worker, or a credit risk. Information about quality is often scarce and expensive, asymmetrically held among the parties in transactions, and subject to guileful manipulation. The buyers and sellers in markets can themselves take steps to overcome these problems. To do so, they sometimes need the help of third parties, such as the government; and the government itself may take direct measures to improve the informational content of markets.

We consider many options for the government in Chapters 3 to 5. Each option entails costs as well as benefits. To say that the government may have a role in these areas is not, of course, to say in a particular case that it should, nor in any case that only it should. Each situation deserves both the creative rethinking of alternatives and careful analysis of benefits and costs. To help stimulate this process, two devices often prove useful. One is the case study, wherein public and private policy makers analyze concrete problems and their successful or failed resolution in other contexts. The second device is the framework for policy analysis. The objective is to provide policy makers with something to guide their debates and inquiries and to stimulate new thinking, rather than a blueprint or a formula.

Chapters 3 and 5 present a framework for considering what buyers, sellers, and governments can do to overcome one category of informational problems (see Table 3-1 and the discussion of it in the appendix to Chapter 5). Chapter 4 contains two case studies, which were analyzed in terms of the framework. The Indian case documents the successful development of a milk market. A key step was the dissemination of a credible process—technological and organizational—for measuring the quality of milk at each step in the marketing chain. In contrast, the Pakistani shrimp case showed both internal and export marketing in disarray because at various stages the quality of the country's shrimp was not credibly and accurately assessed. When information is distorted and incomplete, incentives too go awry.

How can the government provide ways and means for credible information to be developed, elicited, shared, and processed? The alternatives include setting up and enforcing rules of the game that encourage information-sharing and cooperation by reducing transaction costs and risks—for example, laws, weights and measures, and commercial codes. They include various state roles in quality evaluation and control, the development and dissemination of market information, research and development, education (the dissemination of knowledge and also the development of information processing skills, materials, and technologies), communication, and the production of goods and services. The state may intervene directly or indirectly—the latter meaning creating the legal and institutional framework for private parties to solve informational problems by themselves—or both.

It is surprising how often these problems with "free markets" are overlooked in development policy making. For example, a recent World Bank review of all its projects in agricultural marketing from 1974 to 1985 identifies and criticizes a common assumption in Bank work that "the existing marketing system operates satisfactorily." In fact, most markets don't—as these Bank-funded projects eventually discovered. The report laments that "there has been little attempt to improve the efficiency and transparency of private sector marketing mechanisms. This is reflected in lack of attention to market news services, legally defined grades, weightbridges and regulated weights and measures, credit for small traders, and improved market structures." Most Bank-funded projects in agriculture between

1975 and 1985 failed, the report concludes, because the World Bank and the countries receiving these loans seemed to assume that "if it is produced, it will get sold."

> Notable omissions include the lack of any measures for providing a framework within which markets could operate more efficiently—commercial legal code, regulation or inspection. . . . It is striking how little attention seems to have been given to the government's role in providing standardized weights and measures, defining and policing nationally recognized quality grades, collecting and disseminating timely price information, or encouraging competition.[20]

In a similar vein, at the end of a study of markets in Africa and Asia, researchers from the International Food Policy Research Institute concluded that governments should allow private trade "to work freely. Market development policies improving legal and physical facilities and flow of information should be another component of this transition." These policies include "development of marketplaces, dissemination of price and production information, introduction of standard grades and weights, [and] maintenance of law and order in transport channels and markets," among others.[21]

Fair and efficient markets do not occur by accident; they are the products of, among other things, intelligent laws and public policies and environments rich in information. If policy makers and aid donors have tended to overlook this fact, one is tempted to diagnose a visceral reaction to misdirected state interventions and an overdose of elementary economics. Textbook models assume conditions that we have said are often lacking—in particular, perfect information on prices, quantities, and quality. Under these assumptions, unfettered competition guarantees efficiency, and governmental intervention can only foul up the works. When information is imperfect and incomplete, however, the model breaks down. "With perfect information and no nonconvexities, the postulates underlying perfect competition have a certain degree of plausibility, or should I say, at least internal consistency," writes Joseph E. Stiglitz. "The competitive paradigm is an artfully constructed structure: when one of the central pieces (the assumption of perfect information) is removed, the structure collapses."[22]

Structural adjustment means that the role of the state in economic development is cut back. More reliance is placed on market forces. These are, I believe, welcome changes. But adjusting to reality means going beyond elementary models to recognize the shortcomings of markets as they are found in developing countries. It also means that government has a role to play, not just in the "standard" cases of public goods and environmental externalities, but also to help markets become efficient and just. For free markets to work better, the government must also work better.

IMPROVING GOVERNMENTS

Just as the informational perspective provides insights into the problems of markets in developing countries, so too does it suggest approaches to three classic problems of government: inefficiency and adverse incentives, corruption, and decentralization.

Chapter 7 analyzes "incentive myopia," the chronic oversight of the importance of incentives in the public sector. A crisis of public incentives plagues many poor countries. Real wages have fallen and been compressed in ways unimaginable in the industrialized North. Pay and performance are virtually unconnected. The resulting inefficiencies threaten not only public services but also economic reforms themselves.

Politics, custom, and sheer poverty constrain public sector incentives. Public services are notable for the difficulty of defining objectives and measuring results. Civil service rules limit the use of financial incentives. Despite all these obstacles, experience shows that improvement is possible. Chapter 7 presents a framework for analyzing public sector incentives (see Table 7-2). It suggests that leaders work with public employees to redefine the objectives being sought, to generate information about how well the objectives are being met, and to link part of the compensation of public officials to the achievement of those objectives. It discusses various ways to raise the revenues needed to improve incentives. Chapter 7 also describes ingenious success stories of improved public sector incentives, despite all the obstacles.

Chapter 8 discusses the related problem of corruption. Until recently, this subject was virtually taboo in developing countries. But as its cancerous effects have grown, eroding incentives and nourishing a predatory elite, corruption has become impossible to avoid.[23] Many governments are launching initiatives against corruption. International agencies are offering support as never before. In the past two years, international aid organizations such as the World Bank, the U.S. Agency for International Development, Ministère de la Cooperation (France), and the United Nations Development

Programme have initiated seminars and programs dedicated to corruption and what to do about it.

But what *can* be done to reduce bribery, extortion, kickbacks, influence-peddling, fraud, and other illicit activities? Simply declaring a campaign against corruption is no solution.[24] Structural adjustment will presumably help reduce corruption by reducing the state's monopoly powers in economic life. (We should note, however, that privatizing a state monopoly may simply rename the corruption.) Government in any case remains, and its success will determine the success of free-market reforms.

Corruption can never be eliminated, only reduced; our approach is to treat it as a problem of policy and management in addition to one of morality and law. After disaggregating the many forms of corruption, we focus on the structures of incentives and information facing public officials. A framework for policy analysis (Table 8-2) details five categories of tools for controlling corruption between public "agents" (or employees) and "clients" (or citizens):

1. selecting the agents (and training them)
2. altering the incentives facing agents and clients (for both efforts and results)
3. collecting and processing information on the agents' and clients' efforts and results
4. restructuring the agent-client relationship (for example, reducing monopoly powers, clarifying rules and procedures to circumscribe agents' discretion, changing decision making, and indeed, redefining the mission of the organization)
5. raising the moral costs of corruption (for example, with ethical codes and changes in the organizational culture)

Generating reform when many leaders are themselves corrupt is hardly automatic; here aid donors may play a catalytic role. Even in the best of cases, controlling corruption requires political will and great managerial skill. It is not easy, but as the examples cited in Chapter 8 reveal, it is possible. Information and incentives are at the heart of the solution.

Chapter 9 analyzes two examples of administrative reform—the decentralization and integration of public services. Over-centralized government, in part the result of the strategy of state-dominated economic development, is now an obstacle to free-market reforms. But decentralization is not easy or automatic. Experience shows that it often degenerates into inefficiency and chaos. The classic explanations for the failures of decentralization are a lack of local technical and managerial capabilities and insufficient political will. Our analysis focuses instead on information and incentives. When information is plentiful about public services and their results, and when incentives can be linked to such information, then both "agents" and "clients" can be given more authority and discretion over public services. In the opposite case, decentralization is likely to fail.

Administrative integration is one response to the interlinked, holistic nature of development problems. A classic example is integrated rural development, in which various services ranging from agriculture to health to education to infrastructure are administratively combined in a single agency or project. Chapter 9's analysis again emphasizes information and incentives. When both are poor, then administrative integration may be tempting as the only way to induce necessary coordination across activities. But we also saw that the costs of administrative integration have often been greater than foreseen. Many of the benefits of specialization are often sacrificed, and the sought-after coordination often proves elusive. (See the framework for policy analysis in Table 9-1.)

The discussion leads to two general conclusions. First, what to decentralize or integrate, and how, should depend on the environment, in particular on the availability of information and the malleability of incentives. Decentralization is most likely to be successful when information is rich and incentives powerful and linked to results. Under these same circumstances, coordination can be achieved without administrative integration.

Second, beyond adapting to the environment one may try to change it. If information is scarce, how might it be created and shared? If ultimate outcomes are impossible to measure, what short-run proxies might be employed? How can incentives be increased and linked to results? Each of these steps of course entails its own costs, so there is again no magic formula or blueprint for reform.

In our discussion of the failures of government, information and incentives take central stage. "The problem in government is not lack of accountability, as is sometimes suggested," writes public policy professor Steven Kelman, "but the nature of the accountability. Government people do not lead sheltered lives: they are indeed held accountable, often publicly and painfully so, if they violate rules, even if the standards of probity themselves were not violated. . . . What is missing is demand for accountability for the quality of the government's performance."[25]

THE NEW INFORMATION-BASED ORGANIZATION

Management guru Peter Drucker believes that information will become the defining feature of bureaucracy and organization. Although he was speaking of developed countries, his observations are consistent with trends in the poor nations as well.

Very few events have as much impact on civilization as a change in the basic principle for organizing work. . . . In 1946, with the advent of the computer, information became the organizing principle of production. With this, a new basic civilization came into being.

[T]he business, and increasingly the government agency as well, will be knowledge-based, composed largely of specialists who direct and discipline their own performance through organized feedback from colleagues and customers. It will be an information-based organization.

Large organizations will have little choice but to become information-based.

A good deal of the work will be done differently in the information-based organization as a result. Traditional departments will serve as guardians of standards, as centers for training and for the assignment of specialists. The work itself will largely be done by task-focused teams. . . . One thing is clear, though: the information-based organization requires self-discipline and an emphasis on individual responsibility for relationships and for communications.

Perhaps the most important future task of government in a pluralist society is to set standards.

SOURCE: Peter F. Drucker, The New Realities: In Government and Politics/In Economics and Business/In Society and World View (New York: Harper & Row, 1989); 256, 207, 210, 211, 98-9.

Why is accountability so difficult in government, especially in developing countries? Part of the answer lies in difficulties of measurement. Many public sector results are intrinsically harder to gauge than private sector performance. Consequently, we rely on rules and procedures to guide public officials; we measure the inputs rather than the outputs of public systems. Part of the problem is inherent in "publicness"; but not all of it. We have not been aggressive in developing partial and proxy measures of public sector success, or in empowering clients and citizens with marketlike proxies such as vouchers. We have also been unwilling to link pay to performance in the public sector.

If, as we have seen, government's strengths are needed to improve markets, so too are ideas from the market needed to improve government. "Efficient organizational design," writes economist Paul Milgrom, "seeks to do what the system of prices and property rights does in the neoclassical conception: to channel the self-interested behavior of individuals away from purely redistributive activities and into well-coordinated, socially productive ones. The success that a society's institutions have in achieving this objective is a major determinant of its economic welfare."[26] The next decades, I believe, will see a revolution in the provision of transparent information about public performance, and the development of new ways to link incentives to those results. This, in turn, will enable governments to play their appropriate roles in freeing private markets and fostering economic development.

OVERCOMING ETHNIC INEQUALITIES

Information also provides a new perspective on one of the most intractable problems of development—the persistence of ethnic poverty and discrimination. Within most developing countries, as Chapter 10 shows, certain ethnic groups are economically and educationally backward. They tend to remain behind despite efforts at assimilation, despite educational and public health programs, despite affirmative action. Although economic growth and improved public services alleviate ethnic poverty, they do not overcome group inequalities, at least in the short and medium run. Our brief analyses of the cases of Peru, Brazil, and Malaysia in Chapter 11 reveals the stubbornness of ethnic differences in income, employment, and education.

Information plays a dual role in the plight of economically backward groups, as we see in Chapter 12. First, in conditions of imperfect information, markets and merit systems may reinforce rather than remove group differences. When individual information is scarce, economic actors rely on group information. The result is a form of institutionalized discrimination. Second, a profound source of their disadvantage may be informational—they lack data about prices, quantities, and qualities in the markets for goods and labor; they often speak different languages; they lack access to institutional knowledge about laws and regulations; they are removed from modern devices of information transmission (such as telephones); they are measurably poorer in certain learning abilities.

We developed a framework for policy analysis concerning the problem of ethnic inequalities and discrimination (see Table 12-2). It subsumes many alternatives under four categories:

1. Through direct redistribution, reduce group inequalities in social outcomes like power, employment, ownership, and income—or deflect attention from those inequalities.

2. Reduce underlying group differences in behavior, human capital, and culture.

3. Improve information and market functioning.

4. Change or influence where and how economic and political decisions are made. (Preferential treatment programs enter here.)

The third option is attractive. Especially in developing countries, group inequalities are partly the result of imperfect information in both markets and merit systems. Better information on the abilities and achievements of individuals—combined with labor markets and personnel systems that make hiring and firing easy and permit the adjustment of pay to performance—will reduce many kinds of institutionalized discrimination.

EXTENSIONS

"Adjusting to reality" means going beyond free-market economic reforms at the macroeconomic level. Markets involve *institutions*, which must be developed. Buyers and sellers act together in some of these institutions—for example, trade associations and consumer groups—but in even in the freest markets the state plays many roles. We must go beyond debates over state versus market, over the choice between state and market, even over the proper balancing of state and market. The market and the state work together. Even from the narrow perspective of economic development, a priority is to make government work better.

This will mean going beyond many past efforts to improve public administration, which have ignored some of the economic and informational realities of government in developing countries. Past efforts have stressed administrative reform, training, institution building, foreign advisers, and better equipment; they have usually left out incentives for performance. This is analogous to past efforts to boost private sector production without raising producer prices. Incentives are equally crucial in the public sector, especially given the current crisis concerning public sector pay in developing countries.

Improving government will also mean facing up to corruption

as a problem for policy and management—not squeamishly avoiding it as too sensitive, or considering it exclusively a problem of morals, education, or better laws. It will mean redimensioning the overcentralized state apparatus. Effective decentralization and administrative integration will go beyond slogans to a hard-headed analysis of various public activities and functions and the information and incentives attending each.

"Adjusting to reality" also means overcoming taboos about ethnicity, not just for the sake of social stability or to avoid ethnic violence, but for economic development. Policy analyses on this subject must break out of certain intellectual conventions. Ethnic poverty is not just the result of discrimination; on the other hand, discrimination is not just the result of irrational racial hatred but can become institutionalized. Advantaged groups do not necessarily benefit from ethnic disparities; at the same time, competition is not the automatic solution to all forms of discrimination. If our efforts to fight poverty are to bear fruit, they must neither overlook nor misunderstand the ethnic dimensions of disadvantage.

These various calls to action certainly do not exhaust the subject of government and economic development; many important topics are left out.[27] But they do ask us to address new topics and to take new approaches. To do so, the style of policy analysis may itself need to be transformed.

WHAT IS POLICY ANALYSIS?

This book has presented an approach to policy analysis as well as a way of looking at economic development. The approach may perhaps best be described through a comparison.

Consider the way structural adjustment policies are formulated. Government officials, perhaps in collaboration with international aid agencies, recast macroeconomic policies involving interest rates, prices, tariffs, and commerce. In some countries, including Bolivia, key decisions have been made behind closed doors by a handful of senior officials and politicians. Implementing the reforms is of course another matter; but the style of decision making is a centralized, top-down adjustment of certain parameters or changing of laws. United Nations experts have written many national plans; World Bank officials have designed many structural adjustment programs.

Such decisions are the dream of a certain style of policy analysis. The analyst is given the objectives, alternative actions, and constraints; then her or his job is to determine the effects of the various actions. From the analyst's calculations a prescription is derived. The analytical problem is the leap from givens to prescriptions, from the "if" to the "then." This conception borrows from economic theory. Under idealized assumptions, economics is able to derive powerful statements about optimal tariffs and taxes and exchange rates. Seduced, the policy analyst may accept a lot of unrealistic restrictions on the "if" for the thrill of an unassailable "then." And so it is that policy analysis may feed top-down decision making and the exercise of authority, whether of the old planning variety or the new macroeconomic reforms.

But—again at the schematic level, so as to exaggerate the contrast—the issues we have been addressing in this book are different. They tend to be microeconomic, decentralized, and institutionally loaded. They involve information—its creation, dissemination, sharing, and processing. In the case of public sector reforms, we have emphasized the importance of participation by public employees in incentive schemes and the fight against corruption. Because of the richness of the problems and the need to involve those on the line and at the bottom in their solution, a different style of policy analysis is needed. The intellectual problem is transformed: how to discover, how to be more creative about, the objectives, the alternatives, and the constraints. These are no longer given, but are to be generated or enhanced; the analyst's job is to understand, expand, and enrich the "if."

Policy analysis provides not so much a set of answers that politicians should adopt and bureaucrats should implement, but a set of tools and examples for enriching the appreciation of alternatives and their consequences.

This conception of policy analysis has another implication. It has to do with the lamentable reluctance of politicians to adopt and bureaucrats to implement the analyst's advice. "Economic policy professionals are . . . well accustomed to frustration," notes Arnold C. Harberger. "Proposals aimed at improving policy must run a veritable gauntlet of hazards . . . on their way to implementation. Most proposals do not survive, and those that do may emerge so mutilated or distorted that they no longer serve their intended purposes."[28]

In a similar vein, Gerald M. Meier asks:

> But how to gain acceptance of more appropriate
> policies? This remains the most underdeveloped part
> of the development economist's subject. . . . To
> become more persuasive, the development economist

needs to become a student of public policy, and to
determine why particular policies are adopted and not
others. . . . Development economics is on the edge of
politics and the edge of management. To be more
effective in policy making, it must venture more into
each territory.[29]

Under the standard paradigm of policy analysis, it is at first
baffling why one's optimal advice is not pursued—until one notes
that, unlike oneself, policy makers and bureaucrats have selfish
agendas. Aha.

But the resistance of politicians and functionaries—as well as
citizens, labor unions, and business groups—may mean more. It
may be a sign that the analyst has more to learn about the operative
objective functions, alternatives, and constraints. In most real policy
problems, these are not given.

So, when confronted with the reluctance of the real world, the
analyst should not scorn but should listen carefully and learn. The
words and actions of politicians and bureaucrats and citizens provide invaluable clues for appreciating what the objectives and alternatives really are and might be. And, after listening, the analyst's
task is to provide theoretical frameworks and practical examples to
expand and enrich *their* thinking about objectives, alternatives, and
consequences. At least part of the failure of standard policy analysis
to make a difference stems from the way many analysts conceive of
answers in public policy.[30]

Such is the aim of the analyses presented here. Take the treatment of corruption in Chapter 8, for example. One tries to unpack
the concept, even an emotively loaded one; one disaggregates the
types of corruption. One approaches a sensitive subject by highlighting not the moral failures of individuals but the structural failures of information and incentives. One uses a simplifying theory to
obtain, not an optimizing model under restrictive assumptions, but
a framework that stimulates the creativity of policy makers and
managers in their varied and unique circumstances. One searches
for examples of best practice.

How might participation and creativity best be kindled
through policy analysis? I know of little research on the subject.
Theoretical investigations can play a role. For example, at the same
time that policy makers and popularizers rush to apply the simple
model of competitive markets, theorists seem to be finding more and
more things wrong with it. The conditions assumed by elementary
economics are hardly the rule. "Neoclassical economies or econo-

mies that satisfy all the textbook neoclassical assumptions," writes Andrew Schotter, "can be represented as degenerate special cases of institution-assisted economies because the set of institutional rules existing in the information set is null. Clearly, these economies are exceptional cases."[31] Economist Joseph Stiglitz has been one of the most insistent on this point.

> In traditional welfare economics, we did not have to model the government very precisely: we established that no government, no matter how good, could do better than the private market. The results of the recent literature have established that that proposition is not correct: whenever there are information problems (whether of the adverse selection or moral hazard form) there are government interventions . . . which could make everyone better off.

These are useful reminders. But Stiglitz, like most other theorists, stops short of policy recommendations.

> Though recent analysis has identified the nature of the requisite interventions . . . I am not sanguine about the government's ability to effect a welfare improvement . . . Now, our analysis has established that there are interventions which are feasible (within the information structure) which would effect a Pareto improvement. But why should we believe that such improvements would evolve out of our political processes?[32]

The market is imperfect, so government action may be called for; but governments are imperfect, too; and there Stiglitz leaves it.[33] Policy analysis is short-circuited. Economist David M. Newbery provides another example of this tendency:

> The state also has the potential to collect and use information that might allow the creation of new risk-sharing institutions, or that might alleviate problems of asymmetric information—the income insurance scheme, and the collection of area-wide yield figures which facilitate new share contracts are good examples. Again, it is the public good nature of the information that is the cause of the failure of the private market. Having said this, the evidence from the past operation of marketing boards in developing countries and the current operation of farm support

---

THE PEDAGOGY OF AID

Our approach has implications for foreign aid as well. One is that matters thought to be "political" are central to economic development—corruption, public sector incentives, decentralization. Economic negotiations should include governance. Another is that donors' comparative advantage may be informational—providing to poor countries examples from elsewhere, a comparative perspective, the lessons from the donors' own failures. The financial and intellectual dependence of structural adjustment, as induced by leveraged aid, should be progressively replaced by a pedagogical relationship in the fullest sense of the word.

    Consider this analysis by Thomas Bucaille:

> *From this history [of Africa since independence], what is the lesson for the future? The profound depression of raw materials prices, the indebtedness—which postponed the crisis at the same time as it increased its cost—are not the only things responsible for the situation. The crisis is that of passing from one mode of regulation to another. In this sense, it gives birth to the future but, if we are not on guard, the baby risks being stillborn. Calling into question all the constitutive elements of the society, and their cohesion, this crisis can't help but provoke disruptions of great amplitude. A good adjustment policy would ease the difficulties of transition between the two moments of development.*
>
> > *The partners of structural adjustment have recognized it, but in the worst fashion, in putting progressively greater emphasis on "the social dimension of adjustment." The matter is not simply putting in place some sorts of measures to avoid the outbreaks of hunger which one has seen burst forth almost everywhere. It is worth more to*

---

schemes in developed countries does not give much cause for optimism on this front.[34]

Consider sociologist Norman Nicholson's words in a book on institutional development:

> In the face of momentous changes in the Asian economies over the past twenty years, markets have been very slow to react for a variety of reasons. For example, there has been a shift from subsistence to predominantly commercial agriculture within this period. Yet the marketing structures for key inputs and for intermediate-term capital have frequently not responded. . . . It is reasonable to argue that, in many of these countries, public authority has not been directed toward improving market institutions and

> evoke "a political dimension of adjustment," the necessity
> of restructuring, indeed of constructing, a State that
> works, with respect for the law, and deprived at last of its
> predatory reflexes. The problem of corruption is central,
> but neither bilateral aid, because of its bad conscience
> from colonial times, nor multilateral aid, obeying its
> principle of noninterference, has been able to confront this
> obstacle. All the same, aid is a necessary condition for the
> emergence of a new economy. And the donors are the
> ones who will stipulate the ways and means of this new
> departure.
>
> More than ever, aid is a pedagogy, a relation of
> teacher to student more or less acknowledged. So it is
> necessary that, like all liberal education, this pedagogy
> brings forth an emancipation. The risk is double: not to
> assume this pedagogical relationship, or to perpetuate
> dependence. Aid awaits of the donor means and rules, but
> it does not involve initiatives; the master is forbidden the
> commandment, the student a servile apprenticeship. Aid,
> by its conditionality, reconstructs the mechanisms of
> financial dependence, but above all intellectual. One
> witnesses today various processes of veritable
> recolonization by the powerful, strangely similar to those
> that have subjugated Tunisia, Egypt, or the Chinese and
> Ottoman empires. Limited to economic policy, but
> refusing political interference, this new tutelage is
> forbidden its true contractual exigencies, and therefore
> efficiency.

SOURCE: Thomas Bucaille, "Métamorphoses du problème africain: L'économie africaine et la Coopération française depuis 1945," Études 373, no. 1-2 (July-August 1990): 14–16, my translation.

market efficiency. Even more recently, the development goal has been stated—incorrectly I would argue—as one of expanding the private sector, rather than of developing market institutions. We need to understand clearly the character of the public functions and policies that encourage expansion and innovation in a market economy.[35]

These scholars are appealing for an enriched understanding not only of market failures but also of nonmarket failures—the inefficiencies of hierarchical organizations such as corporations and government agencies.[36] Their analysis provides a useful step forward, but one that usually stops short of application.

Perhaps this is as it should be for academic research. But one may also wish to go further. One may wish for case studies of best practice, say of Nicholson's market institutions or Newbery's insurance programs. One may also hope for analytical frameworks that can serve as the basis for participative discussions and brainstorming even if inevitably any single framework can be criticized as inexact and incomplete. Somewhere between history and theory stands the use of examples and models to stimulate creative and necessarily idiosyncratic responses by people solving specific problems.

FURTHER RESEARCH

Each topic opened in this book has barely been touched. The analysis badly needs to be extended and deepened: extended to new topics such as democratization and legal reforms, deepening to subtopics such as credit reforms, market information systems, and the reform of labor markets. More case studies of success and failure would be especially welcome.

More broadly, I am fascinated by what one might call the informational approach to institutions. When we recognize that less-developed countries are characterized by incomplete and imperfect information, we can take a fresh look at features of local economies that are often ascribed to tradition or to forms of class domination. Many rural institutions, such as sharecropping and interlinked markets, can be seen as adaptations to markets with poor information and high risks.[37] "With regard to trade in the ordinary sense—trade of unlike articles between strangers—in primitive society," writes Richard A. Posner, "transaction costs are presumably high because of the costs of information regarding the reliability of the seller, the quality of the product, and trading alternatives (that is, the market price). However, institutions have arisen which reduce these transaction costs," including gift-exchange, "customary" prices, "the transformation of an arms-length contract relationship into an intimate status relationship," and "a buyer's deliberately overpaying a seller in order to induce the seller to deal fairly with him in the future."[38]

So, too, can one analyze the sometimes bizarre institutions of the bazaar. "In the bazaar," says anthropologist Clifford Geertz, "information is poor, scarce, maldistributed, inefficiently communicated, and intensely valued. . . . The level of ignorance about everything from product quality and going prices to market possibilities and production costs is very high, and much of the way in which the bazaar functions can be interpreted as an attempt to reduce such ignorance for someone, to increase it for someone, or to defend someone against it."[39] Geertz emphasizes clientelization (or repeated purchases) and "intensive rather than extensive bargaining" as institutional responses to informational problems.

"Culture" itself can be viewed, if never fully apprehended, through the lens of information. The causality runs in both directions. Culture and its stipulations and conventions can be viewed as providing solutions to market failures, especially when information and enforcement problems make coordination difficult. As information becomes cheaper and more widespread and other systems of enforcement begin to work well—such as the law—then cultural norms start to break down. At least, this is the hypothesis.

Throughout this book we have emphasized information. One key to its effective utilization is information processing capability. For an individual, this capability (or better, capabilities) is a complicated function of many factors: inherited abilities, conditioning, education, and access to information processing technologies, among others. The acquisition and development of these capabilities also depend on how they are rewarded—on features of the economy and political power.

Individuals form organizations and societies. These can also be said to have information-processing capabilities. How well organizations learn is again a function of many variables, including the opportunities to make profits through greater knowledge, technology, power structures, culture, and policy choices.

Since people and organizations and perhaps entire societies differ along these various dimensions, we may expect two things. First, they will adapt differently to problems of imperfect and incomplete information. Given the same structures of information, different processing capabilities will lead to different outcomes and to different adaptive strategies. For example, people or organizations or societies that are less adept at processing information will tend to rely more on rules, conventions, conformity, and hierarchy, other things being equal.

Second, people and organizations and societies will differ in their capabilities to take advantage of a modern, open, information-intensive economy. Confronted with profit opportunities that depend on information-processing capabilities, those with lower capabilities will tend to lag economically.

And so the informational perspective opens new approaches

to the explanation of economic inequalities among people, institutions, cultures, and social systems. Beyond inequalities in capital and labor and natural resources, we should examine information and the capability to process it, each a function of the other, and both developed, conditioned, and invested in as the result of a host of factors, including the role of the state.

NOTES

NOTES TO CHAPTER I

1. This and the quotations below are from my interview with President Paz Estenssoro in Tarija, Bolivia, 7 December 1990.

2. Agreeing with Darcy Ribeiro's observation that Bolivia has often been a model for other countries, Bolivia's current president, Jaime Paz Zamora, said, "In 1952, the first signal is given of being adequate to the times that came with the National Revolution which later, in its main points, has to be copied by countries of Africa and Asia." Speech in *Fondo Social de Emergencia: Seminario de Evaluación: 26 al 29 de Agosto, 1989* (La Paz: Fondo Social de Emergencia, 1990): 293; my translation. Spanish original: "En 1952, se da la primera señal de adecuación a los tiempos que vienen con la Revolución Nacional, que luego, en los puntos fundamentales, ha de ser copiada, por países de Africa y Asia."

3. Country Economics Department, *Adjustment Lending: An Evaluation of Ten Years of Experience*, Policy and Research Series no. 1 (Washington, D.C.: World Bank, December 1988): 56.

4. Alexander Gerschenkron, *Economic Backwardness in Historical Perspective* (Cambridge: Cambridge University Press, 1962).

5. Cynthia Taft Morris and Irma Adelman, "Nineteenth-Century Development Experience and Lessons for Today," *World Development* 17, no. 9 (September 1989): 1419.

6. See, for example, Gerald W. Scully, "The Institutional Framework and Economic Development," *Journal of Political Economy* 96, no. 3 (June 1988): 652–62; and Patrick Conway, "An Atheoretic Evaluation of Success in Structural Adjustment" (University of North Carolina, Department of Economics, October 1990). As most authors readily admit, various technical problems plague econometric efforts to explain economic growth, so such evidence needs to be supplemented with detailed studies of individual countries, as in the forthcoming work of Marc Lindenberg, *The Development Dilemma*.

7. Writing in 1958, Edward S. Mason noted: "Presently underdeveloped areas, as shaped by the past, are overwhelmingly private enterprise economies. The public share in income, wealth, and employment is small. And large areas of economic activity are almost entirely locally independent and relatively untouched by the hand of central government." *Economic Planning in Underdeveloped Areas: Government and Business*, Millar Lectures no. 2 (New York: Fordham University Press, 1958): 12. In the 1950s in countries with per capita incomes of less than $100 per year, the government's share of the national income ran between 6

and 15 percent. Harry T. Oshima, "Share of Government in Gross National Product for Various Countries," *American Economic Review* 27 (June 1957): 381.

8. Morris and Adelman, "Nineteenth-Century Development Experience," 1427.

9. Albert O. Hirschman emphasizes disillusionment with recent experience as a perennial tendency, one that may explain a historical pattern in which societies oscillate between public and private preoccupations. *Shifting Involvements: Private Interests and Public Action* (Princeton, N.J.: Princeton University Press, 1982).

10. For Zeckhauser, no single metaphor sufficiently stresses the lack of a dividing line between state and market. In a single paragraph he writes: "Government activity is inextricably interwoven with that of the private sector . . . their distinctive identities have been eroded. Instead of a jar that contains a mixture of blue and yellow marbles, we have a lumpy soup of varying shades of green. Ours is a mongrel economy. It presents a muddle of public and private responsibilities." Richard Zeckhauser, "The Muddled Responsibilities of Public and Private America," in Winthrop Knowlton and Richard Zeckhauser, eds., *American Society: Public and Private Responsibilities* (Cambridge, Mass.: Ballinger, 1986): 46.

11. "Neoclassical economic theory presumes that the only social loss associated with a distortion introduced by a policy is the deadweight loss associated with it. For instance, the loss due to an import tariff imposed by a country which cannot influence its terms of trade is equated to the value of the resources that could be saved by abolishing the tariff while assuring the consumers *their posttariff level of welfare*. On the other hand, as Buchanan of the public choice school put it, the loss is not confined only to the deadweight loss. For it to be so, the only response of producers and consumers to the tariff must be to shift their production and consumption patterns. But in fact a person or group that is differentially affected, favorably or unfavorably, by a government may: (i) engage in *lobbying efforts* to institute or repeal it; (ii) engage *directly in politics* to secure access to decision-making power; and (iii) *shift resources* in or out of the affected activity. Resources may be employed at all three levels simultaneously while the traditional deadweight loss calculation is confined only to the last level." T. N. Srinivasan, "Neoclassical Political Economy, the State and Economic Development," *Asian Development Review* 3, no. 2 (1985): 42–43, emphasis in original.

12. Mancur Olson, "The Political Economy of Comparative Growth Rates," in Dennis C. Mueller, ed., *The Political Economy of Growth* (New Haven, Conn.: Yale University Press, 1983): 48.

13. Cynthia Taft Morris and Irma Adelman, *Comparative Patterns of Economic Development, 1850–1914* (Baltimore: Johns Hopkins University Press, 1988): 215. "In sum," the authors say in a synthetic article, "the effects of tariff policies are complex and vary greatly across countries in ways depending strongly on resources, institutions, and government strategies." Morris and Adelman, "Nineteenth-Century Development Experience," 1427.

14. See, for example, James E. Anderson, *The Relative Inefficiency of Quotas* (Cambridge, Mass.: MIT Press, 1988); José Antonio Ocampo, "The Macroeconomic Effect of Import Controls: A Keynesian Analysis," *Journal of Development Economics* 27, nos. 1-2 (October 1987): 285–305; and relevant sections of W. Arthur Lewis's essay and Arnold Harberger's comments in Gerald M. Meier and Dudley Seers, eds., *Pioneers in Development* (New York: Oxford University Press, 1984).

15. But one of the exponents of the new approach admits that policy implications have not yet been fully explored. "The new literature on I-O [industrial organization] and trade certainly calls into question the traditional presumption that free trade is optimal. Whether it is a practical guide to productive protectionism is another matter. The models described here are all quite special cases; small variations in assumptions can no doubt reverse the conclusions. . . . It may be questioned whether our understanding of how imperfectly competitive industries actually behave will ever be good enough for us to make

policy prescriptions with confidence. . . . The attempts at quantification described here are obviously primitive and preliminary." Paul R. Krugman, *Rethinking International Trade* (Cambridge, Mass.: MIT Press, 1990): 257, 261. For a critique of the policy relevance of the so-called new trade theory, see Jagdish Bhagwati, *Protectionism* (Cambridge, Mass.: MIT Press, 1988): 105–14.

16. Marc Lindenberg and Noel Ramírez, *Managing Adjustment in Developing Countries* (San Francisco: ICS Press for the International Center for Economic Growth, 1990).

17. Paul P. Streeten, review of Arnold C. Harberger, ed., *World Economic Growth: Case Studies of Developed and Developing Nations* (San Francisco: ICS Press for the International Center for Economic Growth, 1984), in *Journal of Comparative Economics* 12 (1988): 451.

18. For a criticism of the rhetoric, see H. W. Singer, "The *World Development Report 1987* on the Blessings of 'Outward Orientation': A Necessary Correction," *Journal of Development Studies* 24, no. 2 (January 1988): 232–36.

19. Dwight Perkins, "Economic Systems Reform in Developing Countries," Development Discussion Paper No. 307 (Cambridge, Mass.: Harvard Institute for International Development, June 1989): 15–16.

20. A few valuable exceptions exist: Samuel Paul, *Managing Development Programs: The Lessons of Success* (Boulder, Colo.: Westview, 1982); Harberger, *World Economic Growth*; and Lindenberg and Ramírez, *Managing Adjustment in Developing Countries*.

21. Richard A. Musgrave, "A Brief History of Fiscal Doctrine," in Alan J. Auerbach and Martin Feldstein, eds., *Handbook of Public Economics*, vol. 1 (Amsterdam: North-Holland, 1985): 53.

22. For a review of the economics literature on the failures of both markets and governments, see Robert P. Inman, "Markets, Governments, and the 'New' Political Economy," in Alan J. Auerbach and Martin Feldstein, eds., *Handbook of Public Economics*, vol. 2 (Amsterdam: North-Holland, 1987): 647–777. Charles Wolf elucidates this typology of chronic shortcomings:

Market Failures

1. Externalities and public goods
2. Increasing returns
3. Market imperfections
4. Distributional inequity (income and wealth)

Nonmarket Failures

1. Disjunction between costs and revenues: rising and redundant costs
2. Internalities and organizational goals
3. Derived externalities
4. Distributional inequity (power and privileges)

Charles Wolf, Jr., *Markets or Governments: Choosing between Imperfect Alternatives* (Cambridge, Mass.: MIT Press, 1988): 85.

23. Gordon Tullock, *Private Wants, Public Needs: An Economic Analysis of the Desirable Scope of Government* (New York: Basic Books, 1970): vi.

24. B. Caillaud, R. Guesnarie, P. Rey, and J. Tirole, "Government Intervention in Production and Incentives Theory: A Review of Recent Contributions," *RAND Journal of Economics* 19, no. 1 (Spring 1988): 23.

25. Mohsin S. Khan, "Macroeconomic Adjustment in Developing Countries: A Policy Perspective," *World Bank Research Observer* 2, no. 1 (January 1987): 37–38.

26. Paul A. Samuelson, "The Economic Role of Private Activity," in Joseph E. Stiglitz, ed., *The Collected Scientific Papers of Paul A. Samuelson* (Cambridge, Mass.: MIT Press, 1966): 1423.

NOTES TO CHAPTER 2

1. Terms such as "Indian" and even "indigenous" are offensive to some people. To Fausto Reinaga, for example, "Indian is a defamatory word. It defames the person who pronounces it and it defames the person against whom it is pronounced. White racism has injected the venom of racial hate into the conscious and subconscious mind, into the knowledge and customs of the peoples of the world. . . . A nauseating term that today flows through mestizo politics." Fausto Reinaga, *El Pensamiento Amáutico* (La Paz: Ediciones PIB [Partido Indio de Bolivia], 1978): 98, 102, my translation.

Unfortunately, I know of no convenient and widely accepted substitute. People who dislike one term prefer another (Reinaga uses *indio*), so I will follow common usage in Bolivia and employ "indigenous" and "Indians" interchangeably. Similar remarks apply to the use of terms such as "mestizo," "white," "black," and "mulatto."

2. This estimate comes from Dick E. Ibarra Grasso, *Pueblos Indígenas de Bolivia* (La Paz: Librería Editorial Juventud, 1985): 50. The 1976 census categorized 32.7 percent of the population as "white and mestizo (speak only Spanish)." Since, according to the census, 10.1 percent of the population did not yet speak any language, the correct estimate of the proportion of speakers who speak only Spanish is 36.4 percent. Ibarra Grasso points out that some of them are ethnically "indigenous" people who have given up the language of their ancestors.

3. Estimates of Bolivia's infant mortality range from 113 to 169 per thousand—both much higher than other Latin American countries—but among rural indigenous peoples in Bolivia the rate probably exceeds 200 per thousand.

4. Ricardo Godoy, *Peasant Mining in Highland Bolivia* (Cambridge, Mass.: Harvard Institute for International Development, 1988).

5. Preston S. Pattie et al., *Agricultural Sector Assessment for Bolivia* (La Paz: U.S. Agency for International Development, January 1988): 63. This paragraph also draws on Th. Hatzius, *The Agricultural Sector within a Development Strategy for Bolivia* (Heidelberg: Research Centre for International Agrarian Development, October 1987).

6. Pattie et al., *Agricultural Sector Assessment*, 54–55.

7. Harold Osborne, *Bolivia: A Divided Land* (London: Institute of International Affairs, 1964), cited in Spanish in Eduardo Arze Cuadros, *La Economía de Bolivia: Ordenamiento Territorial y Dominación Externa, 1492–1979* (La Paz: Los Amigos del Libro, 1979): 66. Being unable to locate the original, I have converted Arze's translation back into English. [For the Spanish translation: "El elaborado sistema de irrigación y la organización del trabajo colectivo para el transporte de piedras, cultivos y recolección, fue desorganizado y cayó en decadencia, de manera que después de haber sido bajo los Incas una de las tecnologías más avazadas que haya conocido el mundo, la agricultura boliviana se transformó, y se ha mantenido hasta este día, astrasada, primitiva, de subsistencia."]

8. For example, William L. Rodgers and Jonathan E. Smith, *MACA Restructuring Report* (La Paz: U.S. Agency for International Development, August 1987). For examples of such problems handicapping rural development, see World Bank Operations Evaluation Department, *Project Performance Audit Report. Bolivia. Ingavi Rural Development Project, Ulla Ulla Rural Development Project, Omasuyos-Los Andes Rural Development Project* (Washington, D.C., September 1988).

9. Pattie et al., *Agricultural Sector Assessment*, 118, 74.

10. All dollar amounts refer to U.S. dollars.

11. World Bank, *Transport Sector Strategy Paper* (Washington, D.C., 1987), para. 1.21.

12. David Morawetz, *After Tin and Natural Gas, What? Bolivia's Exports and Medium Term Economic Strategy: Prospects, Problems and Policy Options* (Washing-

ton, D.C.: World Bank, August 1986): Table 4. Morawetz concluded: "The difficulty and high cost of shipping goods from Bolivian production centres to markets in the United States, Europe and Latin America is the single most important
problem hindering ALL of Bolivia's exports. Certainly, it rules out manufacturing
exports from the start" (p. 28, emphasis in original).

13. Catherine J. Allen, *The Hold Life Has: Coca and Cultural Identity in an
Andean Community* (Washington, D.C.: Smithsonian Institution Press, 1988): 32.

14. *Presencia* (La Paz), 7 December 1989, 7.

15. *The Economist* (8 October 1988, 22) gives a guess of $375 million for
1987, whereas Samuel Doria Medina estimates the Bolivian value added of cocaine in 1985 as between $367 million and $489 million. Doria estimates that
another $2 billion in coca-related earnings left the country in 1985. Samuel Doria
Medina, *La Economía Informal en Bolivia* (La Paz: Editorial Offset Boliviana, 1986):
175.

16. The prices at Eteramazama are much higher than at the other two
centers—in March 1988, two times higher.

17. Doria Medina, *La Economía Informal*, p. 90.

18. U.S. Agency for International Development, "Micro and Small Enterprise Development Project," Project Paper (La Paz, August 1988): 99.

19. The Economist Intelligence Unit, *Country Profile, Bolivia, 1989–1990*
(London: Economist, 1990).

20. Paul P. Streeten, *What Price Food? Agricultural Price Policies in De-
veloping Countries* (London: Macmillan, 1987); Kevin M. Cleaver, "The Impact of
Price and Exchange Rate Policies on Agriculture in Sub-Saharan Africa," World
Bank Staff Working Paper no. 728 (Washington, D.C.: World Bank, April 1985).

NOTES TO CHAPTER 3

1. Repeatedly buying milk from the same supplier might be a solution.
Apparently, the variation in milk quality at each stage was so large that the buyer
could never be sure that a particular instance of low quality reflected cheating by
the seller or that the milk in the market that day was simply of low quality (or the
actions of previous sellers had rendered it so). We will discuss repeat buying later
in the chapter.

2. For some goods and services, consumers can judge quality before a
purchase. For other goods and services, quality is readily ascertained soon after
the purchase but not before (as it is for canned goods). In still other cases, quality
is difficult to judge even long after the good or service is consumed (as it is for an
educational program). These three kinds of goods have been labeled "search
goods," "experience goods," and "credence goods" in the economics literature.
In what follows we focus on experience and credence goods, although the
dividing lines are imperfect. We will include some agricultural products that
would qualify as search goods if, before they were purchased, sufficient time and
funds were available to scrutinize them, but that become experience goods when
they are bought without being examined individually in advance (for example,
bulk purchases of shrimp).

3. See, for example, J. M. Juran, "Quality Control and the National
Culture," in J. M. Juran, Frank M. Gryna, Jr., and R. F. Bingham, Jr., eds., *Quality
Control Handbook*, 3d ed. (New York: McGraw-Hill, 1974).

4. Consider, for example, the following questions. Why does every company not produce goods of the best quality? Why does every consumer not
procure goods of the very best kind? The answer is that at some point additional
increases in quality, although desirable, are not worth the associated increments
in cost. There is something like an optimal level of quality that considers costs as
well as benefits. (This point may seem more intuitive if one thinks of appropriate

technology: the optimal level of sophistication of a technology in a developing country is not necessarily "the most advanced"). Economic logic therefore suggests that a firm or a public enterprise should calculate an optimal level for the quality of its product, given its market possibilities and its cost structure. (For example, see James E. Austin, *Agribusiness Project Evaluation* [Baltimore, Md.: Johns Hopkins University Press, 1981]: 90 ff.) This is an important calculation, but it is not the problem of "quality and markets" that we shall examine.

5. See, for example, the case studies and generalizations from Japan in JETRO, *Productivity and Quality Control: The Japanese Experience*, Now in Japan, no. 30 (Tokyo: JETRO, 1981).

6. Edward E. Lawler III and Susan A. Mohrman, "Quality Circles after the Fad," *Harvard Business Review* 85, no. 1 (January-February 1985): 65–71.

7. Onid Knudsen and John Nash, with contributions by James Bovard, Bruce Gardner, and L. Alan Winters, "Redefining the Role of Government in Agriculture for the 1990s," Discussion Paper no. 105 (Washington, D.C.: World Bank, November 1990): 3. The authors do a brilliant job of describing nonmarket failures—that is, the shortcomings of government intervention—but disappoint by simply assuming that, left alone, the market would hum along in textbook optimality.

8. William O. Jones, *Marketing Staple Food Crops in Tropical Africa* (Ithaca, N.Y.: Cornell University Press, 1972): 104; Jones cites George J. Stigler, "Competition," *International Encyclopedia of the Social Sciences*, vol. 3, ed. D. L. Sills (New York: Macmillan, 1968).

9. See, for example, George S. Tolley, Vinod Thomas, and Chung Ming Wong, *Agricultural Pricing Policies and the Developing Countries* (Baltimore, Md.: Johns Hopkins University Press, 1982).

10. Bohannan and Dalton's collection of twenty-eight case studies of local marketing in Africa underlines the theme of traders-as-exploiters. P. Bohannan and G. Dalton, eds., *Markets in Africa* (Evanston, Ill.: Northwestern University Press, 1962).

11. Paul A. Baran, *The Political Economy of Growth* (New York: Monthly Review Press, 1957): 171.

12. Consider, for example, this account from Nicaragua: "Ten days of better-build-an-ark rains (21 inches in one day alone!) struck Nicaragua's Pacific coast in late May 1982. . . . Arriving the day after the rains, I found a country outraged at the opportunistic hoarding and speculation by private merchants, especially wholesalers. Public sentiment was so strong that it was easy for the government to move quickly and decisively. The day after I arrived the national police were authorized to inspect food prices and arrest speculators." Joseph Collins, with Frances Moore Lappé and Nick Allen, *What Difference Could a Revolution Make? Food and Farming in the New Nicaragua* (San Francisco: Institute for Food and Development Policy, 1982): 138.

13. For example, Jones, *Marketing Staple Food Crops*; P. T. Bauer, *West African Trade: A Study in Competition, Oligopoly and Monopoly in a Changing Economy*, rev. ed. (London: Routledge and Kegan Paul, 1963); Polly Hill, "Markets in Africa," *Journal of Modern African Studies* 1, no. 1 (December 1963): 441–54; Uma J. Lele, "The Role of Credit and Marketing in Agricultural Development," in *Nural Islam*, ed., *Agricultural Policy in Developing Countries* (London: Macmillan, 1974): 413–41; John W. Mellor et al., *Developing Rural India* (Ithaca, N.Y.: Cornell University Press, 1968): chaps. 12–14. Barbara Harriss criticizes the statistical and logical arguments used by Jones and others in "There Is a Method in My Madness: Or Is It Vice Versa? Measuring Agricultural Marketing Performance," *Food Research Institute Studies* 17, no. 2 (1979): 197–218.

14. Even when traders' margins at first appear high, they often include credit and other services and therefore are "reasonable." For example, in research on the Pakistani shrimp industry (summarized below), several colleagues and I examined the economic role of the middlemen called "mole holders." The

twenty-three mole holders took shrimp from the fishermen, weighed it, and auctioned it to the shrimp processors. This seemed a simple task, and for carrying it out, the mole holders received a commission of 3 percent. This seemed unreasonably high. It turned out, however, that the mole holders had another economic function. Each had his regular suppliers. To about nine-tenths of these fishermen, the mole holder gave credit for fuel, ice, and repairs. My colleagues and I calculated the ratio of the total commission received to the total credit outstanding. It worked out to quite a reasonable implicit interest rate of about 10 percent per year.

Basu cites several examples of similar phenomena in India. In one case, employers in Kerala gave interest-free loans to fishermen on the condition that they would not desert their employers during the peak season. A penalty was imposed if they deserted. Kaushik Basu, "Rural Credit Markets: The Structure of Interest Rates, Exploitation, and Efficiency," in Pranab Bardhan, ed., *The Economic Theory of Agrarian Institutions* (Oxford: Clarendon Press, 1989): 165n. For a general analysis of buyers who offer credit, see Clive Bell and T. N. Srinivasan, "Some Aspects of Linked Product and Credit Market Contracts among Risk-Neutral Agents," in Bardhan, *The Economic Theory of Agrarian Institutions*, 221–36.

15. Baran, *The Political Economy of Growth*, 171.

16. Edward S. Mason, *Promoting Economic Development* (Claremont, Calif.: Claremont College, 1955): 46.

17. Uma Lele, *The Design of Rural Development: Lessons from Africa* (Baltimore, Md.: Johns Hopkins University Press, 1975): 114.

18. Ibid., 114.

19. Joseph E. Stiglitz, "Rational Peasants, Efficient Institutions, and a Theory of Rural Organization: Methodological Remarks for Development Economics," in Bardhan, *The Economic Theory of Agrarian Institutions*, 23.

20. Harold F. Breimyer, *Economics of the Product Markets of Agriculture* (Ames: Iowa State University Press, 1976): 138.

21. Bruce F. Johnston and Peter Kilby, *Agricultural and Structural Transformation: Economic Strategy for Late-Developing Countries* (New York: Oxford University Press, 1975): 51, see also 46–47.

22. Theodore W. Schultz, *Transforming Traditional Agriculture* (New Haven, Conn.: Yale University Press, 1964): 118.

23. Based on an interview with a Zambian official who wished to remain anonymous, August 1987. For a longer account, see my teaching case "Fighting Consumer Exploitation in Zambia" (Cambridge, Mass.: Harvard University, Kennedy School of Government, 1984).

24. For example, the price per kilogram ranged from kwacha 0.65 to 2.00 for onions, K4.00 to K6.60 for "ordinary mince," and from K0.50 to K2.00 for tomatoes. (One kwacha was then worth about $0.56.)

25. "[W]eek-to-week price changes showed signs of serious random disturbances consistent with the hypothesis that traders were poorly informed about episodic changes in the conditions of supply and transport." William O. Jones, "Measuring the Effectiveness of Agricultural Marketing in Contributing to Economic Development: Some African Examples," *Food Research Institute Studies in Agricultural Economics, Trade and Development* 9, no. 3 (1970); cited in Harold M. Riley and Michael T. Weber, "Marketing in Developing Countries," Working Paper no. 6, Rural Development Series (East Lansing: Michigan State University, Department of Agricultural Economics, 1979): 11. Jones cites a number of studies showing "defective market information" in Nigerian and other African markets in *Marketing Staple Food Crops in Tropical Africa*, esp. chaps. 6, 9, and 10.

26. John Kenneth Galbraith and Richard H. Holton, in collaboration with Robert E. Branson, Jean Ruth Robinson, and Carolyn Shaw Bell, *Marketing Efficiency in Puerto Rico* (Cambridge, Mass.: Harvard University Press, 1955): 192–93.

27. Barrington Moore, Jr., *Social Origins of Dictatorship and Democracy: Lord and Peasant in the Modern World* (Boston: Beacon Press, 1966): 467.

28. "The volume of market exchange rises more rapidly than the production of final goods and services owing to (a) the gradual but uninterrupted transfer of function from the household to the market and (b) rising trade in intermediate goods and services that is associated with advancing producer specialization." Johnston and Kilby, *Agriculture and Structural Transformation*, 42.

29. This is true in a broader sense than may be conveyed by this statement by agricultural marketing expert Martin Kriesberg: "Often marketing institutions in developing countries lag behind other programs, even where capital is readily available for marketing facilities, because trained personnel are not available to help staff them. As marketing institutions become more complex—taking on more activities over larger geographical areas, involving more products and people as well as capital—the task of management grows more difficult. In most developing countries, there has been little training in specific marketing functions or in the management of agribusiness firms performing them." Better marketing institutions include a wide variety of informational systems and devices to help overcome problems of quality in markets. Martin Kriesberg, "Marketing Efficiency in Developing Countries," in Dov Izraeli, Dafna N. Izraeli, and Frank Meissner, eds., *Marketing Systems for Developing Countries* (New York: John Wiley & Sons, 1976): 28.

30. Joseph E. Stiglitz and Andrew Weiss, "Credit Rationing in Markets with Imperfect Information," *American Economic Review* 71, no. 3 (June 1981): 393–410.

31. Richard A. Posner, "A Theory of Primitive Society, with Special Reference to Law," *Journal of Law and Economics* 23, no. 1 (1980): 25.

32. Ibid., 25–27. See also Colin Camerer, "Gifts as Economic and Social Symbols," *American Journal of Sociology* 94, Supplement (1988): S180–S214.

33. Clifford Geertz, "The Bazaar Economy: Information and Search in Peasant Marketing," *American Economic Review Papers and Proceedings* 68, no. 2 (May 1978): 30.

34. Ibid., 29.

35. Douglass C. North, "A Framework for Analyzing the State in Economic History," *Explorations in Economic History* 16 (1979): 254. See also the work of Vernon W. Ruttan and his colleagues, summarized in Ruttan, "Institutional Innovation and Agricultural Development," *World Development* 17, no. 9 (September 1989): 1375–87.

36. George A. Akerlof, "The Market for 'Lemons': Quality Uncertainty and the Market Mechanism," *Quarterly Journal of Economics* 84, no. 3 (August 1970): 488.

37. Michael Rothschild and Joseph E. Stiglitz "Equilibrium in Competitive Insurance Markets: An Essay on the Economics of Imperfect Information," *Quarterly Journal of Economics* 90, no. 4 (November 1976): 648.

38. Charles Stuart, "Consumer Protection in Markets in Informationally Weak Buyers," *Bell Journal of Economics* 12, no. 2 (Autumn 1981): 570.

39. For example, Bruce Greenwald, *The Labor Market as a Market for Lemons* (New York: Garland, 1979); Andrew Weiss, "Job Queues and Layoffs in Labor Markets," *Journal of Political Economy* 88, no. 3 (May-June 1980): esp. 533–55; Charles Wilson, "The Nature of Equilibrium in Markets with Adverse Selection," *Bell Journal of Economics* 11 (Spring 1980): 108–30; Boyan Jovanovic, "Favorable Selection with Asymmetric Information," *Quarterly Journal of Economics* 97, no. 3 (August 1982): 535–39; Stuart, "Consumer Protection"; Lawrence R. Glosten and Paul R. Milgrom, "Bid, Ask and Transaction Prices in a Specialist Market with Heterogeneously Informed Traders," *Journal of Financial Economics* 14, no. 1, (March 1985): 71–100. Jean Tirole's magisterial text consolidates this vast literature: *The Theory of Industrial Organization* (Cambridge, Mass.: MIT Press, 1988).

40. An exception is the pioneering work of Joseph E. Stiglitz, who reflects on the importance of the economics of information for development theory in many articles, including "The New Development Economics," *World Development* 15, no. 2 (February 1986); "Economic Organization, Information and Development," in Hollis Chenery and T. N. Srinivasan, eds., *Handbook of Development Economics*, vol. 1 (Amsterdam: Elsevier, 1988); and "Markets, Market Failures, and Development," *American Economic Review Papers and Proceedings* 79, no. 2 (May 1989): 197–203. After I wrote this chapter, two compendia of interest became available: Bardhan, *The Economic Theory of Agrarian Institutions*, which includes several papers cited elsewhere in this chapter; and a special issue of *World Development* 17, no. 9 (September 1989), on the so-called new institutional economics and development. The literature so far is largely theoretical. Stiglitz and others call for further study of ways that governments (and collective action) can improve malfunctioning markets—and of ways to mitigate the defects of those very interventions: which are two of the subjects of this book.

41. Akerlof, "Market for 'Lemons'," 488. See also John W. Pratt, David A. Wise, and Richard J. Zeckhauser, "Price Differences in Almost Competitive Markets," *Quarterly Journal of Economics* 93, no. 2 (May 1979): 189–211; Charles Wilson, "The Nature of Equilibrium in Markets with Adverse Selection," *Bell Journal of Economics* 11, no. 1 (Spring 1980): 108–30.

42. By "effective information" I mean to include the costs of gathering information, processing it, and understanding what is being processed. It is possible that two participants in the market could obtain information about quality at the same cost. Nonetheless, if the first participant is more astute or better trained than the second, his cost of additional units of effective knowledge would, in some meaningful sense, be lower.

43. Keith B. Leffler, "Ambiguous Changes in Product Quality," *American Economic Review* 72, no. 5 (December 1982): 965.

44. Stiglitz and Weiss, "Credit Rationing," 409.

NOTES TO CHAPTER 4

1. An excellent analysis is Samuel Paul's three-part teaching case, "The National Dairy Development Board" (Cambridge: Harvard University, Kennedy School of Government, 1980). A shorter discussion is contained in Paul's *Managing Development Programs: The Lessons of Success* (Boulder, Colo.: Westview, 1982).

2. In 1982 I visited an NDDB processing plant in Ahmedabad and examined the methods used to assess and reward quality. What a farmer received varied markedly with the quality of the milk he or she sold. For example, for 100 kilograms of milk with 3.0 percent butterfat and 8.0 percent solids nonfat (SNF), the price was Rs 168.66. But for milk with 3.5 percent butterfat and 8.5 percent SNF, the price was Rs 224.67. (The exchange rate was Rs 8.9 to the U.S. dollar.) The point of measuring and rewarding quality is not that each farmer should produce the "best" quality of milk. Rather, with appropriate information and quality-dependent pricing, producers can produce the best quality of milk given their cows, inputs, and labor.

3. Michael Halse, "Operation Flood II: The Evolution of a Rural Development Program," Appendix C in Ray A. Goldberg and Richard C. McGinity, *Agribusiness Management for Developing Countries—Southeast Asian Corn System and American and Japanese Trends Affecting It* (Cambridge, Mass.: Ballinger, 1979): 468.

4. George Mergos and Roger Slade, "Dairy Development and Milk Cooperatives: The Effects of a Dairy Project in India," Discussion Paper no. 15 (Washington, D.C.: World Bank, July 1987).

5. For an account of the managerial ingredients of the NDDB's success, see Paul, *Managing Development Programs*. An international leader of the co-op movement observed: "For many thousands of people from all over the world, Anand [the home of AMUL] has become a sort of Mecca to which to journey to have their faith in the cooperative idea strengthened and confirmed."

6. Mergos and Slade, "Dairy Development and Milk Cooperatives," 33.

7. In this case, the people buying and testing the milk had to be credible; their incentives to mislead the sellers had to be minimized. Being members of the same cooperative helped achieve this: a kind of vertical integration.

8. See Mergos and Slade, "Dairy Development and Milk Cooperatives," 18: "The changes perceived by farmers following the establishment of the DCS [dairy cooperative society] were mostly related to the milk market and to the price of milk."

9. For example, in January and February 1975, the average price for Pakistani 21/30 count, white, shell-on shrimp was $2.20 to $2.35 per kilogram. ("Count" refers to the number of shrimp in a kilogram and is thus a measure of shrimp size.) During the same period the average Japanese price for the same shrimp from Indonesia and India was about $2.80 per kilogram. In 1974 the United Nations Food and Agriculture Organization estimated an average difference of about $0.90 per kilogram between Pakistani shrimp and "similar products in the world markets." In April 1974 the processors issued a statement that Japanese buyers were paying 30 percent less than what was being paid for Indian or Indonesian shrimp.

10. The catch of white shrimp had dropped from 10.0 to 6.4 metric tons per year between 1971 and 1974. Over this same period the catch of the very small shrimp had increased from 3.7 to 5.6 metric tons.

11. For example, more shrimp were landed in June 1980 than in April or July, and in 1981 the catch for May was above that for January and only a little short of April's.

12. In fact, by the early 1980s some vertical integration had occurred. Some processors had purchased trawlers. Two mole holders had bought processing plants, and two processors had gone into mole holding. "In this way they can have their pick of the bigger shrimp and make more money," one processor told me in 1982.

13. A. H. Haquani, "Seafood Industry Headed for Doom?" *The Leader*, 30 March 1982, 3.

14. It remains unclear why importers could not use this device to punish poor quality. Perhaps it was easier to lower the import price itself, then keep the 5 percent in exchange for a deal to put 15 percent in non-Pakistani bank accounts. It is also true that gross violations of the kind noted by the FDA would involve losses well beyond 15 percent of the purchase price.

15. In 1982 the government's Certificate of Quality and Origin affirmed only that "this consignment at the time of our inspection was found to be wholesome and fit for human consumption. It is hygienically packed and is of Pakistan Origin."

NOTES TO CHAPTER 5

1. Hernando de Soto, in collaboration with E. Ghersi and M. Ghibellini, *El Otro Sendero: La Revolución Informal* (Buenos Aires: Editorial Sudamericana, 1987): esp. pp. 172–220.

2. Governments may have a role to play in helping such groups become established. For examples of successful public intervention, see Monika Huppi and Gershon Feder, "The Role of Groups and Credit Cooperatives in Rural Lending," *World Bank Research Observer* 5, no. 2 (July 1990): 187–204.

3. Mihail C. Demetrescu, "Comparative Marketing Systems—Conceptual Outline," in Dov. Izraeli, Dafna N. Izraeli, and Frank Meissner, eds., *Marketing Systems for Developing Countries* (New York: John Wiley & Sons, 1976): 111–12.

4. *Cameroon: Agricultural Sector Report,* Report no. 7486-CAM, vol. 1: Main Report (Washington, D.C.: World Bank, November 1989): 73.

5. See, for example, Robert H. Bates, "The Private Sector: The Regulation of Rural Markets in Africa," AID Evaluation Special Study no. 14 (Washington, D.C.: U.S. Agency for International Development, June 1983). Also, the remarkable essay by Odin Knudsen and John Nash, with contributions by James Bovard, Bruce Gardner, and L. Alan Winters, "Redefining the Role of Government in Agriculture for the 1990s," Discussion Paper no. 105 (Washington, D.C.: World Bank, November 1990): esp. 49–82.

6. Clifford Geertz, "The Bazaar Economy: Information and Search in Peasant Marketing," *American Economic Review Papers and Proceedings* 68, no. 2 (May 1978): 29.

7. "To be sure, to the extent which it is derived from direct exploitation of the peasantry, the maintenance of the superabundant mercantile population is supported from the same source. Yet to a large extent it is based on transfers of surplus appropriated by other classes: landowners, foreign enterprises, and domestic industrialists. The diversion of this surplus to the upkeep of a parasitic stratum constitutes a significant drain on capital accumulation." Paul A. Baran, *The Political Economy of Growth* (New York: Monthly Review Press, 1957): 173.

8. Harold M. Riley and Michael T. Weber, "Marketing in Developing Countries," MSU Rural Development Series Working Paper no. 6 (East Lansing: Michigan State University, Department of Agricultural Economics, 1979): 7, 11, 13.

9. Steven Salop and Joseph E. Stiglitz, "The Theory of Sales: A Simple Model of Equilibrium Price Dispersion with Identical Agents," *American Economic Review* 72, no. 5 (December 1982): 1129.

10. Sometimes sellers will include a coupon or chit that is good for a discount on the second purchase of the product. Such practices are analyzed in Jacques Crémer, "On the Economics of Repeat Buying," *Rand Journal of Economics* 15, no. 3 (Autumn 1984): 396–403.

11. Only with an identifiable product will the happy results of quality competition cited by J. M. Juran actually ensue: "In the capitalistic economies, the income of the enterprise is determined by its ability to sell its products, whether directly to users or through an intermediate merchant chain. If poor quality results in excessive returns, claims, or inability to sell the product, the manufacturer stops production until he is able to remedy the poor quality. This severe and direct impact of poor quality on the manufacturer's income has the useful by-product of forcing manufacturers to keep improving their market research and early warning signals, so as to be able to respond promptly in case of trouble." J. M. Juran, "Quality Control and the National Culture," in J. M. Juran, Frank M. Gryna, Jr., and R. F. Bingham, Jr., eds., *Quality Control Handbook,* 3d ed. (New York: McGraw Hill, 1974): 48–49.

12. Mancur Olson, *The Logic of Collective Action* (Cambridge, Mass.: Harvard University Press, 1965).

13. The vast literature on market signaling began with A. Michael Spence, *Market Signaling* (Cambridge, Mass.: Harvard University Press, 1974). A recent review is that by Joseph Stiglitz and Andrew Weiss, "Sorting Out the Differences between Screening and Signaling Models," in M. Bachrach, ed., *Oxford Essays in Mathematical Economics* (Oxford: Oxford University Press, 1991).

14. On the role of reputations in markets, see, for example, Franklin Allen, "Reputation and Product Quality," *Rand Journal of Economics* 15, no. 3 (Autumn 1984): 311–27; and H. Lorne Carmichael, "Reputations in Labor Markets," *American Economic Review* 74, no. 4 (September 1984): 713–25.

15. Barry Newman, "Consumer Protection Is Underdeveloped in the Third World," *Wall Street Journal,* 9 April 1981, 23.

16. Oliver E. Williamson analyzed hierarchical arrangements in business as a response to asymmetric information and the resulting adverse incentives; see *Markets and Hierarchies* (New York: Free Press, 1975). See also Alfred Chandler's history of the rise of vertically integrated organizations, *The Visible Hand* (Cambridge, Mass.: Belknap Press, 1977).

17. An analysis of the practical advantages and disadvantages of vertical integration appears in Michael Porter, *Competitive Strategy* (New York: Free Press, 1980): chap. 10. See also Chapter 9 below.

18. John Kenneth Galbraith and Richard H. Holton, in collaboration with Robert E. Branson, Jean Ruth Robinson, and Carolyn Shaw Bell, *Marketing Efficiency in Puerto Rico* (Cambridge, Mass.: Harvard University Press, 1955): 179.

19. Nancy E. Bocksteel, "The Welfare Implications of Minimum Quality Standards," *American Journal of Agricultural Economics* 66, no. 4 (November 1984): 466–71.

20. Geoffrey S. Shepherd and Gene A. Futrell, *Marketing Farm Products: Economic Analysis,* 7th ed. (Ames: Iowa State University Press, 1982): 185–86.

21. Ibid., 193–94.

22. Operations Evaluation Department, *Agricultural Marketing: The World Bank's Experience, 1974–85,* (Washington, D.C.: World Bank, July 1990): 64.

NOTES TO CHAPTER 6

1. Gordon Tullock, *Private Wants, Public Needs: An Economic Analysis of the Desirable Scope of Government* (New York: Basic Books, 1970): vi, 69.

2. I have only dipped into this fascinating stream. Thomas M. Callaghy's brilliant article, "The State and the Development of Capitalism in Africa: Theoretical, Historical, and Comparative Reflections," suggests how much is to be learned from it (in Donald Rothchild and Naomi Chazan, eds., *The Precarious Balance: State and Society in Africa* [Boulder and London: Westview, 1988]: 67–99). Of particular relevance to today's "developing countries" are Max Weber's classic works on the conditions under which various roles of the state lead to various genres of capitalism. They include *Economy and Society* (Berkeley and Los Angeles: University of California Press, 1978) and *General Economic History* (New Brunswick, N.J.: Transaction Books, 1981).

NOTES TO CHAPTER 7

1. The multiple in Equatorial Guinea in 1985 was about 2. One could not be sure because statistics for both population and national income were uncertain. In its sample of countries, the IMF study found multiples averaging 6.1 for African countries and 4.4 for all developing nations. Nor was Equatorial Guinea's number of government employees particularly large compared to its population and income level: the number was almost exactly that predicted by the IMF study's best regression equation for small nations. Peter S. Heller and Alan A. Tait, *Government Employment and Pay: Some International Comparisons,* OP no. 24 (Washington, D.C.: International Monetary Fund, 1983).

2. The December 1986 draft, mostly crafted by U.N. consultants, anticipated approximately CFAF 23,000 million for salaries of foreign aid workers from 1986 to 1991. Over the same period the government's total investment budget was planned to be less than a quarter as large, CFAF 5,478 million. Although the document did mention that public pay was too low, none of its more than 100 contemplated aid projects would do anything about it.

3. Connoisseurs of irony will appreciate that, back home, the IMF's incentive myopia abates. During negotiations with the IMF in mid-1987, which included a requirement to cut the public payroll, Equatorial Guinea's finance minister received a letter from the head of the IMF's employees' association. It appealed for the Minister's support as a governor of the Fund for the association's plea for pay raises. Surely, the letter asserted, the minister must recognize the need for higher salaries to attract and retain only the best personnel. For more details about Equatorial Guinea, see Robert Klitgaard, *Tropical Gangsters* (New York: Basic Books, 1990).

4. Milton J. Esman and John D. Montgomery, "Administrative Implications of a Basic Needs Development Strategy in Nepal," (Kathmandu: United Nations Development Program, January 1988): 30.

5. Barbara Nunberg, "Public Sector Pay and Employment Policy Issues in Bank Lending: An Interim Review of Experience," draft report (Washington, D.C.: World Bank, 15 July 1987): 22.

6. D. C. E. Chew, "Internal Adjustments to Falling Civil Service Salary: Insights from Uganda," *World Development* 18, no. 7 (July 1990).

7. Arturo Israel, *Institutional Development: Incentives to Performance* (Baltimore, Md.: Johns Hopkins University Press, 1987): 126. The author continued: "A strong argument can be made in many developing countries that high unemployment among unskilled workers is caused by keeping wages at inflated levels for political or social reasons. But with skilled workers and some professional and especially managerial workers the issue is exactly the opposite: political and other social factors have kept their salaries lower than their equilibrium price. This situation . . . is nowhere more pervasive than in the public sector, where attempts to reduce the difference between the highest and lowest remunerations are more intense. Such wage distortions help explain one of the most intractable problems in developing countries, that of attracting and retaining high-quality staff" (p. 126).

8. Nunberg, "Public Sector Pay," 7, 24, 1.

9. West Africa Regional Office, "Technical Assistance and Training: Proposals for Increased Effectiveness," Report of a Regional Task Force (Washington, D.C.: World Bank, November 1986): 2, emphasis in original.

10. Nunberg, "Public Sector Pay," 39. Despite Israel's assertion cited above that pay distortions are a key obstacle to institutional development, he tended to play down financial incentives in favor of professionalization and socialization, without (in my opinion) convincing arguments or supporting data. See, for example, Israel, *Institutional Development*, 64–66, 131, 155.

11. Nunberg, "Public Sector Pay," 10n.

12. Martin L. Weitzman, *The Share Economy: Conquering Stagflation* (Cambridge, Mass.: Harvard University Press, 1984).

13. Alan S. Blinder, ed., *Paying for Productivity: A Look at the Evidence* (Washington, D.C.: Brookings Institution, 1990).

14. For an excellent discussion of the paradigm and its practical problems, see Arnold J. Harberger, "Reflections on Social Project Evaluation," with comments by Partha Dasgupta and Deepak Lal, in Gerald M. Meier, ed., *Pioneers in Development, Second Series* (New York: Oxford University Press, 1987): 151–202.

15. Mancur Olson emphasizes the inherent difficulties of measuring results in the case of public services (for example, *Beyond the Measuring Rod of Money*, forthcoming, chap. 4).

16. For example, an experienced colleague comments that the crisis in public sector incentives is indeed severe in Kenya, a country he knows well. But he avers that in that country "cultural barriers" rule out linking reward and achievement in the public sector.

17. Herbert H. Meyer, "The Pay-for-Performance Dilemma," in Mary G. Minor and John B. Minor, eds., *Policy Issues in Contemporary Personnel and Industrial Relations* (New York: Macmillan, 1977).

18. The argument throughout is one of degree. I am not contending that merit pay in itself is better than other methods of financial reward, nor that financial reward would be the ideal method of motivating public servants, particularly in social services. But many poor countries have fallen off the charts with regard to financial incentives, and the results have been devastating.

Similarly, no doubt in many poor nations government spending needs trimming, and large budget deficits cannot persist. But faced with external economic disequilibriums, it turns out that many poor countries are "correcting" their deficits incorrectly.

19. Neither is employee participation the answer; without incentives, research shows that it, too, tends to fail. "The postulated link between participation and improved efficiency is one of information. . . . To an economist it should not be surprising to find that participatory arrangements, such as quality circles, that are designed to elicit better information from workers without offering any stake in the returns to such information are usually short-lived." (Daniel I. Levine and Laura D'Andrea Tyson, "Participation, Productivity, and the Firm's Environment," in Blinder, ed., *Paying for Productivity,* 186.)

20. For example, as a condition of an export rehabilitation project in Ghana, the World Bank required that the powerful Cocoa Marketing Board lay off a fifth of its employees. Cocobod complied in 1986 and the cost was the remarkable sum of $20 million over a three-year period.

21. Nunberg notes that "Bank sector work has not, by and large, carefully analyzed the connections between public employment reductions and the capacity of either agriculture or the urban labor market to absorb fired government workers. Nor has it assessed the capacity of specific sectors to take on surplus civil servants, or the mechanisms whereby such a redeployment could take place. Such analyses would appear to be specifically important where the private sector is weak." ("Public Sector Pay," 43) The issue simply has not seemed important to many donors and governments; for a stark contrast, see Donald S. Perkins's description of the efforts made by some private companies in the United States to help displaced workers. "What Can CEOs Do for Displaced Workers?" *Harvard Business Review,* 65, no. 6 November-December 1987): 90–93.

22. Esman and Montgomery, "Administrative Implications," 53.

23. Ledivina C. Cariño, "How Can We Use the Bureaucracy We Now Have? Issues as We Search for Means to Set the Public Servant Moving," Occasional Paper no. 86-4 (Manila: College of Public Administration, University of the Philippines, August 1986): 10. Surprisingly, despite their recognition of the poor working conditions and low levels of public pay in poor countries, the World Bank reports by Nunberg, "Public Sector Pay," and the West Africa Regional Office, "Technical Assistance and Training," both overlook the need to link rewards with results.

24. Samuel Paul's path-breaking works on successful public programs in poor countries concluded that economic incentives for public servants may be more effective in economic sectors than in social programs. Nonetheless, even in family planning and health care, successful managers staked out a few, clear objectives among the many and vague possibilities and created rapid, simple, and relevant information systems. See his *Managing Development Programs: Lessons from Success* (Boulder, Colo.: Westview, 1982); and *Strategic Management of Development Programmes,* Management Development Series no. 19 (Geneva: International Labour Office, 1983).

25. Herbert Simon, "Management of Productive Enterprises," (Unpublished ms., September 1987): 11, 17, 9, 12.

26. For a review of the "First World" evidence on employee participation in pay-for-performance schemes, see Levine and Tyson, "Participation, Productivity, and the Firm's Environment," in Blinder, *Paying for Productivity.*

27. A valuable source of ideas is Ronald A. Berk, ed., *Performance Assessment: Methods and Applications* (Baltimore, Md.: Johns Hopkins University Press, 1986).

28. James Q. Wilson, *Bureaucracy: What Government Agencies Do and Why They Do It* (New York: Basic Books, 1989): chap. 9.

29. Paul, *Managing Development Programs.*

30. Samuel Paul, "Accountability in Public Services: Exit, Voice and Capture," CECPS Discussion Paper (Washington, D.C.: World Bank, October 1990): 46.

31. See Linda Darling-Hammond and Barnett Berry, *The Evolution of Teacher Policy* (Santa Monica, Calif.: Rand Corporation, March 1988): 51–68.

32. See Dwight Heald Perkins, "Reforming China's Economic System," *Journal of Economic Literature,* 26, no. 2 (June 1988).

33. For an analysis of a successful Chinese case involving incentive wages, bonuses, and promotion schemes coupled with participatory management, see Anthony Y.C. Koo, "The Contract Responsibility System: Transition from a Planned to a Market Economy," *Economic Development and Cultural Change,* 38, no. 4 (July 1990): 797-820.

34. Rosabeth Moss Kanter, *When Giants Learn to Dance: Mastering the Challenge of Strategy, Management, and Careers in the 1990s* (New York: Simon and Schuster, 1989): chap. 9.

35. Arturo Israel offers fascinating insights into the ways that the nature of the work and the availability of information about its results provide what might be called intrinsic incentives (*Institutional Development,* esp. chap. 5).

36. David J. Gould, *Bureaucratic Corruption and Underdevelopment in the Third World: The Case of Zaire* (New York: Pergamon Press, 1980): 71.

37. In Equatorial Guinea, for example, 10 percent of the salaries paid to foreigners working on aid projects would constitute over 25 percent of the entire public payroll.

38. Gabriel Roth, *The Private Provision of Public Services in Developing Countries* (New York: Oxford University Press, 1987).

39. As Charles Wolf, Jr., recognizes in the text but not in the title of his *Markets or Governments: Choosing between Imperfect Alternatives* (Cambridge, Mass.: MIT Press, 1988).

40. Deepak Lal, *The Poverty of "Development Economics"* (Cambridge, Mass.: Harvard University Press, 1985): 107, referring to Frances Stewart and Paul Streeten, "New Strategies for Development: Poverty, Income Distribution, and Growth," in Streeten, ed., *Development Perspectives,* (London: Macmillan, 1981).

NOTES TO CHAPTER 8

1. Jane Perlez, "As Tanzania Debates Corruption, Officials Say It Makes Ends Meet," *New York Times,* 4 March 1990, 8.

2. Marta Altolaguirre, "Cuando Sucede . . . ," *La Prensa* (Guatemala City), 22 February 1990, my translation.

3. Robert Wade, "The Market for Public Office: Why the Indian State Is Not Better at Development," *World Development* 13, no. 4 (1985): 480.

4. Jean-François Bayart, *L'État en Afrique: La Politique du Ventre* (Paris: Fayard, 1989): esp. 87–138. See also Mark Gallagher, *Rent-Seeking and Economic Growth in Africa* (Boulder, Colo.: Westview, forthcoming).

5. United Nations, *Corruption in Government,* TCD/SEM. 90/2 INT-89-R56 (New York: United Nations Department of Technical Co-operation for Development, 1990): 4, 6, 12.

6. United Nations, *Corruption in Government,* 12.

7. Susan Rose-Ackerman, *Corruption: A Study in Political Economy,* (New York: Academic Press, 1978); T. N. Srinivasan, "Neoclassical Political Economy, the State and Economic Development," *Asian Development Review* 3, no. 2 (1985);

Robert P. Inman, "Markets, Government, and the 'New' Political Economy," in Alan J. Auerbach and Martin Feldstein, eds., *Handbook of Public Economics*, vol. 2 (Amsterdam: North-Holland, 1987); and Gerald M. Meier, ed., *Politics and Policy Making in Developing Countries: Perspectives on the New Political Economy* (San Francisco: ICS Press, 1991).

8. Paul Milgrom and John Roberts, "An Economic Approach to Influence Activities in Organizations," *American Journal of Sociology* 94, Supplement (1988); Paul Milgrom, "Efficient Contracts, Influence Activities, and Efficient Organizational Design," *Journal of Political Economy* 96, no. 1 (1988).

9. For example, David J. Gould, *Bureaucratic Corruption and Underdevelopment in the Third World: The Case of Zaire* (New York: Pergamon Press, 1980); Marcela Márquez, Carmen Antony, José Antonio Pérez, and Aida S. de Palacios, *La Corrupción Administrativa en Panamá* (Panama City: Instituto de Criminología, Universidad de Panamá, 1984); John T. Noonan, Jr., *Bribes* (New York: Macmillan, 1984); Ledivina V. Cariño, ed., *Bureaucratic Corruption in Asia: Causes, Consequences, and Controls* (Quezon City, Philippines: JMC Press, 1986); and Robert Klitgaard, *Controlling Corruption* (Berkeley and Los Angeles: University of California Press, 1988).

10. David J. Gould and José A. Amaro-Reyes, *The Effects of Corruption on Administrative Performance: Illustrations from Developing Countries*, World Bank Staff Working Paper no. 580, Management and Development Series (Washington, D.C., 1983): abstract, 34.

11. Another example is an article by the Bangladeshi economist Harendra Kanti Dey: "Understanding the microeconomic basis of corruption is the aim of this paper, not suggesting ways of fighting it. Yet a few remarks about the general lines of attack seem to be in order"; followed by a paragraph of schematic advice. "The Genesis and Spread of Economic Corruption: A Microtheoretic Interpretation," *World Development* 17, no. 4 (April 1989): 510.

12. Gunnar Myrdal,"Corruption as a Hindrance to Modernization in South Asia," in Arnold J. Heidenheimer, Michael Johnson, and Victor T. LeVine, eds., *Political Corruption: A Handbook* (New Brunswick, N.J.: Transaction Publishers, 1989): 406–7 (this is an excerpt from Myrdal's *Asian Drama* [1968]).

13. A speech by S. Rajaratnam, in Arnold J. Heidenheimer, ed., *Political Corruption: Readings in Comparative Analysis* (New York: Holt, Rinehart & Winston, 1970): 542.

14. Ledivina V. Cariño, "Tonic or Toxic: The Effects of Graft and Corruption," in Cariño, *Bureaucratic Corruption in Asia*, 168.

15. Noonan, *Bribes*, 702–3.

16. Thomas C. Schelling, "Command and Control," in James W. McKie, ed., *Social Responsibility and the Business Predicament* (Washington, D.C.: Brookings Institution, 1974): 83–84.

17. For example, Stanley Karnow ascribes corruption in the Philippines to the *compradazgo* system, a ritual network of relatives and adopted relatives that commands the loyalty of Filipinos more than any formal institution, and the cultural trait of *utang na loob*, "the debt of gratitude." Stanley Karnow, *In Our Image: America's Empire in the Philippines* (New York: Random House, 1989).

18. Samuel Huntington, "Modernization and Corruption," in Monday U. Ekpo, ed., *Bureaucratic Corruption in Sub-Saharan Africa: Toward a Search for Causes and Consequences* (Washington, D.C.: University Press of America, 1979): 318 (this is an excerpt from Huntington's *Political Order in Changing Societies* [1968]). Weber was reluctant to attribute causation but was "inclined to think the importance of biological heredity was very great." Max Weber, *The Protestant Ethic and the Spirit of Capitalism*, trans. Talcott Parsons (New York: Charles Scribner's Sons, 1958 [1904–5]): 31.

19. See Klitgaard, *Controlling Corruption*, 7–9, 62–67.

20. More complicated versions of this calculation are presented in the literature on criminal behavior; for example, in James Q. Wilson and Richard J.

Herrnstein, *Crime and Human Nature* (New York: Simon and Schuster, 1985): 41–62 and 531–35.

21. Security expert Bob Curtis argues that only by changing employees' sense of identification with the organization could corruption be controlled. He recommended the participation of employees in managerial decisions. (*How to Keep Your Employees Honest* [New York: Lebbar-Friedman Books, 1979].)

22. The pioneering analysis of the supply and demand conditions is Rose-Ackerman, *Corruption*.

23. More generally, "by being party to contracts and being able to set rules and constraints, LDC governments can change the nature and role of transaction costs and information costs, either reducing their importance or magnifying them and thereby creating additional sources of opportunistic behavior." Mustapha K. Nabli and Jeffrey B. Nugent, "The New Institutional Economics and Its Applicability to Development," *World Development* 17, no. 9 (September 1989): 1341.

24. Useful references include Oliver Williamson, *The Economic Institutions of Capitalism* (New York: Free Press, 1985); Oliver Hart and Bengt Holmstrom, "The Theory of Contracts," in Truman Bewley, *Advances in Economic Theory— Fifth World Congress* (Cambridge: Cambridge University Press, 1987); Paul Milgrom and John Roberts, "Economic Theories of the Firm: Past, Present, and Future," *Canadian Journal of Economics* 21, no. 3 (August 1989): 444–58; and Bengt Holmstrom and Jean Tirole, "The Theory of the Firm," in R. Schmalensee and R. Willig, *Handbook of Industrial Organization* (Amsterdam: North Holland, 1989).

25. Steven Kelman emphasizes the efficiency costs of reducing official discretion in public sector procurement in the name of controlling corruption. He proposes "experiments in eliminating most procurement rules in favor of a regime with only two broad procedural requirements—written justification for each procurement decision, and multiple-member evaluation panels to reach decisions." Kelman's research was concerned with computer procurement in the U.S. government, a government where, he says, there is little corruption and, in any case, procurement rules in the U.S. context do little about it. Steven Kelman, *Procurement and Public Management: The Fear of Discretion and the Quality of Government Performance* (Washington, D.C.: American Enterprise Institute, 1990): 91, 95–99. While agreeing with his qualitative point and favoring evaluation by results whenever possible, I fear that the trade-off is different in developing countries where corruption is rampant.

26. For more details, see Klitgaard, *Controlling Corruption*, chap. 3.

27. Susan Rose-Ackerman, "Reforming Public Bureaucracy through Economic Incentives?" *Journal of Law, Economics, and Organization* 2, no. 1 (Spring 1986): 131.

28. See Klitgaard, *Controlling Corruption*, chap. 4.

29. Amitai Etzioni, "The Fight against Fraud and Abuse," *Journal of Policy Analysis and Management* 2 (Fall 1982): 26–38.

30. Adam Smith, *An Inquiry into the Nature and Causes of the Wealth of Nations* (Oxford: Oxford University Press, 1976 [1776]): 678.

31. For a review of the literature, see Daniel J. B. Mitchell, David Lewin, and Edward E. Lawler III, "Alternative Pay Systems, Firm Performance, and Productivity," in Alan S. Blinder, *Paying for Productivity: A Look at the Evidence* (Washington, D.C.: Brookings Institution, 1990).

32. For example, Inman, "Markets, Government, and the 'New' Political Economy"; *Politics and Policy Making in Developing Countries*, ed. Meier; Gallagher, *Rent-Seeking and Economic Growth in Africa*; and on a complementary note, Frank A. Cowell, *Cheating the Government: The Economics of Evasion* (Cambridge, Mass.: MIT Press, 1990).

33. The reader wishing to explore these dimensions can find no better place to start, and perhaps to end, than Noonan's *Bribes*. Bayart's *L'État en Afrique* is of more than African interest.

NOTES TO CHAPTER 9

1. Cited in Dele Oluwu, "The Failure of Current Decentralization Programs in Africa," in James S. Wunsch and Dele Olowu, eds., *The Failure of the Centralized African State: Institutions and Self-Governance in Africa* (Boulder, Colo.: Westview, 1990): 76.

2. "Certainly the centralization of power in the imperial presidency that one found in the French Constitution was well suited to traditional African leadership concepts of the strong chief. No doubt it had the further advantage of satisfying the ambitions of many of the new chiefs of state. The French centralization of state power also provided a degree of national cohesion though its administrative networks to loosely formed, artificial states." Francis Terry McNamara, *France in Black Africa* (Washington, D.C.: National Defense University Press, 1989): 93.

3. World Bank, *World Development Report 1990: Poverty* (New York: Oxford University Press, 1990): 42.

4. Julius Nyerere, interview with *Third World Quarterly* 6, no. 4 (1984): 828, 830; cited in Oluwu, "The Failure of Current Decentralization Programs," 80.

5. Jerry M. Silverman, "Public Sector Decentralization: Economic Policy Reform and Sector Investment Programs," Public Sector Management Division Study Paper no. 1 (Washington, D.C.: World Bank, Africa Technical Department, November 1990): 58, 69.

6. For example, Jean-François Bayart, *L'État en Afrique: La Politique du Ventre* (Paris: Fayard, 1989); Sheldon Gellar, "State Tutelage vs. Self-Governance: The Rhetoric and Reality of Decentralization in Senegal," in *The Failure of the Centralized African State*; Oluwu, "The Failure of Current Decentralization Programs"; Amos Sawyer, "The Development of Autocracy in Liberia" and "The Putu Development Association: A Missed Opportunity," both in Vincent Ostrom, David Feeny, and Hartmut Picht, eds., *Rethinking Institutional Analysis and Development* (San Francisco: ICS Press for the International Center for Economic Growth, 1988).

7. Steven Kelman, *Procurement and Public Management: The Fear of Discretion and the Quality of Government Performance* (Washington, D.C.: American Enterprise Institute, 1990): 27–28.

8. Robert H. Jackson and Carl G. Rosberg, *Personal Rule in Black Africa: Prince, Autocrat, Prophet, Tyrant* (Berkeley and Los Angeles: University of California Press, 1982): 10, referring to Montesquieu, Friedrich, and Rawls, among others. On the same page the authors say, "The opposite of institutional rule—obviously—is non-institutionalized government, where persons take precedence over rules, where the officeholder is not effectively bound by his office." Fear of this "personal rule," even at the level of local bureaucrats, is one source of attempts to limit official discretion.

9. Samuel Paul, *Strategic Management of Development Programmes* (Geneva: International Labour Office, 1983): 84.

10. See Samuel Paul, *Managing Development Programs: Lessons of Success* (Boulder, Colo.: Westview, 1982).

11. Paul, *Strategic Management of Development Programmes*, 86.

12. Fernando Campero, "Desarrollo Institucional del FSE," in *Fondo Social de Emergencia: Seminario de Evaluación* (La Paz: Fondo Social de Emergencia, 1990): 45. All translations below are mine.

13. Gary E. Hansen, "Rural Development in Indonesia," in Inayatullah [sic], ed., *Approaches to Rural Development: Some Asian Experiences* (Kuala Lumpur: Asian and Pacific Development Administration Center, 1979).

14. Ibid., 46.

15. Fernando Campero and Gerardo Avila, *Mitigando los Costos Sociales del Ajuste: La Experiencia del Fondo Social de Emergencia*, August 1990 draft of forthcoming book, 71.

16. Ibid., 72.

17. Ibid., 84.

18. Adolfo Navarro Flores, "Principales Logros del FSE," in *Fondo Social de Emergencia*.

19. Virginia Osso and Molly Pollack, "Resumen y Conclusiones," in *Fondo Social de Emergencia*.

20. Here other sorts of hygienes and motivators must be brought into play. See, for example, Arturo Israel, *Institutional Development: Incentives for Performance* (Baltimore, Md.: Johns Hopkins University Press, 1987); and Paul, *Managing Development Programs*.

21. John Cohen, "Integrating Services for Rural Development" (Unpublished ms., Lincoln Institute of Land Policy and Kennedy School of Government, September 1979): 100, 41.

22. Vernon W. Ruttan, "Integrated Rural Development Programs: A Skeptical Perspective," *International Development Review* 17, no. 4 (1975): 14.

23. Samuel Paul, "The Indonesian Population Program," pts. A and B, teaching case prepared at the Kennedy School of Government (Cambridge, Mass.: Harvard University, 1980).

24. John Cohen, "Rural Development in Ethiopia: The Chilalo Agricultural Development Unit," *Economic Development and Cultural Change* 22, no. 4 (July 1974).

25. Kevin M. Denny, *A Review of Alternative Approaches to Health Care Delivery in Developing Countries* (Cambridge, Mass.: Management Sciences for Health, 1974): chap. 9.

26. Edilberto C. de Jesus, R., "Masagana 99: Davao del Sur," pts. A and B, teaching case prepared at the Asian Institute of Management (Manila, 1978).

27. For example, *degrees* of or devices for integration might include meetings, joint training, coordinating committees, exchanges of personnel, task forces, joint staffs, integrating roles or jobs, collocation, common hierarchical structures, and network or matrix organizations. *Functions* that might be integrated include planning and programming, finance, organizational rules and procedures, personnel systems, research and development, evaluation, logistics, field workers, and so forth. By *hierarchical location*, integration might take place at the village, district, provincial, regional, national, or international levels.

28. From such holistic visions as farming systems research in anthropology, notes Parker Shipton, "slowest to emerge has been a coherent contribution to anyone's planning." His remarks are applicable beyond anthropological borders: "Systems researchers have produced no shortage of convoluted flow diagrams, exemplified within some recent interdisciplinary collections, showing (in case anyone doubted it) that in African rural poverty everything is related to everything else. Mere complexity, however, is seldom as welcome to planners as to scholars. Every rural African knows that some causes and effects (or combinations of them) are more important than others. The next challenge is to compare the local variations. The idea should be to observe more (or more finely nuanced) causal links, and more variety, as part of the search for truth, while elsewhere, for the use of practitioners, paring them down to the most general or essential." Parker Shipton, "African Famines and Food Security: Anthropological Perspectives," *Annual Review of Anthropology 1990* 19: 357.

29. Alan H. Alderman, "Colombian Friendship Groups: Constraints on a Rural Development Acquisition System," *Journal of Developing Areas* 15, no. 3 (April 1981): 458. FEDERACAFE includes "not only research on experimental farms to develop most productive systems of coffee cultivation (production and research components), but also the design of processing and handling equipment (production and supply); the creation, administration, or stimulation of coffee warehouses, agricultural supply stores, cooperatives, and savings and credit banks (supply, marketing, and governance); formal and non-formal education programs for adults and youth (education); the establishment of health centers and campaigns to improve nutrition, drinking water, and general hygiene

(health care); and the provision of economic and technical assistance for works of common utility, such as community roads, water systems, schools, and housing (personal maintenance, education, and supply)."

30. Robert Wade, "Leadership and Integrated Rural Development: Reflections on an Indian Success Story," *Journal of Administration Overseas* 17, no. 4 (Fall 1978): 253.

31. Robert Chambers, *Managing Rural Development* (Uppsala, Sweden: Scandinavian Institute of African Studies, 1974): 24–25.

32. Ibid., 153.

33. Schematically, we are searching for estimates of positive cross-partial derivatives in the production function, as in, for example:

$$\delta^2 A / \delta F \delta W > 0,$$

where A is agricultural production, F is amount of fertilizer, and W is amount of water.

34. At the height of the integrated rural development "movement," a review prepared for the U.S. Agency for International Development concluded: "A major constraint on implementing integrated rural development strategies is the difficulty of determining the most effective combination of inputs for promoting growth with equity. . . . Although much has been written about techniques for increasing agricultural production, little is known about the best combinations of technical, social, economic, and administrative functions for promoting rural development." Dennis A. Rondinelli and Kenneth Ruddle, "Urban Functions in Rural Development: An Analysis of Integrated Spatial Development Policy" (Washington, D.C.: U.S. Agency for International Development, 1976, photocopy): 62.

35. Arthur T. Mosher, "Thinking about Rural Development" (New York: Agricultural Development Council, 1976). The same point has been made by Ruttan, "Integrated Rural Development Programs," 16; and Wade, "Leadership and Integrated Rural Development," 252.

36. "Previously, the thana representatives of government departments, including agriculture, education, and health as well as police and other organizations, lived and worked in comparative isolation in a variety of places in the thana and often lacked adequate transport even in the form of bicycles. . . . [After collocation] this focus of thana activity immediately improved the impact of individual programs; it also improved their coordinated effectiveness in relationship with each other." George F. Gant, *Development Administration: Concepts, Goals, Methods* (Madison: University of Wisconsin Press, 1979): 183.

37. See, for example, Michael Porter, *Competitive Strategy* (New York: Free Press, 1980): 313–14.

38. "Bearing in mind that we are essentially comparing projects with each other, we feel that differences in these external effects, which are not in any case allowed for in our type of cost-benefit analysis, will seldom make a significant difference." I. M. D. Little and J. A. Mirrlees, *Project Appraisal and Planning for Developing Countries* (New York: Basic Books, 1974): 348–49.

39. James G. March and Herbert H. Simon, *Organizations* (New York: John Wiley & Sons, 1958): 159.

40. Chambers, *Managing Rural Development;* Harry Blair, "Rural Development, Class Structure, and Bureaucracy in Bangladesh," *World Development* 6, no. 1 (1978).

41. Richard Huntington, "Popular Participation in the Abyei Project: A Preliminary Report" (Khartoum: Development Studies and Research Centre, University of Khartoum, photocopy, 1979).

42. Tibor Scitovsky, "Two Concepts of External Economies," *Journal of Political Economy* 62, no. 2 (April 1954): 149.

43. John P. Kotter, Leonard Schlesinger, and Vijay Sathe, *Organization:*

Text, Cases, and Readings on the Management of Organizational Design and Change (Homewood, Ill.: Irwin, 1979): 133, emphasis in original

44. David C. Korten, "Integrated Approaches to Family Planning Services Delivery," Development Discussion Paper no. 10 (Cambridge, Mass.: Harvard Institute for International Development, 1975): 24.

NOTES TO CHAPTER 10

1. A word about terminology. Many people would agree that an ethnic group is defined by some or all of the following: (1) a specific language or dialect, (2) association with a particular territory, (3) a common religion, (4) a history as a group, (5) similar behavioral traits, and (6) shared physical characteristics. See Nathan Glazer and Daniel Patrick Moynihan, eds., *Ethnicity: Theory and Experience* (New York: Praeger, 1975): Introduction.

As explained in Chapter 2, note 1, descriptors of ethnic groups such as "Indian" or "black" or "member of a tribe" can themselves be controversial. My usage of such terms means no offense; it is only because they still reflect common usage and no agreed-upon replacements are available.

Certain terms, such as "backward," are used in a strictly descriptive and technical sense to indicate that a group is, on average, educationally and economically behind in measurable ways. There is no presumption that in other ways—such as culturally, religiously, or humanly—such comparisons have any meaning.

2. A recent exception is the World Bank, *Bolivia Poverty Report*, Report no. 8643-BO (Washington, D.C., October 1990): 20–21.

3. Walker Connor, "Nation-Building or Nation-Destroying?" *World Politics* 24 (April 1972): 320.

4. Mario C. Vázquez, "Immigration and Mestizaje in Nineteenth-Century Peru," in Magnus Mörner, *Race and Class in Latin America* (New York: Columbia University Press, 1970): 93. See in general Magnus Mörner, *Race Mixture in the History of Latin America* (Boston: Little, Brown, 1967).

5. For this reason the continent is not included in Donald Horowitz's massive work on ethnicity. The problem Horowitz and much of the literature address is ethnic conflict, not ethnic inequalities or the ethnic dimensions of poverty. Donald L. Horowitz, *Ethnic Groups in Conflict* (Berkeley and Los Angeles: University of California Press, 1985).

6. In Brazil, which prides itself on its racial democracy and whose situation we examine in more detail below, because of "an obsession with whiteness and blackness and the shades in between, with a concomitant emphasis on features such as people's hair texture, nose shape, and size of lips, there exist further race and colour break-downs to the point where Brazilians have more than twenty different expressions to distinguish colour variations between the two extremes of black and white." Anani Dzidzienyo, "The Position of Blacks in Brazilian Society," in *The Position of Blacks in Brazilian and Cuban Society*, Report no. 7 (London: Minority Rights Group, 1981): 4. According to one Costa Rican critic, his country contains "latent racism" with regard to its mestizo background and the half a percent of the population considered "indigenous." "The prevailing racism within the relationships of domination that are exercised over the indigenous minority is not, in Costa Rica, a phenomenon of individual psychopathology but of a collective one." Mayobanex Ornes, *Los Caminos del Indigenismo* (San José: Editorial; Costa Rica. 1983): 132, my translation. Three U.S. authors conclude that Costa Rica's myth is just that, a myth of racial homogeneity and tolerance. Richard Biesanz, Karen Zubris Biesanz, and Mavis Hiltunen Biesanz, *The Costa Ricans* (Englewood Cliffs, N.J.: Prentice-Hall, 1982): 64–70.

7. Seymour Martin Lipset, "Racial and Ethnic Tensions in the Third

World," in W. Scott Thompson, ed., *The Third World: Premises of U.S. Policy*, (San Francisco: ICS Press, 1978): 129–30.

8. Bernard E. Segal, "The Politics of Unanticipated Trickle: Penetration, Permeation, and Absorption in Peru," in Raymond L. Hall, ed., *Ethnic Autonomy–Comparative Dynamics: The Americas, Europe and the Developing World* (New York: Pergamon, 1979): 371.

9. H. W. O. Okoth-Ogendo, "Ethnicity and Constitutionalism in Kenya: A General Survey" (Paper presented at the Ford Foundation workshop on Structural Arrangements to Ease Ethnic Tensions, September 1981): 6; Y. Bromlei, *Los Procesos Etnicos* (Moscow: Progress Publishers, 1978): 99.

10. Lipset, "Racial and Ethnic Tensions," 133–36, contains a number of examples.

11. I cannot resist inserting a wonderful parallel from the Caribbean, as conveyed in Derek Walcott's poem, "The Spoiler's Return":

> In all them project, all them Five-Year Plan
> what happen to the Brotherhood of Man?
> Around the time I dead it wasn't so,
> we sang the Commonwealth of caiso,
> we was in chains, but chains made us unite,
> now who have, good for them; and who blight, blight;
> my bread is bitterness, my wine is gall,
> my chorus is the same: "I want to fall."

Derek Walcott, *The Fortunate Traveller* (New York: Farrar Straus Giroux, 1981): 58.

12. R. N. Ismagilova, "The Ethnic Factor in Modern Africa," in I. R. Grigulevich and S. Y. Kozlov, eds., *Races and Peoples: Contemporary Ethnic and Racial Problems* (Moscow: Progress Publishers, 1974): 214. Ismagilova notes that the ethnic side of African poverty is played down by African leaders. "Some of them categorically deny the existence of ethnic problems in their countries, others underestimate their importance, while still others who admit the role of the ethnic factor, reduce the whole complex of these complicated problems to mere tribalism, by which they understand inter-tribal enmity. In most cases ethnic problems are given a very narrow treatment, and their connection with social and economic processes is not brought out. Moreover, in many countries the nature and essence of ethnic conflict are often concealed" (p. 213).

13. J. Craig Jenkins and Augustine J. Kposowa, "Explaining Military Coups d'Etat in Black Africa, 1957–1984," *American Sociological Review* 55, no. 6 (December 1990).

14. Lipset, "Racial and Ethnic Tensions," 136.

15. S. I. Bruk, N. N. Cheboksarov, and Y. Y. Chesnov, "National Processes in Asiatic Countries Outside the USSR," in *Races and Peoples*, 192, paragraphing added.

16. "A fast rate of inter-racial metisation, impossible in any other animal species, not only at the edges but even at the center of race area [*sic*], resulted in a situation where more and more human populations formed, disintegrated, or became transformed long before they could be consolidated into new races. . . . Nevertheless mixed populations, which had absorbed different racial components over a long period of complete or nearly complete isolation, always tended eventually to develop into separate races, no less consolidated than other races formed from genetically more homogeneous populations. Such was the case with Japan. . . . Similar processes took place in Hindustan." N. N. Cheboksarov, "Human Races and Populations," in *Races and Peoples*, 58.

17. Ibid., 56–57.

18. B. K. Roy Burman, "Social Ecology of Ethnic Groups, Inter-ethnic Relations and Social Action in India" (Paper presented at the Ford Founda-

tion workshop on Structural Arrangements to Ease Ethnic Tensions, September 1981): 9.

19. "When Nordindids ('Indo-Afghans') began to penetrate into India from the north-west from about 1500 B.C. onwards, and came into contact with various peoples differing from themselves in physical features as well as in culture, social barriers against free hybridization were set up and the 'caste' system gradually evolved. This was perhaps the most elaborate and effective barrier against the mixing of contiguous ethnic taxa that the world has ever known." John R. Baker, *Race* (New York: Oxford University Press, 1974): 12.

Baker notes, as we should as well, the danger of linking skin color to race. At best, there is a correlation. Ibid., 158–60.

20. Thomas Sowell, *The Economics and Politics of Race: An International Perspective* (New York: Morrow, 1983): chap. 2.

21. Thomas Sowell evaluates the results of preferential policies in a variety of third world countries in *Preferential Treatment: An International Perspective* (New York: William Morrow, 1990). He finds that they failed to reduce ethnic differences as much as hoped and had higher costs than anticipated.

NOTES TO CHAPTER II

1. *Jornal do Brasil*, 1 December 1984, 9 (my translation).

2. V. I. Lenin, "La Revolución Socialista y el Derecho de las Naciones a la Autodeterminación," in *Lenin: Obras Escogidas* (Moscow: Editorial Progreso, 1980): 160, my translation.

3. Victor Alba, *Peru* (Boulder, Colo.: Westview, 1977): 169.

4. For example, intermarriage in the Huatsani district reached a total of only 7 percent in the period from 1968 to 1972, according to Alberto Chirif and Carlos Mora, *Atlas de Comunidades Nativas* (Lima: SINAMOS, 1976): 16–17.

5. Bernard E. Segal, "The Politics of Unanticipated Trickle: Penetration, Permeation, and Absorption in Peru," in Raymond L. Hall, ed., *Ethnic Autonomy–Comparative Dynamics: The Americas, Europe and the Developing World* (New York: Pergamon, 1979): 373–79.

6. *Constitución del Perú*, Arts. 261, 262, and 264. The duties of the Regional Assembly include the election of a regional president and a regional council, and the approval of the Regional Budget and the Regional Development Plan (Art. 265).

7. See Giorgio Alberti, *Basic Needs in the Context of Social Changes: The Case of Peru* (Paris: Organisation for Economic Co-operation and Development, 1981), 311ff; and Peter Cleaves and Martin Scurrah, *Agriculture, Bureaucracy, and Military Government in Peru* (Ithaca, NY.: Cornell University Press, 1980): 110.

8. Susan C. Bourque and David S. Palmer, "Transforming the Rural Sector: Government Policy and Peasant Response," in Abraham F. Lowenthal, ed., *The Peruvian Experiment: Continuity and Change under Military Rule* (Princeton, N.J: Princeton University Press, 1975): 198.

9. Bourque and Palmer, "Transforming the Rural Sector," 196.

10. Cited in English in ibid., 179.

11. For an analysis of the military government's first national plan, see Robert Klitgaard, "Observations on the Peruvian National Plan for Development, 1971–1975," *Inter-American Economic Affairs* 25, no. 3 (Winter 1971).

12. Michael Painter reviews the literature in "Agricultural Policy, Food Production, and Multinational Corporations in Peru," *Latin American Research Review 18*, no. 2 (1983). See also José María Caballero, "Agriculture and the Peasantry under Industrialization Pressures: Lessons from the Peruvian Experience," *Latin American Research Review 19*, no. 2 (1984): 4, 19, from which the data in the next paragraph are culled.

13. Cynthia McClintock in Peru survey, *Le Monde Dimanche*, 30 November 1981 (I am indebted to David Rossington for a translation); Cynthia McClintock, "Post-Revolutionary Agrarian Policies in Peru," in Stephen M. Gorman, ed., *Post-Revolutionary Peru* (Boulder, Colo.: Westview, 1982): 150–51.

14. Robert A. Drysdale and Robert G. Myers, "Continuity and Change in Peruvian Education," in *The Peruvian Experiment*, 278; quotation from p. 272.

15. Charles W. Anderson, "The Concepts of Race and Class and the Explanation of Latin American Politics," in Magnus Mörner, ed., *Race and Class in Latin America* (New York: Columbia University Press, 1970): 253.

16. For example, Jorge A. Flores Ochoa, "Mistis and Indians: Their Relations in a Microregion of Cuzco," in Pierre Van den Berghe, ed., *Class and Ethnicity in Peru* (Leiden, The Netherlands: E. J. Brill, 1974).

17. The data in this paragraph are drawn from Richard Webb, *Government Policy and the Distribution of Income in Peru* (Cambridge, Mass.: Harvard University Press, 1977): 6, 16, 38–43. .

18. Elena Alvarez, *Política Agraria y Estancamiento de la Agricultura, 1969–1977* (Lima: Instituto de Estudios Peruanos, 1980), as summarized in Painter, "Agricultural Policy," 204.

19. Caballero, "Agriculture and the Peasantry."

20. Julio Cotler, "The New Mode of Political Domination in Peru," in *The Peruvian Experiment*, 65.

21. Cristóbal Key, "Achievements and Contradictions of the Peruvian Agrarian Reform," *Journal of Development Studies*, 18, no. 2 (January 1982): 161; Cleaves and Scurrah, *Agriculture, Bureaucracy, and Military Government*.

22. Caballero, "Agriculture and the Peasantry," 5, 19.

23. Drysdale and Myers, "Continuity and Change," 258–59.

24. Approximately the same ratios held for those living in rural areas. But since Indians tend to reside in rural areas and rural areas have lower rates of education than urban areas, the ethnic inequalities reported in the text would be even larger if calculated on a national basis.

25. Jorge Cándido, "Perfil Histórico-Cultural de Discriminação Racial e da Violencia Urbana," *Estudos Afro-Asiáticos*, no. 8-9 (1983): 165.

26. Abdias do Nascimento, *O Genocidio do Negro Brasileiro* (Rio de Janeiro: Paz e Terra, 1978).

27. Donald Pierson, *Negroes in Brazil: A History of Race Contact at Bahia* (Chicago: University of Chicago Press, 1942). The quotation is from page xv.

28. Gilberto Freyre, *The Masters and the Slaves: A Study in the Development of Brazilian Civilization*, trans. Samuel Putnam, abridged ed. (New York: Knopf, 1964): 255.

29. "As for the reaction of the black Brazilian himself to a critical assessment of his position, it must be remembered that black and dark Brazilians have been colonized and brought up to accept the 'new world in the tropics' myth, so that they show signs of discomfort at any open and controversial discussion of the subject. More importantly, they have been encouraged to believe that they are the most fortunate blacks in the New World—especially in comparison with the 'poor black North American'—and perhaps for that reason, they faithfully observe the 'etiquette' of race relations and will readily point out the brotherly feelings which exist between them and white Brazilians." (Anani Dzidzienyo, "The Position of Blacks in Brazilian Society," in *The Position of Blacks in Brazilian and Cuban Society*, Report no. 7 (London: Minority Rights Group, 1981): 7.

30. Ibid., 3.

31. The analyses are my own. A key source of information was Nelson do Valle Silva, "Côr e o Processo de Realizaçao Sócio-Econômica," *Revista de Ciências Sociais* 24, no. 3 (1981).

32. For example, Florestan Fernandes, "Immigration and Race Relations in São Paulo," in *Race and Class in Latin America*, ed. Mörner. In a later work

Fernandes summarized the reasons for the deterioration: "First, because the ex-slave did not get any type of monetary help for his survival; second, because suddenly blacks had to compete with the whites in a small market without qualifications." Florestan Fernandes, in *Folhetim*, no. 177, 8 June 1980, 6; I am grateful to Luisa Fernandes for a translation.

33. Florestan Fernandes, *A Integração de Negro à Sociedade de Classes* (São Paulo, 1964), 8; cited in English in Octavio Ianni, "Research on Race Relations in Brazil," in *Race and Class in Latin America*, 271.

34. Dzidzienyo, "The Position of Blacks," 9.

35. Fernandes, "Research on Race Relations in Brazil," 261.

36. For numerous examples, see Thomas Sowell, *Preferential Policies: An International Perspective* (New York: William Morrow, 1990).

37. Marc Galanter, *Competing Equalities: Law and the Backward Classes in India* (Berkeley and Los Angeles: University of California Press, 1984).

38. Donald L. Horowitz, *Ethnic Groups in Conflict* (Berkeley and Los Angeles: University of California Press, 1985): 656.

39. Sunil Bastian, "University Admission and the National Question," in *Ethnicity and Social Change in Sri Lanka* (Colombo: Karunaratne & Sons, 1984): 166–78.

40. Mahathir Mohamad, *The Malay Dilemma* (Singapore: Times Books International, 1970): 96, 85, 133.

41. The term *bumiputera* (or *bumiputra*) is officially used to cover not only the Malays but other indigenous groups called *Orang Asli*, mainly the Ibans and Kadazans of Sarawak and Sabah. As is common practice in Malaysia, I use "Malay" and "ethnic Malays" interchangeably with *bumiputera*. In 1989 the projected population of peninsular Malaysia for 1990 was 14.71 million, of Sabah 1.54 million, and of Sarawak 1.77 million, for a total of 18.01 million. Of the total population, 62 percent were Malays and other *bumiputera*, 29 percent Chinese, and 8 percent Indian. (*Mid-Term Review of the Fifth Malaysia Plan, 1986–1990* [Kuala Lumpur: National Printing Department, 1989]: 83.)

42. Viswanathan Selvaratnam, "Ethnicity, Inequality, and Higher Education in Malaysia," *Comparative Education Review* 32, no. 2 (May 1988): 174.

43. Tun Tan Siew Sin, cited in Viswanathan Selvaratnam, "Intercommunal Relations and Problems of Social-Economic Development: The Malaysian Dilemma," in *Ethical Dilemmas of Development in Asia*, ed. Godfrey Gunatilleke, Neelan Tiruchelvam, and Radhika Coomaraswamy (Lexington, Mass.: Lexington Books, 1983): 111.

44. See Robert Klitgaard and Ruth Katz, "Overcoming Ethnic Inequalities: Lessons from Malaysia," *Journal of Policy Analysis and Management* 2, no. 3 (1983), and the references cited therein.

45. James W. Gould, *The United States and Malaysia* (Cambridge, Mass.: Harvard University Press, 1969): 241; cited in Selvaratnam, "Intercommunal Relations," 101–2.

46. Interestingly, the government has adopted a different strategy toward the *Orang Asli*, or non-Malay *bumiputera*. These small minority groups, even more economically and educationally backward than the Malays, are not given explicit preferential treatment. Instead, the strategy is more like Peru's: "The government does feel an obligation," writes the Rand Corporation's John Haaga, "to do something for them as a group (the Malays grab all the places reserved for *bumiputra* in general). . . . The policy is to encourage assimilation (Malay language, settled farming, Muslim religion and names, etc.) rather than to set up quotas within quotas" (personal communication, April 1989).

47. Selvaratnam, "Intercommunal Relations," 116–17, referring to Senu Abdul Rehman, ed., *Revolusi Mental* (Kuala Lumpur: Penerbitan Utusan Malaya, 1971).

48. Selvaratnam, "Ethnicity, Inequality, and Higher Education in Malaysia."

49. *Mid-Term Review of the Fifth Malaysia Plan*, 68.

50. Selvaratnam, "Ethnicity, Inequality, and Higher Education in Malaysia," 187.

51. Various Malaysia plans and mid-term reviews.

52. *Fifth Malaysia Plan,* 105; *Mid-Term Review of the Fifth Malaysia Plan,* 67.

53. Kamil Salih and Zainal Aznam Yusof, "Overview of the New Economic Policy and Framework for the Post-1990 Economic Policy" (Paper presented at the National Conference on Post-1990 Economic Policy, Kuala Lumpur: Malaysian Institute of Economic Research, 1989): 10

54. *The Economist,* 11 March 1989, 40.

55. Data are always problematic in longitudinal comparisons, but for the 1979 data there appears to be a major discrepancy. In the *Mid-Term Review of the Third Malaysia Plan,* the government gave different figures for the 1979 average household monthly income of Chinese than did the *Fifth Malaysia Plan.* In constant 1970 Malaysian dollars, the former figure was 659, the latter 565. Because of the other studies cited in Klitgaard and Katz, "Overcoming Ethnic Inequality," the former figure seems more reasonable; but the latter is obviously more recent. Unable to untangle this discrepancy, I have omitted 1979 data from Figure 11-3.

56. Various Malaysia plans and mid-term reviews; Klitgaard and Katz, "Overcoming Ethnic Inequalities"; Sowell, *Preferential Policies.*

57. Sowell, *Preferential Policies,* 157.

58. Selvaratnam, "Ethnicity, Inequality, and Higher Education in Malaysia," 192.

59. Salih and Yusof, "Overview of the New Economic Policy," 3, 5.

60. Ibid., 3.

61. *Economist,* 11 March 1989, 40.

62. Donald L. Horowitz, "Cause and Consequence in Public Policy Theory: The Malaysian System Transforming Itself," *Policy Sciences* 22 (1989): 249–87.

63. See *Mid-Term Review of the Fifth Malaysia Plan,* esp. 68–73.

64. *Fifth Malaysia Plan 1986–1990* (Kuala Lumpur: National Printing Department, 1986): 123–24.

65. *Mid-Term Review of the Fifth Malaysia Plan,* 78

NOTES TO CHAPTER 12

1. Edward Tower, *Development Economics* (Durham, N.C.: Eno River Press, 1980). The avoidance of the topic in the political science literature on development is documented in Walker Connor, "Nation-Building or Nation-Destroying?" *World Politics* 24 (April 1972).

2. Jan Tinbergen, "Development Cooperation as a Learning Process," in Gerald M. Meier and Dudley Seers, eds., *Pioneers in Development* (New York: Oxford University Press, 1984): 321–22.

3. Emilia Viotti da Costa, "The Portuguese-African Slave Trade: A Lesson in Colonialism," *Latin American Perspectives* 12, no. 1 (Winter 1985): 48. See also P. J. Marshall and Glyndwyr Williams, *The Great Map of Mankind: Perceptions of New Worlds in the Age of Enlightenment* (Cambridge, Mass.: Harvard University Press, 1983).

4. Viotti da Costa, "The Portuguese-African Slave Trade," 49.

5. Some authors have defined colonialism in racial terms. According to Georges Balandier, for example, colonialism is "the domination imposed by a foreign authority, racially (or ethnically) and culturally different, acting in the name of racial (or ethnic) superiority dogmatically affirmed, and imposing itself on an indigenous population constituting a numerical majority but inferior to the dominant group from a material point of view." Georges Balandier, "The Colonial Situation: A Theoretical Approach," in Immanuel Wallerstein, ed., *Social Change: The Colonial Situation* (New York: John Wiley & Sons, 1966): 54.

6. Severo Martínez Peláez, *La Patria del Criollo: Ensayo de Interpretación de la Realidad Colonial Guatemalteca*, 8th ed. (Ciudad Universitaria "Rodrigo Facio," Costa Rica: Editorial Universitaria Centroamericana, 1981): 568, 570, my translation, emphasis in original.

7. Mayobanex Ornes, *Los Caminos del Indigenismo* (San José: Editorial Costa Rica, 1983): 10, my translation.

8. Robert Klitgaard, "Institutionalized Racism: An Analytical Approach," *Journal of Peace Research* 8, no. 1 (1972); reprinted in William Barclay, Krishna Kumar, and Ruth P. Simms, eds., *Racial Conflict, Discrimination, and Power: Historical and Contemporary Studies* (New York: AMS Press, 1976).

9. Richard B. Freeman, "Decline of Labor Market Discrimination and Economic Analysis," *American Economic Review Papers and Proceedings* 63, no. 2 (May 1973): 284.

10. Gary Becker, *The Economics of Discrimination* (Chicago: University of Chicago Press, 1957). George Akerlof later showed that the size of the market is crucial for the forces of competition to eliminate "prejudiced" employers. He provided a model of a "small" market in which searching for an employee was costly, and in such a market one cannot count on competition from a few unprejudiced employers to drive away the prejudiced ones. George A. Akerlof, "Discriminatory, Status-based Wages among Tradition-Oriented, Stochastically Trading Coconut Producers," *Journal of Political Economy* 93, no. 2 (April 1985): 265–76.

11. In the large economic literature on discrimination, the best piece known to me is Thomas C. Schelling's "Discrimination without Prejudice: Some Innocuous Models," distributed as a discussion paper by both the Harvard Institute for Economic Research and the Kennedy School of Government in 1972. Schelling derived a cost curve, or cumulative performance disadvantage curve, as the number of group B workers increases. He showed that the shape of this curve is crucial. Depending on the exact nature of this curve and the proportion of B workers in the relevant pool, performance differences may induce complete segregation of groups in the workplace, complete integration, or various mixes in between. This means that the effects in terms of segregation of (1) the fact that members of group B tend to be less productive than members of group A or (2) the fact that an employer has a "distaste" for workers from group B depend on the proportions of Bs and As in the pool and the exact way that the performance disadvantage, or the distaste, varies as a function of how many Bs and As are hired.

12. Ijaz Nabi's study of labor productivity in a small-scale industry in Pakistan found that, holding constant education, experience, and other factors, members of the *lohar bradri* or "caste" enjoyed higher wages than members of other castes. "This may, of course, represent merely a human capital proxy, since workers belonging to the *lohar bradri* are supposed to be 'born into the profession' and may in fact be more skilled in manufacturing agricultural machinery." *Entrepreneurs and Markets in Early Industrialization: A Case Study from Pakistan* (San Francisco: ICS Press for the International Center for Economic Growth, 1988): 50.

George Mergos and Roger Slade's statistical analysis of Operation Flood in India found that "the milk output of lower caste households is about 10 percent lower than households of higher caste given the same factor endowments," including education, agricultural inputs, land, irrigation, and membership in a cooperative. "Dairy Development and Milk Cooperatives: The Effects of a Dairy Project in India," World Bank Discussion Paper no. 15 (Washington, D.C., July 1987): 73–75.

13. See Donald L. Horowitz, *Ethnic Groups in Conflict* (Berkeley and Los Angeles: University of California Press, 1985): chap. 4; the quotation is from p. 156, emphasis added.

14. Horowitz concluded: "The comparison of backward and advanced groups proceeds from their juxtaposition in a common environment. . . . Colo-

nial policy inadvertently helped sharpen group juxtapositions and clarify the field in which comparisons were made. Measures taken by European rulers to make sense of a new environment, to create order, and to facilitate colonial administration had the effect of sharpening the contrasts and evaluations that emerged with group disparities. Although the balance of these forces varied from colony to colony, overall the response of the groups themselves to opportunities that opened up seems to have been more influential in producing disparities than was anything the colonial rulers did by way of disparate treatment of groups." *Ethnic Groups in Conflict,* 150, 151, 160.

Consider also this passage from Ernest Gellner, *Nations and Nationalism* (Ithaca, N.Y: Cornell University Press, 1983): 61: "In the old days it made no sense to ask whether the peasants loved their own culture: they took it for granted, like the air they breathed, and were not conscious of either. But when labour migration and bureaucratic employment became prominent features within their social horizon, they soon learned the difference between dealing with a co-national, one understanding and sympathizing with their culture, and someone hostile to it. This very concrete experience taught them to be aware of their culture, and to love it (or, indeed, to wish to be rid of it) without any conscious calculation of advantages and prospects of social mobility. In stable self-contained communities culture is often quite invisible, but when mobility and context-free communication come to be the essence of social life, the culture in which one has been *taught* to communicate becomes the core of one's identity" (emphasis in original).

15. Florestan Fernandes, "Immigration and Race Relations in São Paulo," in Magnus Mörner, ed., *Race and Class in Latin America* (New York: Columbia University Press, 1970): 131.

16. Examples are provided in Seymour Martin Lipset, "Racial and Ethnic Tensions in the Third World," in W. Scott Thompson, ed., *The Third World: Premises of U.S. Policy* (San Francisco: ICS Press, 1978): esp. 144–48; Malcolm Cross, "Colonialism and Ethnicity: A Theory and Comparative Case Study," *Ethnic and Racial Studies* 1, no. 1 (January 1978): esp. 40–41; and Donald L. Horowitz, "Patterns of Ethnic Separatism," *Comparative Studies in Society and History* 23, no. 2 (April 1981): esp. 173–78.

17. Donald L. Horowitz, *Ethnicity and Development: Policies to Deal with Ethnic Conflict in Developing Countries,* a report to the Agency for International Development under grant AID/OTR-C-1835 (Washington, D.C.: Smithsonian Institution, March 1981): 20.

18. These conclusions are based on Horowitz, *Ethnicity and Development,* 5–35.

19. Marx/Engels, *Werke,* Bd. 17, S. 558, cited in P. N. Fedoseyev, "Racialism–An Imperialist Ideology," in I. R. Grigulevich and S. Y. Kozlov, *Races and Peoples: Contemporary Ethnic and Racial Problems* (Moscow: Progress Publishers, 1974): 279.

20. Still among the best studies is Christopher Jencks et al., *Inequality* (New York: Basic Books, 1972).

21. My calculations, based on the regression equations in Nelson do Valle Silva, "Côr e o Processo de Realização Sócio-Econômica," *Revista de Ciências Sociais* 24, no. 3 (1981).

22. For a useful compendium, see Ronald A. Berk, ed., *Handbook of Methods for Detecting Test Bias* (Baltimore, Md.: Johns Hopkins University Press, 1982).

23. For examples from the United States and a methodological discussion, see Arthur Jensen, *Bias in Mental Tests* (New York: Free Press, 1980).

24. Robert Klitgaard, *Elitism and Meritocracy in Developing Countries* (Baltimore, Md.: Johns Hopkins University Press, 1986): chaps. 5 and 7.

25. *Sinhalayage Adisi Hatura* ("The Unseen Enemy of the Sinhalese"), Feb-

ruary 1970, chaps. 6 and 7, as excerpted in English in "The Mathew Doctrine," *Race & Class* 26, no. 1 (Summer 1984): 131, 133.

26. Cited in Gemeenschappelijk Overleg Medefinancierings Organisaties, "Memorandum on Human Rights Violations and Ethnic Violence in Sri Lanka" (The Netherlands, December 1983), reprinted as "Human Rights Violations in Sri Lanka," *Race & Class* 26, no. 1 (Summer 1984): 129.

27. The report was reprinted as "Sri Lanka: Myths and Realities," authored by the Committee for Rational Development, in *Race & Class* 26, no. 1 (Summer 1984): 139–57. The quotation is from p. 146.

28. This calculation would be carried out as follows. First, compute the distributions of predicted performance for each group A and B. Second, combine the groups into a single pool T. Given the number N and the proportion p_i to be selected, calculate the cut score C_T, such that N candidates fall above C_T. Third, calculate the difference in cut scores for groups A and B that would be needed to have various desired proportions p of group B among those selected. (This is done by calculating what cut score yields p times N candidates from group B given the distribution of group B's predicted performance, then calculating what cut score yields $1 - p$ times N candidates from group A given the distribution of group A's predicted performance.) This difference in predicted performance is the marginal cost of preferential treatment in order to get p selectees from group B.

29. Law professor Marc Galanter's study of India contains an excellent summary of the pros and cons of greater representation. *Competing Equalities: Law and the Backward Classes in India* (Berkeley and Los Angeles: University of California Press, 1984): 81–82. See also the discussion in Klitgaard, *Elitism and Meritocracy*, chaps. 3 and 5.

30. In *Justice and Reverse Discrimination* (Princeton, N.J.: Princeton University Press, 1979), Alan H. Goldman argues that the "most qualified" job applicant has the "right" to the job.

31. On the possibility of positive incentives for both groups under "stratified contests," see Mary O'Keeffe, W. Kip Viscusi, and Richard J. Zeckhauser, "Economic Contests: Comparative Reward Schemes," *Journal of Labor Economics* 2, no. 1 (Winter 1984). If students "invest" in their capabilities in part as a function of the probability of being accepted, then preferential treatment can have counterproductive effects. Stephen Coate and Glenn Loury develop a model where students in the educationally backward groups respond to affirmative action by lowering their investments in themselves, thereby perpetuating both their lower qualifications and the perception by other group members of their "inferiority." ("Affirmative Action as a Remedy for Statistical Discrimination," unpublished draft, Kennedy School of Government, Harvard University, October 1990.)

32. Robert Klitgaard, *Choosing Elites* (New York: Basic Books, 1985): chap. 8. See also *Elitism and Meritocracy*, chap. 5.

33. Klitgaard, *Elitism and Meritocracy*, chap. 6.

34. As mentioned above and detailed in *Elitism and Meritocracy*, this idea of efficiency is highly limited, and the benefits and costs of preferential treatment are multidimensional. This analysis illuminates only one part of the problem.

35. Ibid., chaps. 5 and 6; Klitgaard, *Choosing Elites*, chap. 8.

36. Klitgaard, *Elitism and Meritocracy*, chap. 5.

37. Galanter, *Competing Equalities*, 417.

38. Ibid., 536.

39. Thomas Sowell has provided a breathtaking international review of one class of policies in his *Preferential Policies: An International Perspective* (New York: William Morrow, 1990).

40. Thomas Sowell, *The Economics and Politics of Race* (New York: William Morrow, 1983): 249.

41. Glenn C. Loury, "Why Should We Care about Group Inequality?" *Social Philosophy and Policy* 5, no. 1 (Autumn 1987); Glenn C. Loury, "A Dynamic Theory of Racial Income Differences," in P. A. Wallace and A. LaMond, *Women, Minorities and Employment Discrimination* (Lexington Books, 1977).

42. Anatoli Gromyko, "The National Question: The Soviet Experience," in his *Africa Today: Progress, Difficulties, Perspectives* (Moscow: "Social Sciences Today" Editorial Board, USSR Academy of Sciences, 1983): 125, 128–29

43. John M. Echols, "Racial and Ethnic Inequality: The Comparative Impact of Socialism," *Comparative Political Studies* 13, no. 4 (January 1981). The socialist states studied included the Soviet Union, Czechoslovakia, Roumania, and Yugoslavia, with brief analyses of China and Cuba.

NOTES TO CHAPTER 13

1. Interview with the author, Tarija, Bolivia, 7 December 1990.

2. I have no litmus test for the intensity of ideology, but as noted in Chapters 1 and 6, many economists emphasize the pragmatic rather than ideological nature of the choice between state and market and various mixes thereof. Compare also sociologist Talcott Parsons: "The balance between governmentally controlled and free-enterprise industry is to a far larger degree than is generally held a pragmatic question and not one of fundamental principles." "Some Reflections on the Institutional Framework of Economic Development," in Alfred Bonné, ed., *The Challenge of Economic Development* (Jerusalem, 1958): 110.

3. Arturo Israel, "The Changing Role of the State: Institutional Dimensions," WPS 495 (Washington, D.C.: The World Bank, August 1990).

4. Markets allow more economic dynamism than state control, but, Daniel W. Bromley argues, it is wrong "to attribute this flexibility to the existence of markets rather than to the real cause, which is a legal environment that recognizes new opportunities, and that allows individual agents (individuals or firms) to capitalize on those opportunities. Markets do not cause adaptation to new conditions; they allow responses to the situations that are permitted by the legal foundations of the economy. . . . By recognizing both commodity transactions and institutional transactions, the economist will be able to see markets as manifestations of the legal foundations of the economy, and economics will then be seen not only as the study of the exchange processes that are defined by those foundations, but also as the study of those very foundations." *Economic Interests and Institutions: The Conceptual Foundations of Public Policy* (Oxford: Basil Blackwell, 1989): 49.

5. Philip Heymann and Robert Klitgaard et al., *Dealing with Corruption and Intimidation in Criminal Justice Systems: Cases and Materials* (Cambridge, Mass.: Harvard Law School, 1991).

6. Mükerrem Hiç, "The Mixed Economic System and the Role of the State in the Developing Countries," in Mükerrem Hiç, ed., *Turkey's and Other Countries' Experience with the Mixed Economy* (Istanbul: University of Istanbul, 1979): 32–33.

7. An additional piece of evidence comes from economist Vernon W. Ruttan's review of the literature on the relationship between government and economic development. "The only empirical generalization for the presently developed countries that appears relatively secure is the apparent association between authoritarian political organization and rapid economic growth at the beginning of the development process. Reasonably firm evidence to support this view is found in both the economic development and the political development literature. It also seems apparent, although the empirical basis for the generalization is less secure, that highly centralized political systems became an obstacle to economic growth as countries evolve toward middle-income status." ("What Happened to Political Development?" *Economic Development and Cultural Change*

39, no. 2 (January 1991): 284. The first conclusion is questioned in the United Nations Development Program's *Human Development Report 1991* (New York: UNDP, 1991), whose statistical research finds that democracy is not harmful to development at any stage.

8. For example, Shantayanan Devarajan shows that the usual method of computing the effective rate of protection leads to large errors of magnitude and even of sign. See, among other papers, Shantayanan Devarajan and Chalong-phob Sussangkarn, "Effective Rates of Protection When Domestic and Foreign Goods Are Imperfect Substitutes: The Case of Thailand" (Cambridge, Mass.: Harvard University, Kennedy School of Government, January 1991). For other criticisms of conventional trade theory and its policy implications, see Paul R. Krugman, *Rethinking International Trade* (Cambridge, Mass.: MIT Press, 1990).

9. Gustav Ranis, "A Comparison of the Import Substitution Experience of the Philippines and Taiwan" (Paper prepared for the Department of State, n.d.): 55–56.

10. Jagdish Bhagwati, *Protectionism* (Cambridge, Mass.: MIT Press, 1988): 98, emphasis added. He argues that successful interventions use "prescriptions" rather than "proscriptions," meaning the specification of the positive ends to be sought rather than the prohibition of particular means. Such prescriptions leave "large areas open for initiatives" by the private sector, while the proscriptions encourage corruption (p. 100).

11. Uma Lele, *Agricultural Growth and Assistance to Africa: Lessons of a Quarter Century* (San Francisco: ICS Press for the International Center for Economic Growth, 1990).

12. Carl K. Eicher and Doyle C. Baker, *Research on Agricultural Development in Sub-Saharan Africa: A Critical Survey*, International Development Paper No. 1 (East Lansing: Michigan State University, Department of Agricultural Economics, 1982): 257–58.

13. Robert P. Inman, "Markets, Governments, and the 'New' Political Economy," in Alan J. Auerbach and Martin Feldstein, eds., *Handbook of Public Economics*, 2 (Amsterdam: North-Holland, 1987): 672.

14. Uma Lele, *The Design of Rural Development: Lessons from Africa* (Baltimore, Md.: Johns Hopkins University Press, 1975): 114.

15. William O. Jones, "Measuring the Effectiveness of Agricultural Marketing in Contributing to Economic Development: Some African Examples," *Food Research Institute Studies in Agricultural Economics, Trade and Development* 9, no. 3 (1970); cited in Harold M. Riley and Michael T. Weber, "Marketing in Developing Countries," Working Paper no. 6, Rural Development Series (East Lansing: Michigan State University, Department of Agricultural Economics, 1979): 11. Jones cites a number of studies showing "defective market information" in Nigerian and other African markets in *Marketing Staple Food Crops in Tropical Africa* (Ithaca, N.Y.: Cornell University Press, 1972): esp. chaps. 6, 9, and 10.

16. Raisuddin Ahmed and Narendra Rustagi, "Marketing and Price Incentives in African and Asian Countries: A Comparison," in Dieter Elz, *Agricultural Marketing Strategy and Pricing Policy* (Washington, D.C.: World Bank, 1987).

17. See, for example, Alfred Chandler, *Scale and Scope: The Dynamics of Industrial Capitalism* (Cambridge, Mass.: Harvard University Press, 1990); and Oliver Williamson, *Markets and Hierarchies: Analysis and Antitrust Implications* (New York: Free Press, 1975).

18. Andrew Schotter emphasizes information problems as the origin for social norms and rules. "Social and economic institutions are informational devices that supplement the informational content of economic systems when competitive prices do not carry sufficient information to totally decentralize and coordinate economic activities." *The Economic Theory of Social Institutions* (New York: Cambridge University Press, 1981): 109. See also Robert Sugden, *The Economics of Rights, Co-operation and Welfare* (Oxford: Basil Blackwell, 1986).

19. On the variety of definitions of "information" in economics, see Fritz

Machlup and Una Mansfield, eds., *The Study of Information* (New York: John Wiley & Sons, 1983).

20. Operations Evaluation Department, *Agricultural Marketing: The World Bank's Experience, 1974–85*, World Bank Operations Evaluation Study (Washington, D.C., July 1990): 47, 48, 2, 3. Another recent World Bank study, this one of markets in Africa, makes similar points. "Finally, the conditions needed for the private sector to operate efficiently, including free entry, information, and factor mobility, access to credit and transport of private traders and small producers must also be considered. The paper documents that it is not so much the principle of privatization as the sequencing, phasing, and pace of privatization and price liberalization that have been the problematic issues. Donors—who indiscriminately supported the growth of the public sector in the 1970s—have not shown adequate appreciation of the preconditions necessary for the private sector to operate competitively or of the steps needed to be taken by the public sector to ensure the competitiveness of the private sector." Uma Lele and Robert E. Christiansen, "Markets, Marketing Boards, and Cooperatives in Africa: Issues in Adjustment Policy," MADIA Discussion Paper 11 (Washington, D.C.: World Bank, December 1989): 4.

21. Raisuddin Ahmed and Narendra Rustagi, "Marketing and Price Incentives in African and Asian Countries: A Comparison," in Dieter Elz, *Agricultural Marketing Strategy and Pricing Policy* (Washington, D.C.: World Bank, 1987): 115–16.

22. Joseph E. Stiglitz, "Information and Economic Analysis: A Perspective," *Economic Journal, Supplement*, 95 (1985): 26.

23. Of course, the predatory state is hardly new. "It is of course possible to imagine or to construe an economy and a State which aim at the satisfaction of the people's needs. But in reality the essence of economy and State is by no means given by such an aim. The contrary can be observed over and over again: the State often does not set out at all to manage economically, it sets out to waste, to rob Peter in order to pay Paul, to be poor in order not to have to give." Rudolf Goldsheid, "A Sociological Approach to Problems of Public Finance," trans. Elizabeth Henderson, in Richard A. Musgrave and Alan T. Peacock, eds., *Classics in the Theory of Public Finance* (New York: Macmillan, 1958): 205. The piece is an extract from Goldsheid's "Staat, öffentlicher Haushalt und Gesellschaft, Wesen und Aufgaben der Finanzwissenschaften vom Standpunkte der Soziologie," in W. Gerloff and F. Meisel, eds., *Handbuch der Finanzwissenschaft*, vol. 1 (Tübingen, 1925): 146–185.

24. "Coups by generals have given way to coups by colonels, captains, flight lieutenants and, finally, sergeants and corporals. A weary sameness sets in: each regime denounces the previous one and promises an early return to civilian government after it 'cleans up' and 'reforms' the government. Too often the military regime has indeed 'cleaned up,' but not in the way it promised." James S. Wunsch and Dele Oluwu, "The Failure of the Centralized African State," in Wunsch and Olowu, eds., *The Failure of the Centralized African State: Institutions and Self-Governance in Africa* (Boulder, Colo.: Westview, 1990): 1.

25. Steven Kelman, *Procurement and Public Management: The Fear of Discretion and the Quality of Government Performance* (Washington, D.C.: American Enterprise Institute, 1990): 14–15.

26. Paul Milgrom, "Employment Contracts, Influence Activities, and Efficient Organizational Design," *Journal of Political Economy* 96, no. 1 (February 1988): 58–59.

27. For example, only tangentially have we discussed the role of law, property rights, democracy, the fostering of civil society, and popular participation. Limits of space and my competence are responsible for these omissions; but I will add the thought that the informational perspective we have been using will lead to valuable insights about these topics.

28. Arnold C. Harberger, "Economic Policy and Economic Growth," in Harberger, ed., *World Economic Growth* (San Francisco: ICS Press, 1984): 428.

29. Gerald M. Meier, *Emerging from Poverty: The Economics That Really Matters* (New York: Oxford University Press, 1984): 223, 229, 230

30. For a pessimistic account of the yield of policy analysis in the United States, see Thomas C. Schelling, "Policy Analysis as a Science of Choice," in R.S. Ganapathy et al., *Public Policy and Policy Analysis in India* (New Delhi: Sage, 1985). Schelling, too, calls for a richer conception of policy analysis: "If policy analysis is the science of rational choice among alternatives, it is dependent on another more imaginative activity—the invention of alternatives worth considering. . . . The point I would make is that policy analysis may be doomed to inconsequentiality as long as it is thought of within the paradigm of rational choice" (pp. 27–28).

31. Schotter, *The Economic Theory of Social Institutions*, 131.

32. Joseph E. Stiglitz, "Information and Economic Analysis: A Perspective," *Economic Journal, Supplement*, 95 (1985): 27, 28. In his classic article on quality problems in markets, George A. Akerlof exhibits the same ambiguity: "It should be perceived that in these markets social and private returns differ, and therefore, in some cases, government intervention may increase the welfare of all parties. Or private institutions may arise to take advantage of the potential increases in welfare which accrue to all parties. By nature, however, these institutions are nonatomistic, and therefore concentrations of power—with ill consequences of their own—can develop." "The Market for 'Lemons': Quality Uncertainty and the Market Mechanism," *Quarterly Journal of Economics* 84, no. 3 (August 1970): 488.

33. On other occasions Stiglitz has turned "the one hand and the other" in a different direction. "These examples also provide a cautionary note on government intervention: in some cases, special interests have diverted price stabilization schemes and export-marketing cooperatives to serve their narrow interests. But the fact that government policies have sometimes been used in this way does not mean that government interventions are necessarily bad. Government intervention has played a critical role in successful development efforts." Joseph E. Stiglitz, "Markets, Market Failures, and Development," *American Economic Review Papers and Proceedings* 79, no. 2 (May 1989): 202.

34. David M. Newbery, "Agricultural Institutions for Insurance and Stabilization," in Pranab Bardhan, ed., *The Economic Theory of Agrarian Institutions* (Oxford: Clarendon Press, 1989): 294–95.

35. Norman Nicholson, "The State of the Art," in Vincent Ostrom, David Feeny, and Hartmut Picht, eds., *Rethinking Institutional Analysis and Development* (San Francisco: ICS Press for the International Center for Economic Growth, 1988): 36.

36. Thus the final paragraph of one of Joseph E. Stiglitz's articles: "Market failures are particularly pervasive in LDCs [less developed countries]. Good policy requires identifying them, asking which can be directly attacked by making markets work more effectively (and in particular, reducing government imposed barriers to the effective working of markets), and which cannot. We need to identify which market failures can be ameliorated through nonmarket institutions (with perhaps the government taking an instrumental role in establishing these nonmarket institutions). We need to recognize both the limits and strengths of markets, as well as the strengths, and limits, of government interventions aimed at correcting market failures." "Markets, Market Failures, and Development," 202.

37. See Bardhan, ed., *The Economic Theory of Agrarian Institutions*.

38. Richard A. Posner, "A Theory of Primitive Society, with Special Reference to Law," *Journal of Law and Economics* 23, no. 1 (1980): 25–27. See also Colin Camerer, "Gifts as Economic and Social Symbols," *American Journal of Sociology* 94 (Supplement 1988): S180–S214.

39. Clifford Geertz, "The Bazaar Economy: Information and Search in Peasant Marketing," *American Economic Review Papers and Proceedings* 68, no. 2 (May 1978): 30, 29.

ABOUT THE AUTHOR

Robert Klitgaard is currently a visiting professor of economics at the University of Natal, Pietermaritzburg, South Africa. He is in the midst of a multiyear research project on how development policies and management might be improved by taking cultural diversity into account, with a special focus on Africa. Formerly a professor at Harvard and Karachi universities, he has done research and served as a consultant in twenty-two countries of Asia, Africa, and Latin America.

INDEX

Abyei Development Organization
(Sudan), 163
Achieving Society, The (McClelland),
148
Adam Smith Effect, 112
Adelman, Irma, 4, 9
Administrative integration, 89,
152–67
of agencies, 153
attitudes and studies, 152–53
backward integration, 49, 80, 82,
164
complementarity among
services, 157, 159–61
conclusions, 166–67
costs, 156, 164–66, 244
examples (figures), 154, 155
financial diversification
facilitated by, 164
forward integration, 49, 55, 78,
82, 164
of health services, 153
information and incentive
linkages, 165–67, 244
monopoly creation, 163–64
policy analysis framework
(table), 158–59
production functions, 53–55,
156–57, 244
of public services, 153, 161–63
structural adjustment
implications, 248
transaction costs overcome via,
164
types and mechanism of, 153–56
of workers, 153
Administrative reform, 89, 243, 247
Adverse incentives, 151, 236
Adverse selection
definition, 44

market mechanism, 56, 59, 236,
238
market regulation to overcome,
49, 82
Advertising rules, 49, 74, 77, 215
Aeta people, 173
Africa
agriculture studies, 234–35
ethnic diversity, 171–72
ethnic inequalities, 213
ethnic tensions, 169, 227
ghost workers, 111
market studies, 39, 241
overcentralized government,
72–73, 139–41
political corruption, 116, 119
price exploitation, 237–38
structural adjustment policies, 3,
5, 232, 252–53
See also specific countries
Agency for International
Development (U.S.), 29, 169,
242
Agricultural markets
Bolivia, 27, 29
as model of perfect competition,
33
price information, 37–40
quality information. *See*
Information/quality/market
system linkages
trader and middleman actions,
33–37, 68, 238
Agricultural Promotion Law of 1980
(Peru), 180
Agricultural sector
Africa, 234–35
Bolivia, 20–22, 86
grading standards, 81
information remedy, 35, 37

293

ICEG Academic Advisory Board